Class and the Corporation

Graeme Salaman has been senior lecturer in sociology at the
Open University since 1978. He graduated from Leicester
University and gained his doctorate from Cambridge. Before
joining the Open University in 1971, he lectured at the
Polytechnic of the South Bank and was on the scientific staff of
the National Institute of Industrial Psychology.

He is the co-editor of *People and Organizations* (1973), *People
and Work* (1975), *The Politics of Work and Occupation* (1980),
Control and Ideology in Organizations (1980) and *The
International Yearbook of Organizations* (1980); and author of
Community and Occupation (1974) and *Work Organizations*
(1979)

Fontana New Sociology

Editor: Gavin Mackenzie, lecturer in sociology at the University of
Cambridge and fellow of Jesus College, Cambridge

Published

Social Mobility   Anthony Heath

Class and the Corporation   Graeme Salaman

Culture   Raymond Williams

Forthcoming

Education and the Reproduction of Inequality   Paul Corrigan
The Sociology of Trade Unions   Colin Crouch
Corporatism and Modern Capitalism   Leo Panitch
Race   John Stone

Class and
the Corporation
Graeme Salaman

Fontana Paperbacks

First published by Fontana Paperbacks 1981
Copyright © Graeme Salaman 1981
Set in 10/11½ pt Lasercomp Plantin
Made and printed in Great Britain by
William Collins Sons & Co. Ltd, Glasgow

To Rena, Sophia and Alexandra

Contents

Acknowledgements

A number of people have been important and influential in the preparation of this book, even if they weren't aware of it. And while it must be clear that I alone must be answerable for the arguments I advance, it would be wrong and ungracious not to take this opportunity to thank those people who have given me the benefit of their ideas, research, support and attention. I would like to thank the course team members of two Open University courses – *People and Organizations* and *People and Work* – and my sociologist colleagues at the Open University: David Dunkerley for his lively and well-informed interest; Craig Littler for his scholarly and thorough approach to the subject matter of this book. Most of all I would like to thank Gavin Mackenzie, the series editor. That he interprets the role of editor in a most thorough, patient and thoughtful way has played a major part in producing what strengths the book has. When the idea for this book was first raised he was enthusiastic and supporting; when, at a later stage, criticisms and suggestions were necessary he supplied them. Throughout this venture he has remained a source of intellectual stimulation and academic assistance.

G.S.

Editor's Preface

This series is designed to provide comprehensive and authoritative analyses of issues at the centre of contemporary sociological discussion. Each volume will therefore present and evaluate both the major theoretical standpoints and the empirical findings relevant to specific problems within sociology; but, in addition, each volume will itself be an original contribution to our understanding of that topic. So the series will be of value to laymen and professional sociologists alike.

The focus will be on contemporary Britain, although comparison with the institutional orders of the other advanced societies and, indeed, with pre-capitalist social formations, will form an integral part of each book. Analyses of the division of labour, its structure and consequences, of social class and other forms of inequality, and of the institutions and the distribution of power in politics and in industry, will dominate the collection. Yet this emphasis will not preclude discussion of other aspects of contemporary British society, such as the family, urbanism or law-breaking.

The series is based on three premises. First, the primary concern of sociology as an academic discipline is the analysis of *social structure* – of the institutions and social processes characteristic of advanced industrial societies. Second, the distinction between 'sociological theory' and 'empirical sociology', found so often within the subject, is false. Finally, sociological explanation incorporates historical explanation; and 'social' institutions cannot be examined in isolation from 'economic' or 'political' ones. Indeed, one of the most important changes now taking place in the social sciences is the recognition that the boundaries which hitherto have separated one discipline from another are artificial. On these premises, the series determines to help us understand the functioning of the society in which we live.

Gavin Mackenzie
Jesus College, Cambridge

Introduction

At this stage in history, in the last quarter of the twentieth century, there is little need to argue about the significance and social impact of large-scale employing organizations. We are familiar with their social, economic and political power. We know that some organizations are wealthier – and more powerful – than some nation states. For example, it is no surprise to learn that the wages bill of Ford Motor Company approaches in size the Irish Republic's gross national product, or that the economies – and politics – of the underdeveloped, or developing nations are frequently dominated by the capital, personnel and policies of multinational corporations. Similarly, we are probably alive to the political implications of the social and economic supremacy of these large corporations. Numerous sociologists have expressed concern at the increasingly social domination of anonymous, faceless bureaucrats and corporation spokesmen, often far removed from democratic, or even parliamentary, control. Similarly, industrial sociologists have for some time shown a concern to record and assess the extent of work-based deprivations experienced by many of those who sell their labour to large organizations.

Probably these three areas of activity and significance – the economic, political and social – are those which currently attract most attention. But they appeared more radically striking and remarkable to the social theorists of the nineteenth century, who witnessed the emergence of these entirely new phenomena. It is worthwhile considering their early assessments of the new organizations of the early industrial period, for we shall find that the analyses offer a depth of understanding that has not been equalled, and that their fresh reactions to new forms of organization and work design emphasize many original qualities which, a century or more later, may appear 'normal' to many sociologists, and therefore are regarded as unworthy of note or explanation. But this process of 'normalization' of many features of large-scale employing organizations is itself a systematic product of the organizations themselves, which strive to present themselves as the mere instruments of society's needs and dictates.

It is not surprising that the early sociologists devoted attention to the new work institutions they saw developing, for these institutions constituted a central element in the overall process of industrialization, which, numerous sociologists have argued, itself constituted one – and probably the major – spur to the development of sociology as a discipline. As Nisbet remarks:

The fundamental ideas of European sociology are best understood as responses to the problem of order created at the beginning of the nineteenth century by the collapse of the old regime under the blows of industrial and revolutionary democracy . . . The Industrial Revolution, the power of the bourgeoisie, and the rise of the proletariat may or may not have been all that Marx thought them to be, but the fact remains that apart from his *conception* of them there is no way of accounting for perhaps the major intellectual and social movement in the subsequent history of the West. (Nisbet, 1967: 21–2.)

Nisbet's argument is that sociology as an intellectual tradition revolves around certain core ideas or areas of interest – community, authority, status, the sacred and alienation – which demonstrate considerable importance, continuity and generality, and which constitute the early social thinkers' efforts to comprehend the social, economic and political changes occasioned by the breakup of the old order in Europe. It has been criticized on the grounds that it pays insufficient attention to competing traditions within the discipline, which, while they may originate in reactions to the transformations he describes, represent different interpretations of, and assessments of, those changes.

These opposed interpretations may be seen as giving rise to competing brands of sociological theory. Dawe (1971) takes issue with the widespread notion, which he attributes, *inter alia*, to Nisbet, that the early sociologists' reactions to the transformations of the nineteenth century took the form of a concern with the problem of social order – how is social order achieved in the face of the breakup of traditional constraint and regulation? Dawe insists that this concern, which leads to a preoccupation with the ways in which society as a structure or system regulates the activities of its members and organizes the inter-relationships of its constituent elements, represents only one tradition within the discipline. To start with a concern with the problem of order results in an emphasis on the ways in which individual members of society are controlled and socialized by that society. But, he maintains, there is another tradition within sociological theory which emphasizes the ways in which individuals *create* social structure and institutions through the emergent patterning of their actions. According to this approach, the apparent structure of social life is the result, the outcome, of individuals' decisions and negotiations. There are, then, Dawe concludes, two sociologies which, because they are based on different problems and different approaches, cannot be reconciled except by implicitly accepting the essential premisses of one of them.

However, despite these important reservations, Dawe does not wish to question the point of greatest pertinence here: the origins of the (as he sees it, various and competing) elements of the sociological tradition. The point at issue for Dawe is one of the content of the ideas, not their origin. Dawe argues that the sociological concern for human control over the increasingly oppressive and autonomous institutions developed alongside a concern for re-establishing new forms of external constraint. This confirms the central importance of the original development of the institutional and societal transformations of the nineteenth century which were seen to pose such a threat to social order and to individual freedom and control: viz., the process of industrialization itself.

Sociology, then, can be seen in all its variety as an intellectual and moral attempt to understand and assess the various large-scale changes conventionally subsumed under the expression, the Industrial Revolution – the Great Transformation. More particularly, much of the theorizing of the classic nineteenth-century sociologists was addressed to one of the most important elements in this social transformation: the grouping together of workers in new work organizations with all its implications for family and community life, and for social and political attitudes. This was a development which, while it might appear normal to us today, struck the nineteenth-century observer – or worker – as quite revolutionary and remarkable.

As such it elicited considerable critical attention. The three major founding fathers of sociology – Marx, Weber and Durkheim – advanced ambitious and distinctive theories of modern industrial organizations and their place in, and implications for, modern society. Together, these theories supply the parameters of a sociological understanding of modern organizations; but separately each theory offers a distinctive, and, to some variable degree, competing, analysis.

The theories of organization supplied by Marx, Weber

and Durkheim are highly relevant to a current analysis of organizations since their analyses concern three issues of continuing importance. Clearly the theories differ in direction and precise content. But to a striking degree we can see that each writer was in broad terms concerned with the same questions, even if these elicited different answers. Each writer was concerned with three inter-related issues: the impact of organizational hierarchy and the design of work on employees – what we may call the pathologies of industrial/organizational work; the determinants and principles of modern organizational structure – what we may describe as a theory of organization; and the origins and implications of differentiation and inequality within organizations – what we may describe as theory of class, or stratification within organizations. Each writer tends to treat these three questions in a consistent manner, but clear differences between each approach are also evident.

These theories are still highly relevant today precisely because the questions around which they centre still constitute the major problematics of a sociology of organizations. They are influential, as we shall see, in the development of distinctive modern forms of organization theory, which, if they do not explicitly acknowledge their origin in nineteenth-century theory, still employ the concepts and assumptions drawn from these seminal analyses.

However, we shall find that the relationship between modern forms of organization theory and research and the earlier theories is uneven and distorted. The work of some of the founding fathers has proved more attractive to modern writers than others. Until recently, forms of more or less primitive neo-Durkheimianism were much more appealing to organizational researchers – particularly American writers – than Marxist approaches. Weber has also been influential, but both Weber and Durkheim have been misunderstood in ways which suggest that much modern organization theory is concerned to establish the neutrality of organizations, their origins in societal agreement (about organizational goals and products) and their relative harmlessness for their employees. Frequently Durkheim and Weber are regarded as the authorities for such notions. And while there is some basis for such attribution, nevertheless, the employment of the analyses of Weber and Durkheim to develop such an anodyne approach to organizations systematically distorts the fact that Weber saw organizations as reflecting not the need for efficiency, but the cultural principle of *rationality*. Durkheim, while encouraging the emphasis on the Industrial Society, and its distinctive form of integration, was well aware of the problems of moral collapse – of normlessness and anomie – as a result of modern economic institutions and what he called the forced division of labour.

The manner in which much modern organization theory has selectively, and sometimes confusedly, drawn upon the works of the founding fathers reveals a great deal about its ideological priorities and sectional identifications. However we shall find that recent years have seen the re-emergence of a sociology of organizations deriving from the works of Marx and from a more accurate understanding of Weber, which directly confronts the bland assumptions and findings of conventional organizational theory, i.e. that the design of work, the hierarchy of organization, the differentiation of employees, and their relationships, emerge from the application of neutral, and socially legitimated technology to agreed objectives.

One of the major points of the book is that there is no sociology of organizations without some theory of organizational structure and process. Those who profess a practical, common-sense interest in organizations must, nevertheless, deploy some set of theoretically based assumptions about the origins of organizational structure, about the nature of inter-group relations, about the origins of organizational inequalities, and so on. Obviously, in some cases, where the search for practical outcomes is most intense, or where common sense is most celebrated, their theoretical underpinnings might be notably slipshod and ill-thought out. Frequently in such cases, common sense, and the flight from theory actually employ some simple-minded version of a neo-Durkheimian approach, as we shall see. The point here, however, is merely to stress that no understanding of organizations is possible without some theory of organizations. In the main such theories derive from the founding fathers. In the main the issues that preoccupy current researchers are versions of those that preoccupied the founders of the discipline. This makes it all the more important that their seminal analyses be clearly articulated and compared, and their relationship to current schools and traditions considered. This is the major aim of this study.

The book is organized as follows. Chapter 1 briefly outlines the major elements of the new forms of work organization which emerged in the nineteenth century and which constituted an element of the great industrial transformation which led to the development of early theories of organization. A brief historical account serves to remind us how radical these organizational developments were. It was these developments which encouraged the emergence of the classic theories of organization. Chapter 2 considers the major features of these classic theories of organization and bureaucracy, and pays particular attention to similarities and differences between the three theories discussed there. Chapters 3 and 4 consider theories of alienation and anomie and their relationship to current studies of work satisfaction. These chapters illustrate the manner in which 'practical' and sectional interests have caused the development of what Horton has described as an alienated sociology – the transformation, within the language of alienation and anomie, ' . . . from radical to conformist definitions under the guise of value-free sociology' (Horton, 1964: 283). Chapter 5 relates theories of the pathologies of work to theories of organization, isolates three classic traditions of organizational analysis deriving from Marx, Weber and Durkheim, and relates these to their current disciples. Chapter 6 continues this interest in theories of organization through an analysis of theories of organization control. Organizations are structures of control. Any theory of organization centres around a distinctive theory of the origins and ramifications of processes. This chapter delineates the major differences between the three theoretical traditions, while demonstrating their influence on recent work. Chapter 7 focuses on theories of class and stratification within organizations. Starting with a consideration of inequalities within organizations it passes to an analysis of three distinctive theoretical traditions in class analysis and demonstrates their strikingly different conceptions of group relationships and inter-relationships.

Within each section the relevant analyses of the theories treated in this book are presented and considered. This presentation strives to be fair and balanced. Each position is presented, and each is criticized. Nevertheless, it is the author's conviction that these theories are not of equivalent usefulness. In particular, it is argued that organization theory and research which articulates a version of neo-Durkheimian perspective fails to come to grips with the essentially political nature of organizations – with the fact that within capitalism, employing organizations are structured around the accumulation of profit, that they reveal the priority of profit, and the consequent need for control of alienated labour. Similarly, much neo-Weberian analysis, by mis-reading Weber, centres around an unexplored and naive conception of efficiency (a conception which is not found in Weber's own analysis). This too offers an apolitical view of organizations, as beyond choice, alteration, or human agency. A more representative and critical Weberianism is however apparent. This focuses not on the concept of efficiency, but on *rationality*, and explores, as Weber himself did, the emergence of rationality as an oppressive and alienating cultural principle in both capitalism (the rationality of the market) *and* bureaucracy. A Marxist approach to organization offers a thoroughly political approach. Now organizations are seen to reflect not the *techniques* of production, but the *relationships of production*: that one group employs another to make profit. Such a view, spelt out in detail in the book, offers a fruitful approach to organizations. But here, too, there are problems: how far are the characteristic features of organizations a result of capitalism *per se*, and how far do they result from the need for coordination and differentiation within any large-scale coordinated enterprise? And how can the concepts and distinctions of Marxist theory be translated into actual social categories and organizational processes? How can we differentiate the functionalism of neo-Durkheimianism from the functionalism of Marxism? And how can we choose from the various Marxist analyses of the bases of class within organizations? This last point is of particular importance, since, for Marxism, a theory of organizations revolves, ultimately, around the theory of class. These issues will be raised throughout the book and in the last chapter. The point here is simply to note that while every effort will be made to present each approach fairly, it would be disingenuous to deny that, for the author, some are more useful than others.

1 The Emergence of New Work Forms

Any general account of the emergence of new work forms during the period of industrialization is likely to be hazardous and misleading for a number of reasons. First, in any such historical account, it is impossible to separate the empirical developments themselves from the conceptual and theoretical categories within which they are organized and classified. The facts do not speak for themselves. These difficulties are all the more acute when the purpose of the history, as in this case, is to supply the context for the development of theories which have as their subject matter the actual historical developments. There is a constant interplay between the theories of Marx, Weber and Durkheim, and the developments which they attempted to explain. For not only, in each case, did each theorist select and exaggerate the empirical developments which he found most significant, but our 'knowledge' of these developments has been coloured by these theories. As Kumar notes, the 'nineteenth-century image of industrialism has great force.' (Kumar, 1978: 112.) And if, as he notes, this image was 'in many ways remarkably accurate in its projection of the main tendencies of that society' (Kumar, 1978:112), it has also been responsible for a 'distorting legacy'.

A principal feature of this distortion constitutes the second major problem in generalizing about the development of new work forms: that any generalization involves a compression of numerous different forms, and a compression of time-periods. Looking back from the vantage point of the 1970s it may make sense to talk of the emergence of bureaucracy, or the rationalization of work, of new forms of control and employment. But at the time, these developments were piecemeal, sporadic, inchoate. Frequently they were opposed, or emerged through periods of resistance and negotiation. Sometimes their full flowering was not achieved until very recently. It is possible to argue that British management is still not completely bureaucratized, for example. And sub-contract was by no means eliminated in this country by the beginning of the First World War.

The compression of the historically specific into categories of general trends and developments not only compresses variation and collapses time-periods. It also, as Kumar notes, attaches an obviousness and coherence to these changes which is spurious. Change, as he notes, is presented as 'an orderly process of development or evolution through growth, differentiation and maturation' (Kumar, 1978: 117). This danger is exemplified in much writing on the emergence of new work forms, which, in asserting the bureaucratization and rationalization of the enterprise, ignores the extent to which, as Littler points out, the development of new forms of control, new philosophies of employment and work design, took place sporadically, intermittently and slowly, and was the subject of constant struggle and negotiations: 'change was slow and hesitant. Top management failed to move quickly completely to restructure shopfloor control because new ideas and new managerial practices had not congealed into an integral theory of management in Britain.' (Littler, 1980: 168.)

As Kumar has argued, the early sociologists whose work is described in the next chapter were reacting to various aspects of the development of industrialization by attempting a 'premature conceptualization'. They were reacting to

what were, at the time, incomplete, undeveloped transformations, by attempting an analysis of 'a whole new
system within which they could be comprehended and
described.' (Kumar, 1978: 132.) What is extraordinary is
that the theories of class and of organization which each
developed on the basis of incomplete and partial changes,
should have proved to have such continuing relevance to
understanding the organization of work. The remainder of
this book is about the relevance of these theories, and their
relative value.

Inevitably, then, the historical account which follows
will approach the empirical developments of most significance to the emergence of sociological theories of
industrialization and the development of new work forms
through the conceptual routes plotted by the theorists. It
could not be otherwise. The embryonic form became the
foci of the conceptual and theoretical constructions of
Marx, Weber and Durkheim. These theories and concepts
will guide the selection of relevant empirical changes.

These changes were certainly sporadic, uneven and
variable. Some industries developed more rapidly than
others. Some elements of the new form of work organization were evident much earlier than others. Some early,
pre-industrial forms persisted long into the stage of
advanced capitalism, and some characteristic modern
elements can be discerned in pre-capitalist forms of
organization. Pollard, for example, describes how some
pre-industrial organizations approximated in various
respects to the characteristic organization of the industrial
period (Pollard, 1965: 26–60). Littler (1980) demonstrates
the persistence of sub-contract well into the twentieth
century, and notes the slow bureaucratization of British
management. Melman (1951) notes the slow development
of bureaucratization in general, as measured by the
proportion of administrative to production staff. Indeed,
Kumar argues, 'On almost all the important features of

industrialism, English development was slow and fragmentary, delaying until the very end of the nineteenth
century the full working out of the tendencies of the
Industrial Revolution.' (Kumar, 1978: 133.)

This chapter, then, is necessarily about the beginnings of
these 'tendencies', not their completion.

Despite the uneven rate of development of organizations
within the industrial period, and the fact that some early
enterprises anticipated the innovations of the period, it is
legitimate and useful to speak of the tendencies which can
be seen as characteristic of the early industrial organization. There was, as Pollard notes, a 'common thread
running through that process of economic transformation'
(Pollard, 1965: 103). First and foremost under industrial
capitalism work became organized around profit. Labour
power was bought and sold like any commodity, organized
around the pursuit of profit by capital. It is true, as many
commentators have remarked, that the gradual emergence
of wage labour in the service of capital preceded the full
development of the industrial system, as feudal work
arrangements broke down and the small handicraft shop
was replaced, via a number of routes, by the employed
worker creating products and profits for his employer – a
merchant, a middle-man, or another, more astute producer. As guild handicraft gave way to the domestic system
of production, work became increasingly subject to the
control of capital, and the worker lost his independence.
Even before those changes and innovations in technique
and work organization which are associated with the
industrial period and which permitted the flowering of the
capitalist system, work had begun to display the prime
feature of work in capitalism: that it involved the sale and
purchase of labour power in pursuit of profit, with all its
attendant implications for the emergence of class relations
between buyer and seller, the owner of capital and the seller
of labour. In the industrial period the subordination of

production to capital and the pursuit of profit not only became more widespread and obvious; it became the principle which ultimately guided the design of work organizations, employment relations and work technology as well as the principle determining relations between employed and employers – although, as we see, this principle of employment was not automatically and entirely realized in actual relations, and prior forms of work and employment persisted for many years. It took some time for both parties to learn 'the rules of the game', as Hobsbawm called them. But whether the participants sought to define the employment relationship entirely in terms of the new principle or not (and as the nineteenth century proceeded they became increasingly concerned to define it in pure market terms), the essential nature of the employment relationship was established. Indeed it even preceeded the industrial period (see Hobsbawm 1968: Ch. 17).

The next most obvious feature of the organization of the industrial period was the concentration of the work force – with all the implications for its standard of living – and the organization of work and control. The significance of the concentration of workers did not lie in the subsequent size of the enterprise. Pre-industrial organizations, using the putting-out system, had sometimes involved thousands of workers. The key significance lay in the possibilities of dividing work, and in the implications of this for control and discipline. Divided work must also be coordinated and re-integrated work. The flow of work and the integration of divided processes required management and a disciplined work force. Herein lay the major feature of the factory system, which gave rise to the need for new work habits and a new conception of time – 'by the division of labour; the supervision of labour; fines; bells and clocks; money incentives; preachings and schoolings, the suppression of fairs and sports – new labour habits were formed, and a new time-discipline was imposed.' (Thompson, 1967: 90.) As numerous writers have noted, although the characteristic development of the factory from the putting-out system, which in turn developed from the handicraft shop, cannot be applied to all industries (for some were entirely new, and others missed the putting-out stage) in general this model applies.

Marx, for example, discusses two ways in which factory manufacture arises. In one, the capitalist brings together a variety of discrete trades each of which, before, separately contributed to the construction of one item. He gives the example of the manufacture of carriages which required contributions from a number of independent crafts. The other way occurs when the capitalist employs a number of people who do the same work. Each worker previously constructed (possibly with some assistance) the complete product. Soon, when the workers are together, the work is divided and redistributed; just as in the first case, the independent craftsmen soon lost their control over the whole area of their craft and became 'confined in one groove'. In both cases, the work becomes divided so that it becomes the product of a 'unión of artificers' who perform just one of the required operations (Marx, 1954: 318–19).

The advantages to be gained by gathering the workers together and dividing labour were striking and, to the entrepreneur, attractive. For one thing, as Pollard notes, the putting-out system's great advantage over handicraft was the opportunities it offered the organizing merchant/entrepreneur to initiate some division of labour. By the same token, the factory offered the opportunity to take this division of work even further. Production in a single factory also had the advantage that it enabled 'a much closer supervision of the work in process than was possible with the domestic system' (Dobb, 1963: 145). And once production was organized and dominated by capital – whether in the form of merchant capital, or by some of the producers themselves – the capitalist merchant-manufacturer had an increasingly close interest in promoting improvements in the instruments and methods of production. 'The very division of labour . . . prepared the ground from which mechanical invention could eventually spring.' (Dobb, 1963: 145.)

Landes supports this view of the development of the factory system – that it offered an opportunity to the entrepreneur to take advantage of new forms of technology and at the same time to cope with some of the more severe inadequacies and internal contradictions of the older forms of production, the most serious of which was the problem of control. With the putting-out system, the entrepreneur found it difficult to control the behaviour and, most importantly, the level of output of his dispersed, home-based workers.

He had no way of compelling his workers to do a given number of hours of labour; the domestic weaver or craftsman was master of his time, starting and stopping when he desired. And while the employer could raise the piece rates with a view to encouraging diligence, he usually found that this actually reduced output. The worker . . . preferred leisure to income after a certain point. (Landes, 1969: 59.)

So, just when the entrepreneur wanted an increase in production he found himself frustrated by the 'irrational' traditionalism of the workers. Wage cuts were equally ineffective. These simply resulted either in the workers leaving, or in their embezzling even more of the merchant's raw materials. It was this inherent inadequacy of the putting-out system in the face of increased demand that led in turn to the entrepreneurs' demand for new work technologies and new opportunities for control and work organization and integration offered by the factory system.

But, as Landes remarks, the factory was not simply a larger work unit; it was a

system of production, resting on a characteristic definition of the
functions and responsibilities of the different participants in the
productive process . . . the specialization of productive functions
was pushed further in the factory than it had been in shops and
cottages; at the same time, the difficulties of manipulating men
and materials within a limited area gave rise to improvements in
layout and organization. (Landes, 1969: 2.)

And these improvements in turn were closely related to the
employment of machines. Machines not only replaced – or
reorganized (see below) – manual labour; they made the
concentration of workers in factories necessary and
profitable. By demanding more energy than domestic
supply could provide and by being more productive than
hand labour these machines caused not only the concentration of labour, but also its employment as 'hands', as
machine operators rather than craftsmen.

One can overdo this argument. Certainly, even prior to
the industrial period, there had been considerable division
of labour within the putting-out system. And even during
the industrial period, and right up to the end of the
nineteenth century, pre-industrial work arrangements
persisted in some areas. Nevertheless, the main tendency is
overwhelmingly clear: the organization of production
altered radically during industrialization. The factory, as
Landes puts it, was a 'bridge between invention and
innovation', and as such constituted the transformation of
the organization of work.

Clearly the relationship between factory concentration
and the design and installation of machines was two-way:
each encouraged the other, and the same is true of the
relationship between the development of machine-based
factories and the organization of work; the factories made
possible, and took advantage of, the increasing specialization of labour. As Dobb remarks:

. . . revolution in technique acquired a cumulative impetus of its own, since each advance of the machine tended to have as its consequence a greater specialization of the units of its attendant human team; and division of labour, by simplifying individual work-movements, facilitated yet further inventions whereby these simplified movements were imitated by a machine. (Dobb, 1963: 268.)

Allied to these mutually supporting developments were two others which also fuelled the cycle of specialization and mechanization: the growing productivity of labour, and therefore of capital for further investment, and the increasing concentration of production and ownership.

The mechanization and specialization of work in the early factories undoubtedly resulted in increased labour productivity. But from the employees' point of view they resulted in the large-scale reduction of work skills – the de-skilling of factory work, and the transformation of the worker's relationship to his product, his tools, his materials, his work itself. If, on the one hand, there was 'the employer, who not only hired the labour and marketed the finished product, but supplied the capital equipment and oversaw its use', there was, on the other 'the worker, no longer capable of owning and furnishing the means of production and reduced to the status of a hand' (Landes, 1969: 2).

With the introduction of fragmented, specialized work and mechanization on a large scale, the entrepreneur found himself with a new major problem. Solutions to this problem constitute one of the most important influences on factory organization. They have an impact on every aspect of work design, management structure and employment practices. The problem was that of control, coordination and discipline.

In the early days of the industrial period, the problem of control had a number of aspects: recruitment; training and work control; work discipline in general (or of the new work ethic, as it is sometimes known).

Recruitment was a problem not only because of shortage of labour, but because of potential employees' unwillingness to enter the new factories. Numerous commentators of the period noted the '. . . aversion of workers to entering the new large enterprises with their unaccustomed rules and disciplines' (Pollard, 1965: 160). So great was the resistance, even among the landless and dispossessed, that coercion was often used: convict labour was impressed, for example, in Welsh lead mines; and the establishment of workhouse-manufactories and the forcible use of pauper labour, particularly pauper apprentices, was necessary for 'the pauper children represented the only type of labour which in many areas could be driven into them, and even then it was usually by force and in ignorance of conditions.' (Pollard, 1965: 165.)

That the early employers used such forced labour – of convicts, paupers, beggars and other impressed persons – not only reflects the strength of resistance to the new manufactories with their new principles of work and employment, but had direct implications for the processes of internal control and regulation. The new factories had a great deal in common with the new prisons. As Foucault asks:

Is it surprising, therefore, that the cellular prison, with its regular chronologies, forced labour, its authorities of surveillance and registration, its experts in normality who continue and multiply the functions of the judge, should become a modern instrument of penality? Is it surprising that prisons resemble factories, schools, barracks, hospitals, which all resemble prisons? (Foucault, 1977: 228.)

Indeed, Foucault argues that the development of prisons (in place of the more direct, physical – and public – punishments of previous eras) can only be seen in terms of the need, within capitalist society, for disciplined and trained workers. Certainly the problems of control and discipline loomed very large indeed for the early entrepreneur/employer, as did the associated problem of legitimacy. We can distinguish two inter-related aspects: discipline and work control.

The first priority with the new, factory work force was to encourage the employees to develop 'appropriate' and 'responsible' attitudes towards work regulation and discipline, and towards the new form of employment relationship based on the cash nexus. The widespread concern with sexual morals, drinking habits, religious attitudes, bad language and thrift was an attempt on the one hand to destroy pre-industrial habits and moralities, and on the other to inculcate attitudes of obedience towards factory regulations, punctuality, responsibility with materials and so on. It was considered necessary to change – or improve – the worker's character before he would become amenable to factory regulations and factory inducements: 'A man who has no care for the morrow, and who lives for the passing moment, cannot bring his mind to indulge the severe discipline, and to make the patient and toilsome exertions which are required to form a good mechanic.' (Quoted in Pollard, 1965: 196.) What was required by the new factories was a 'new breed of worker', broken to the inexorable demands of the clock (Thompson, 1967), and willing to react obediently and appropriately to the employers' manipulation of controls and sanctions. Traditional attitudes and priorities had to be replaced by modern rationality.

The preoccupation with the workers' character, morality, sexual habits, religious devotions, etc. might, as Pollard notes, 'seem to today's observer to be both impertinent and irrelevant to the worker's performance, but in fact it was critical, for unless the workmen *wished* to become "respectable" in the current sense, none of the other incentives would bite.' (Pollard, 1965: 269.)

It was appreciated that if 'Idleness, Extravagance, Waste

and Immorality' were to be reduced it was necessary to achieve an entirely new morality. The employees' work and out-of-work lives had to be improved. Hence the frequency of efforts both inside and outside the factory to improve the levels of 'morality' and respectability among the new working class. As Pollard writes:

The worker who left the background of his domestic workshop or peasant holding for the factory, entered a new culture as well as a new sense of direction. It was not only that 'the new economic order needed . . . part humans: soulless, de-personalized, disembodied, who could become members, or little wheels, rather, of a complex mechanism.' It was also that men who were non-accumulative, non-acquisitive, accustomed to work for subsistence, not for maximization of income, had to be made obedient to the cash stimulus, and obedient in such a way as to react precisely to the stimuli provided.
(Pollard, 1965: 254.)

Such efforts were accompanied by intra-factory attempts to regulate and direct the work of the hands. Factory work required regularity and integration. If jobs were now sub-divided, each hand was now interdependent to an entirely new extent. Previously, if a craftsman wished to regulate his own speed and amount of work he affected no one but himself. But with divided and mechanized labour, regularity of effort and of intensity of effort became crucial. Pre-factory work involved a variety of tasks, and an irregularity of levels of effort and of performance. It entailed periods of intense labour followed by periods of licence. And even when such work took the form of employment, it would not place a predominant value on maximizing levels of rewards. All this was incompatible with the factory system. It is worth quoting at length the assessment of a contemporary commentator, Andrew Ure:

The main difficulty did not to my apprehension, lie so much in the invention of a proper self-acting mechanism for drawing out and twisting cotton into a continuous thread, as in the distribution of the different members of the apparatus into one cooperative body, in impelling each organ with its appropriate delicacy and speed, and above all, in training human beings to renounce their desultory habits of work, and to identify themselves with the unvarying regularity of the complex automaton. (Ure, quoted in Bendix, 1963: 59.)

Factory work involves specialization, sub-division and fragmentation. Decisions about the general rules and procedures and detailed work specifications are vested in experts, managers or machinery. The speed and quality of work cannot remain with the individual workers. Levels and standards of effort and intensity must be carefully controlled, coordinated and monitored. These features required a new 'rational' work ethic on the part of the hands. Much of the structure and history of the early factories must be regarded as various managerial efforts to resolve the problem of control, a problem which was exacerbated by the resistance and obduracy of the employees as they struggled to resist attempts to regulate them, strove to develop 'strategies of independence', or to push back the 'frontier of control'. All forms of employment contain the potential for conflict. But the type of employment relationships characteristic of the factory system created a greater potential than any previous system had created. The need, within the new order, for discipline and orderliness; the need to destroy traditional work habits and speeds; the attack on traditional work relationships and skills; the emergence of the cash-nexus as a basis of employment; the sheer fact of exploitation and degradation, all encouraged the development of a new form of conflict – *class* conflict (see Thompson, 1968; Foster, 1974; Morris, 1979). For at the same time that conditions deteriorated and deprivations increased, skills were demolished and the employment relationship came to be defined by both parties as one characterized by the market criterion: the cash nexus.

Such were the major innovations of the factory system in its early stages: concentration of workers, specialization and division of work, the use of machinery, and a related concern both inside and outside the factory with inculcating the 'proper' attitudes of compliance to factory discipline and installing control systems to achieve the regularity and predictability of wage labour. In themselves these were tremendous changes in the nature of work; and, as such, as shall be seen, they attracted the attention of the early theorists. Towards the end of the nineteenth century other characteristic features emerged – features which may be regarded as typical of the mature factory system: the development of management and bureaucracy, and the increasing emergence of rationalized, direct control systems. These two features are closely connected.

With the increasing size of the enterprise the entrepreneur was faced with a serious problem – how to manage the factory. In previous periods, and during the years prior to the industrial period, shortage of managers and of management procedures was a major blockage to expansion. Where entrepreneurs relied on managers or agents they more often than not found themselves faced by embezzlement, incompetence, theft and various dishonest practices. When managers were left in control, the question was how they in turn might be controlled.

Yet by the time the increased division of labour, technological innovations and the use of inanimate power sources made concentration attractive, it was obvious that the function of management had to grow to take over decisions previously left to individual craftsmen, to carry out their specialist management functions, and to achieve control and coordination.

The work of this new specialism of management contained two elements: the management and organization of the work of shop-floor employees, and specialist management services. To some degree these two functions supported each other; as for example, the imposition of increasingly direct control of employees, and of efforts to measure and regard increases in work effort assisted, among other factors, the development of more ambitious accountancy and planning departments, as well as facilitating the expansion of management *per se*.

Gradually the problem of control of the managers themselves was resolved by the adoption of what are now known as bureaucratic systems. Whereas in the early stages the agent was likely to see his position as a resource to be exploited for what he could get out of it, gradually a manager's job became distinguished from his personal property and his rewards were defined in terms of regular salaries. Again, while at the end of the eighteenth century managers were frequently chosen from within the entrepreneur's family (in an effort to gain trustworthiness), by the middle of the nineteenth century, 'the trustworthiness of managers and their professional standing had risen sufficiently to make their appointment less agonizing. Indeed, the replacement of nepotism by merit became one of the more significant aspects of the growing rationalization of industry.' (Pollard, 1965: 146.) This tendency, which Pollard exaggerates (see Nichols, 1969), was assisted by the development of increasingly relevant technical training. Although training in management itself did not emerge during the period, specialist and technical training improved considerably.

During the course of industrialization, as factories grew in size and the management function grew, we can find evidence of another innovation on a considerable scale: the formalization of rules and procedures. Some entrepreneurs went to surprisingly detailed extremes in their attempts to anticipate, and legislate for, work events and exigencies, as they systematized impersonal rules and procedures to replace more ad hoc regulations.

As Pollard remarks, 'Work rules, formalized, impersonal and occasionally printed, were symbolic of the new industrial relations. Many rules dealt with disciplinary matters only, but quite a few laid down the organization of the firm itself.' (Pollard, 1963: 258.)

Furthermore, as the division of manual work increased, and grew more differentiated and specialized, as work became increasingly divided, or fragmented, management was required to develop new, coordinating and integrating functions. Litterer (1961) suggests that in North America managerial responses to this problem were to instigate procedures to achieve vertical and horizontal integration, such as production-control systems, cost accountancy, information systems and the installation of policies and procedures which were used to guide and constrain the decisions of subordinate managers. He also makes the point that these various procedures are identical to the conditions that Weber (see below) cited as major elements of the process of bureaucratization of the enterprise: clear definition of functions and relationships, clear lines of communication, centralized information etc. Bureaucracy was a method of control, or as Goldman and Van Houten put it: 'Specifically bureaucratic mechanisms, notably the detailed division of labour, formalized hierarchy, and the isolation of technical knowledge from workers, proved the most successful means of effecting both social control and efficiency.' (Goldman and Van Houten, 1980: 113.)

Alongside the development of management and of bureaucracy went another key development – the move from *indirect* to *direct* control and employment, which was allied to the increasing intensification of the employment contract. This tendency in particular must not be exaggerated. Certainly the shift towards direct control and employment was critical to the development of the factory system. It is a key tendency, articulating as it does the priorities and problems of profit and accumulation. But the change did not happen overnight. Littler (1980) argues convincingly for the sporadic and uneven and lengthy emergence of direct control – of the way in which, in the early work organizations, the priorities of capitalism were 'funnelled through, and limited by, the social continuities from the pre-industrial period' (Littler, 1980: 160). Furthermore, as Foster (1974), Morris (1979), Thompson (1968) and Hobsbawm (1968), among others, point out, the transition from pre-industrial to the characteristic features of capitalist work organization was resisted by those who found themselves consequently de-skilled and disadvantaged.

Although the work organizations of the early industrial period demonstrate many of the features of present-day organizations, in one significant respect they retained pre-industrial aspects. This is particularly true of the nature of employment relations in the early factories. Initially much employment in the factories was sub-contracted to foremen who arranged the employment, control and payment of his workers. This system of sub-contract continued for many years. From the employers' point of view, in the early stages of industrialization it offered the great attraction that it helped to resolve the problems of management by avoiding them. They were the responsibility of the sub-contractor. And since he very often was able to maintain a more or less traditional relationship with his employees, he too was able to avoid problems of man-management. As Bendix (1963) notes, there is an inverse relationship between the diminishing strength of these traditional relationships between sub-contractor and employees and the increasing division of labour in, and bureaucratization of, the technical and administrative organization of industrial enterprises.

But in the early days the traditional attitudes of labour that so infuriated the entrepreneur eager to take advantage of increased demand actually assisted the management of labour through sub-contract, because traditional ties and relationships between employers and employees persisted. As Bendix expresses it: the 'sub-contractors, whose middle-man role often depended upon their technical skills, could manage the work force of the early enterprise more or less on the basis of the existing and cumulative traditions of the master-apprentice relationship.' (Bendix, 1963: 55.) Employment relations in the early factory were, largely because of sub-contract, characterized by traditional ties, and, as far as the entrepreneur was concerned, coloured by traditional conceptions of the responsibility of the master for his hands. They were permeated by what Mill called the 'theory of dependence' whereby the poor are seen as children unable to think for themselves, who require the protection of their superiors so long as they demonstrate deference and virtue. But this is not to say that these relations were not exploitative, arbitrary and harsh. Personal relations can encourage personal arbitrariness and exploitation (Littler, 1980). Indeed, many contemporaries had occasion in the early stages of industrialization to note and condemn the manner in which middlemen and contractors exploited their workers.

The point is, however, not the extent of deprivation, insecurity and exploitation suffered under this system of indirect control and management, but the type of relationship itself. For this indirect employment, allied frequently to persistent traditional attitudes on the part of entrepreneur, sub-contractor and hand, was to give way to a new philosophy, a new conception of the employment relationship, which in turn was tightly linked to new forms of exploitation, new and tighter forms of control.

Gradually, as industrialization got under way, and early entrepreneurs were replaced by their sons, or agents, a new conception of the employment relationship began to emerge, replacing the traditionalism of the theory of dependence with the rationality of capitalist accountancy.

Under this new philosophy, management control could not be exercised via the channels of traditional master-apprentice relations. It required something new: both sides had to define the relationship in terms of naked self-interest, in market terms. The new generation of industrialists did not believe that their workers' work performance could be controlled on a personal basis: 'rather they tended to regard the workers as factors of production, *whose cost could be calculated*.' (Bendix, 1963: 57; emphasis in the original.)

From the entrepreneurs' point of view traditionalism was an obstacle to the efficient and rational organization of the enterprise. While it facilitated management in the early stages when recruitment was a major problem, and staggering improvements in productivity could be achieved simply by concentrating the work force and organizing the integration of tasks and specialisms, and by introducing machinery, by the middle of the nineteenth century entrepreneurs, faced with a declining rate of profit, were anxious to use their labour more efficiently and systematically. The extensive use of labour, through long hours of work, was gradually replaced by the intensive use of labour, as hours of work shortened, but the amount, and the sort of effort required, was increasingly controlled. The new factory system involved the substitution of formal, centralized controls for the emergent, traditional, decentralized, sub-contracted controls of the early factory. As Nelson has demonstrated, this process had three elements:

a technological dynamic, as technical innovation produced, often inadvertently, fundamental changes in the factory environment and in the human relationships that derived from it; a managerial dynamic, as administrators attempted to impose order and system on the manufacturing organization; and a personnel dynamic, as managers began deliberate efforts to organize and control the factory labour force. (Nelson, 1975: ix.)

We are discussing here the emergence of modern work forms. Although it is true that the processes and mechanisms of control and discipline within (and without) the enterprise have, in some cases, become more subtle – and in many cases have become more 'normalized' as work-based disciplines spread into other areas and institutions of social life, and specialist techniques and 'disciplines' (psychology, social work, O and M, personnel etc.) – control, however disguised and insidious it has become, is direct and intensive, especially on the shop-floor.

Sub-contract employment was gradually replaced by direct employment. Within the enterprise the number of salaried, white-collar and managerial employees grew as managerial, administrative and technical functions developed, and subdivided. A new scale, and type of business enterprise was born. Most important of all was the new philosophy of management and employment. Partly as a result of the new scale of business, partly because of falling rates of profit, increasing attention was given to rationalizing work and employment in the drive for a higher pace of work. This search was based upon the application of market principles to employment, bureaucratic and direct control principles and mechanisms to supervision and management, and engineering principles to work design. Systematic management – soon to be institutionalized in the work and teaching of F. W. Taylor with his Scientific Management – was the engineer's response to the problems posed by inefficiency and the increasing scale of employing organizations. It found its reflection in the developing 'instrumentality' of the employees.

As Babbage noticed, the early days of traditional attitudes had their advantages for employers, not least of which was the consequent cheapness of labour (Hobsbawm, 1968; Babbage, 1835) but a major disadvantage was the difficulties such attitudes posed for the installation of more intensive and efficient work forms. By the middle of the nineteenth century both managers and men were developing more market-oriented attitudes towards the employment contract. Both parties learnt to adjust their behaviour to the 'rules of the game', the worker's attitude towards the employment relationship and the wage/effort bargain becoming characterized by market rather than by traditional criteria. Not surprisingly this had repercussions for the development and manifestation of industrial conflict: more heavily bureaucratized and rationalized companies became interested in defining the employment relationship in terms of a wage/effort bargain. This resulted in increasing conflict around the question of job control and productivity.

These, then, in very general terms, are the major features and developments of the new work organizations of the nineteenth century. How were these conceptualized and theorized about by the early social theorists?

2 Classic Theories of Bureaucracy

We shall restrict our attention to the relevant works of Durkheim, Weber and Marx. It will be seen that each theorist developed an analysis of the major principles of the new organizations which connects directly with his conceptualization of the society within which they emerge. Each theorist also assesses the social and personal implications of the new forms of organization, and advances a theory of organizational structure.

Durkheim and the division of labour

For Durkheim the important point about the increasing differentiation and specialization of the division of labour was not the principles underlying the new work forms, but the implications of the new differentiation for social solidarity. The difference between Durkheim and the other theorists is one of degree. Both the other theorists were concerned with the possibility of societal instability followed by the development of conflict relations between privileged (or exploiting) and negatively privileged (or exploited) classes. Nevertheless, Durkheim's preoccupation with the significance of the division of labour for societal stability and order distinguishes him from the other theorists as surely as do the conclusions he draws.

Durkheim's prime concern was with how it is that

societies hold together. He distinguishes two different kinds of solidarity, one based on the high degree of resemblance of the individuals, wherein the individual is absorbed into the society to such a degree that individuality itself is barely developed. Members are very similar to each other. This is mechanical solidarity. In the other type, organic solidarity, the parts of the society and individuals are differentiated and individualized. Here solidarity comes from functional interdependence and exchange-relationships.

Organic solidarity – in which society is held together by the interdependence of differentiated units, operating separately but always on the basis of some shared pre-contractual morality – is a consequence of the development of the division of labour. Durkheim insists that there is no necessary threat to stability in the growth of individualism or of specialization or of market relations. These simply change the basis of social solidarity, they do not destroy it.

The conception of the 'isolated individual', entering into exchange relationships in order to maximize his personal returns, is itself, according to Durkheim, a product of social development and presupposes a moral order . . . the spread of the ideals of individualism is not a symptom of a pathological condition of society, but on the contrary is the 'normal' and healthy expression of the social transformations that are engendering a new form of social solidarity.
(Giddens, 1978: 10–11.)

This is not the place for a thorough statement and critique of Durkheim's theory of the relationship between the division of labour and social solidarity (see Lukes, 1973; and Eldridge, 1971). The important point is that Durkheim argued that the function of generating social solidarity was, in primitive societies, performed by certain factors and institutions which had, in modern society, been replaced by the division of labour, which far from signalling the end of solidarity and morality, merely represented a new method of creating social solidarity. This new form was based on functional interdependence and relations of exchange. It gives rise to rules which govern the peaceful and regular relationships between the differentiated elements. Therefore, the increasing development and differentiation of the division of labour was a source not of instability and conflict but of stability and social solidarity. Such a view is in marked contrast to Marx's and, to a lesser degree, Weber's assessment of the consequences of new work relationships and forms. It would also seem to be in conflict with observable events and tendencies. Since Durkheim was not unaware of the empirical facts of industrialization and the implications of new work organizations and relationships, he found it necessary, in order to save his thesis, to devote some analysis to what he called 'abnormal forms' of the division of labour. These occur when the process of development of the division of labour as it should naturally develop is obstructed and distorted by various factors. The thesis is saved in face of strongly contrary evidence – that the division of labour frequently produces conflict, instability and division, not solidarity – by defining the conditions under which these 'abnormal' consequences emerge as in some way atypical or unhealthy, i.e. as deviations from the expected which require explanation by reference to special, pathological factors rather than to the fact of the division of labour itself. Furthermore, as Eldridge notes,

. . . when Durkheim writes of abnormal forms of division of labour it is in the most general sense a recognition that the desirable congruence between system integration (of the parts of the society) and the social integration of the individual (into the society) is not always present in modern industrial societies. Organic solidarity, that is to say, is only imperfectly realized. (Eldridge, 1971: 76.)

These 'abnormal' forms are the result, argues Durkheim, of three conditions. First, the division of labour is often not 'spontaneous', that is to say,

> . . . by spontaneity we must understand not simply the absence of all expressed violence, but also of everything that can even indirectly shackle the free unfolding of the social force that each carries in himself . . . In short, labour is divided spontaneously only if society is constituted in such a way that social inequalities exactly express natural inequalities.
> (Durkheim, 1964: 377.)

Durkheim is aware, then, that despite the formal freedom of workers in industrial societies, numerous circumstances operate to limit freedom of choice and equality of opportunity. He notes the importance of class and inherited privilege in distorting the spontaneity of the division of labour. If the division of labour is to be characterized by spontaneity, then individuals' aptitudes and preferences need to be matched by the demands of their work. The 'normal' division of labour, as Lukes remarks, is a 'perfect meritocracy'. Furthermore, exchange relations must also be free from constraint: no one party should be able (because of his resources or position) to exploit or dominate the other party. Contract must, if it is to generate the solidarity described by Durkheim, be free from constraints. There must be ' . . . absolute equality in the external conditions of conflict (or struggle)' (Durkheim, 1964: 377). Such equality was obstructed by the existence of classes: ' . . . there cannot be rich and poor at birth without their being unjust contracts.' (Durkheim, 1964: 3.)

Secondly, the division of labour can produce abnormal effects because it is 'anomic'. The anomic division of labour is regarded as a result of the uneven development of economic conditions and social solidarity, of the rapidity of industrialization which has moved ahead of the necessary developments in social regulation. As a result, the economy is unregulated and liable to crises, work is increasingly specialized and mechanized, with serious consequences for the workers. Yet the appropriate forms of organization and instruction of the workers into the importance of their specialized activities has failed to develop, as has the regulation of industrial conflicts and disputes. The problems of industrial organization are attributed not to the system *per se*, with its inherent priorities and relationships, but to the fact that the organization of work in its entirety has developed so fast that it is largely unregulated and not governed by bodies of moral rules and procedures. From this 'anomic' (i.e. lacking regulation and moral control) condition the 'pathologies' of industrialization stem.

Finally, the third factor responsible for 'abnormal' development of the division of labour concerns the fact of organization itself. Durkheim ascribes some of the problems of industrialization to the inefficiency and inadequacies of management and organization. When functional specialization and interdependence within the enterprise are so poorly designed and coordinated as to allow 'incoherence and disorder', then such conditions will not give rise to smooth integration at the societal level. This is a problem of work design, of management, or, indeed, of coordination. Durkheim was confident that with time, increased functional differentiation would bring about increased solidarity at work. (In fact, as more than one writer has pointed out, increased specialization and differentiation at work has decreased solidarity and increased the deprivation of the worker and, often, his hostility to his employer.)

For Durkheim, most of the personal pathologies of the new industrial order were attributed to the prevalence, within that order, of anomie. As we have seen, one abnormal form of the division of labour was described as anomic. As a result of the rapidity of industrialization, relationships within the enterprise and the individual employee's aspirations lost their moral character, i.e. were no longer bound by acceptable rules. They became unregulated, meaningless, anomic. So long as organization was inadequate and planning was insufficient, the moral character of work did not develop. Work lost its traditional meaning, was no longer imbued with symbolic significance.

Elsewhere Durkheim developed his use of the concept anomie to describe the ills of the industrial society. As many sociologists have suggested, in some ways Durkheim's development and use of the concept anomie can be compared to Marx's use of the concept alienation, though the two concepts differ drastically in the assumptions of human nature employed (Lukes, 1967) and in political direction and sociological implications of the analysis (Horton, 1964). For Durkheim, anomie resulted from the lack of social control; alienation, on the other hand, *results* from certain sorts of social control. Horton describes anomie as follows: 'Cultural constraints are ineffective; values are conflicting or absent, goals are not adjusted to opportunity structures or vice versa, or individuals are not adequately socialized to cultural directives.' (Horton, 1964: 285.)

Durkheim saw modern economic life as characterized by constant and pervasive anomie. Anomie, remarks Horton, has become institutionalized as self-interest and the unchecked search for self-interest dominates economic life. Traditional restraints have been overwhelmed. The result is a characteristic pathological mental condition of the citizen, or employee, whose aspirations are unlimited, and whose lot is meaningless egotism.

Weber

Weber regarded the organizational developments described earlier as constituting the development of *bureaucracy*, a type of organization which articulated a wholly new principle of organization and which represented a radical departure from traditional organizational forms in a number of respects, namely, the basis of authority within the organization, the methods and principles of control, and the basis of decision-making and planning.

All systems of coordinated social action require some mechanism of control and coordination, and some element of 'voluntary submission'. Such submission of the subordinate and controlled to the dominant controller rests upon the attitudes of the subordinate and his perception of the nature of the relationship and the characteristic of his superior. Such attitudes, Weber argues, are of three broad sorts: rational, traditional, and charismatic.

The notion that obedience is due to the superior, or the rules he had promulgated, because such control represents, and derives from, the 'legally established impersonal order' clearly constitutes a major departure from more traditional or personal bases of control and obedience. It rests, Weber argues, on the acceptance of a series of ideas concerning the nature and origin of the underlying legal norms. The concrete realization of this rational-legal authority in administrative and organizational form demonstrates various characteristics described by Weber. In the main these consist of organization on the basis of impersonal rules, the elimination of personal, subjective factors from decision-making or selection, the clear and formal specifications of responsibilities, and the organization of the offices hierarchically. Incumbents of bureaucratic positions are controlled by 'strict and systematic' discipline, are subject to elaborate systems of rules and procedures, are rewarded by regular salaries, and are involved in bureaucratic careers, i.e. they are expected to rise (according to merit and performance) through the hierarchically arranged offices.

Weber sees bureaucracy as characteristic of many aspects of social life – 'the Church and state, of armies, political parties . . . ' He also sees it as characteristic of economic enterprises. The development of capitalism has been marked, he writes, by the progressive expropriation of workers from the means of production, by the increase in size of the enterprise, by increased specialization and mechanization, and the increase in the functions and size of management. With the introduction of capital accounting, which makes possible a rational assessment of profits and losses in money terms, the extensive, essentially traditional utilization of labour gives way to more systematic, rational and intensive use of labour: 'All the non-human means of production become fixed or working capital; all the workers become "hands" . . . even the management itself becomes expropriated and assumes the formal status of an official.' (Weber, 1964: 259.)

Furthermore, not only are capitalist enterprises increasingly bureaucratic, but ' . . . the capitalistic system has undeniably played a major role in the development of bureaucracy.' And, Weber continues, that development,

largely under capitalistic auspices has created an urgent need for stable, strict, intensive, and calculable administration . . . capitalism in its modern stages of development strongly tends to foster the development of bureaucracy, though both capitalism and bureaucracy have arisen from many different historical sources. Conversely, capitalism is the most rational economic basis for bureaucratic administration and enables it to develop in its most rational form . . . (Weber, 1964: 338.)

According to Weber, capitalism and bureaucracy both

depend on the same basic principle or attitude: that of rationality. In order to understand what is meant by this it is necessary briefly to outline Weber's analysis of the nature and origins of capitalism (Weber, 1930).

Capitalism, Weber insists, is not the same as the drive for profit. Capitalism as an economic system or attitude is distinctive for its 'pursuit of profit, and forever *renewed* profit, by means of continuous rational capitalistic enterprise' (Weber, 1930: 17). Capitalism must be distinguished from traditional, pre-rational attitudes and economic systems.

. . . it is one of the fundamental characteristics of an individualistic capitalistic economy that it is rationalized on the basis of rigorous calculation, directed with foresight and caution towards the economic success which is sought in sharp contrast to the hand-to-mouth existence of the peasant, and to the privileged traditionalism of the guild craftsman and of the adventurers' capitalism, oriented to the exploitation of political opportunities and irrational speculation. (Weber, 1930: 76.)

Weber locates the origins of this capitalist rationality in the personal psychological consequences and anxieties of Calvinism. Briefly he argues that the empirical relationship between Protestantism and early capitalist activity is not the result of the formal doctrine of Protestantism but of the impact of Protestant beliefs and practices upon the believer. Thus he emphasizes the distinctive features of rational capitalism – the vigorous and systematic pursuit of wealth coupled with a reluctance to consume the profit thus generated in conspicuous consumption or personal pleasures – and relates these to Protestantism's emphasis on asceticism and on the individual's whole-hearted commitment to his calling. Supplying the motive power for these involvements is the individual's anxiety about his personal salvation, exacerbated by his relative lack of institutional supports within the formal Church.

These are the origins of the 'spirit of capitalism' – an attitude which was necessary to the development of capitalism as a distinctive form of economy based on the pursuit of profit through the use of formally free labour.

Also necessary was the emergence of institutions which could further the capitalist pursuit of profit through rational means, i.e. capital accounting and bureaucracy. These institutions are based on the same rational principles. Both are essential to the development of capitalism as an economic system. It was in conjunction with the emergence of the spirit of capitalism that the rational institutions of the industrial societies achieved their full potential. The rationality of capitalism had to be echoed by the rationality of bureaucracy and the anti-traditionalism of capital accountancy. What, then, was this rationality that it characterized all these separate developments?

When Weber described an institution – say capital accounting, or bureaucracy, or the English legal system – as rational, he was making a number of precise points: (a) he was distinguishing the institution or behaviour pattern sharply from traditionalism, in ways specified below; (b) he was describing the institution, not evaluating it. Rationality for Weber, whatever its current implications in normal usage, was not synonymous with 'sensible', efficient or modern, although it could be related closely to these other conditions; (c) rationality itself was of two forms – 'formal' and 'substantive'. Whereas the first refers to the installation (or possibility) of accurate calculations of the nature – costs; quantities, profits, results etc. – of decisions, or to the organization of conduct around certain explicit, formalized rules and principles, the second refers to the relationship between results and overall, general guiding principles.

In these terms bureaucracy, capital accounting and modern capitalism as institutionalized economic activity

are rational in the formal sense, because of their employment of explicit rules and principles which make possible
exact quantitative assessment of the impact and costs of
decisions. The combination of formally rational institutions and the spirit of modern capitalism has created the
modern capitalist economy: 'Exact calculation – the basis of
everything else – is only possible on the basis of free
labour.' (Weber, 1930: 22.)

Once two types of rationality are distinguished, conflict
between them becomes possible. Weber himself notes, for
example, that the achievement of high standards of formal
rationality within an economy is dependent on a number of
factors, of which one is the expropriation of the individual
worker from the means of production, and his exposure to
'a stringent discipline . . . controlling both the speed of
work and standardization and quality of products' (Weber,
1964: 246–7). Thus formal rationality depends on the
management's extensive control over shop-floor personnel
and functions. Such control must, if it is to maximize
formal rationality, be unhampered by restrictions or
'irrational obstacles', such as 'the existence of [workers']
rights to participate in management'. But such formally
rational procedures contravene other, generally held values
about desirable ways of treating workers, of democracy etc.
It may be that ' . . . the maximum of formal rationality in
capital accounting is possible only where the workers are
subjected to the authority of business management.' But,
continues Weber, 'This is a further specific element of
substantive irrationality in the modern economic order.'
(Weber, 964: 248.)

The same conflict between formal and substantive
rationality is apparent within bureaucracies. Weber
recognizes the achievements of modern bureaucracies.
'Experience tends universally to show,' he writes, 'that the
purely bureaucratic type of administrative organization . . .
is, from a purely technical point of view, capable of

attaining the highest degree of efficiency and is in this sense formally the most rational known means of carrying out imperative control over human beings.' (Weber, 1964: 337.) But he recognizes that bureaucratic rationality and efficiency may conflict. The expression 'efficiency' must be seen against some commitment to certain values and goals. These may be held by some members of the organization, but not by others. An obvious possibility is for formally rational procedures to conflict with the interests of subordinate members of the organization. Or formally rational procedures may obstruct the achievement of substantive rationality. Clearly, Weber's notion of substantive rationality cannot usefully be used without some analysis of the values underlying such assessments, and the social location of such values. According to *which* group's interests and values, for example, can the formal rationality of the division of labour within modern capitalism, as analysed by Weber, or the hierarchic and detailed structure of work and control within modern bureaucracies, be regarded as substantively rational?

To summarize: Weber's analysis of the nature of the new organizational forms of the nineteenth century focused attention on:

(a) the development of organizations with radically new forms and mechanisms of control, which he called bureaucracies. These were distinctive for their use of direct, detailed and specific control, represented in elaborate and strict rules and procedures. Incumbents of positions within these bureaucracies were selected and treated on the basis of their merit, performance and knowledge, not on the basis of personal attributes. They were rewarded by fixed salaries and the promise of careers within the bureaucracy;

(b) these new organizations involved a totally new basis of authority. Orders, and superiors, were obeyed because they were seen by subordinates to reflect acceptable rational-legal norms. Personal and traditional ties between leader and led are irrelevant to the bureaucracy;

(c) these new organizations are described as rational, and this rationality which is also found in other institutions of modern society, is closely related to, and supportive of the developing spirit of capitalism. This rationality constitutes a decisive break with traditional attitudes and values. In its formal manifestation it consists of systems of calculable, quantifiable and explicit procedures and rules. These formally rational procedures are responsible for the achievements bureaucracy supplies for capitalism. But Weber acknowledges the likelihood of conflict between the procedures designed to achieve formal rationality and other societal values. In particular he notes the problems that may attend the development of specialized division of labour, and tight supervision and control.

In general, Weber's interest is in the changes in values and priorities which accompanied the process of industrialization, particularly the gradual transcendence of traditionalism. Weber's analysis also focuses on the emerging structure of organizational control and the establishment, at both management and shop-floor levels, of systems of direct control over personnel and performance. As management developed, so the managers found themselves involved in structures of bureaucratic control.

Weber's work is not applicable only to white-collar and managerial levels. He is aware that the new industrial organizations require – if they are to be formally rational – the expropriation of workers from traditional areas of discretion and autonomy, their subjection to strict and stringent discipline, the fragmentation and specialization of their jobs.

The social and personal consequences of the new organizations are revealed in three ways: through classes, and their inter-relationships, which, being based on an individual's ability to sell goods or services within an economic order, develop; in Capitalism, from the position or function of employees of the new work organizations; through the process of rationalization of all aspects and institutions of modern society of which the development of bureaucracy is a major part, and which Weber sees as an emerging feature of Western society; and through the progressive expropriation of employees, workers, managers and officials – from their work, their product, their personal preferences and judgements. We shall consider each of these.

Weber distinguishes various types of stratification or inequality of which class is one. Class refers first to ownership and non-ownership, and to the probability that people vary significantly in the circumstances of their lives, i.e. 'their provision with goods, external conditions of life and subjective satisfactions'. These variations in 'life chances' are economically determined; that is to say, they are the consequence of the individual's position within the economic order. 'They are dependent,' writes Weber, 'on the kind and extent of control or lack of it which the individual has over goods or services and existing possibilities of their exploitation for the attainment of income or receipts within a given economic order.' (Weber, 1964: 424.)

Within capitalism, the dominant economic order is based on the market. This gives rise to 'acquisition classes', based on the determination of individuals' 'life chances' by their opportunity to sell their skills or services on the market. In general Weber notes that class structures under various historical conditions have demonstrated a sharp distinction between positively and negatively privileged groups, determined by ownership or non-ownership of various forms of property. Under capitalism these categories are composed of, respectively, entrepreneurs of various types, and workers. While Weber notes both these categories must be sub-divided on the basis of the differing goods, skills or services that each group buys or sells, he also notes that capitalistic work organizations tend to result in the relative reduction of differences within classes, and the relative increase in factors, such as the concentration of workers, and mechanization, which produced organized class solidarity and action. He writes, for example, that the 'working class' is an example of a social class, and that it 'approaches this type the more completely mechanized the production process becomes' (Weber, 1964: 427). The process of mechanization has this effect because of its consequences for the type of labour demanded by modern work organizations.

As Giddens and others have noted, the emergence of new forms of 'rational' organization is an integral part of the overall process of rationalization which Weber saw as increasingly dominating all aspects of Western society and culture. Typically, this rationalization of the world was, in the first place, anti-traditional. It disenchanted the world by sweeping aside magic and superstition and replacing them with clear, consistent, explicit and, finally, scientific and calculable principles. The progress is apparent in many aspects of institutional and cultural life. It is most clearly revealed in the emergence of new forms and principles of organization. Freund describes Weber's notion of rationalization as follows:

It is . . . the product of the scientific specialization and technical differentiation peculiar to Western culture . . . It might be defined as the organization of life through a division and coordination of activities on the basis of an exact study of men's relations with each other, with their tools and their environment, for the purpose of achieving greater efficiency and productivity. (Freund, 1968: 18.)

Rationalization has devastating consequences for the lives and attitudes of individuals, for it means 'that there are no mysterious incalculable forces that come into play, but rather that one can, in principle, master all things by calculation.' (Gerth and Mills, 1948: 139.) The result is the disenchantment of the world: 'Reality has become dreary, flat and utilitarian, leaving a great void in the souls of men which they seek to fill by furious activity and through various devices and substitutes.' (Freund, 1968: 24.) Of great importance in the spread of this rationalization has been the emergence and dominance of bureaucratic organizations.

These organizations also affect the lives of individuals directly, by controlling and dominating them through their employment. We have already noted that for Weber, employment within capitalist organization meant the increasing control of the employees as employers attempted to achieve organizational rational systems and procedures in the pursuit of profit. As Parsons, in his introduction to Weber's *Economic Sociology*, remarks, Weber argued that within capitalism production is carried out within large organizations, and these can only operate rationally with 'formally free' labour which has no ownership of, or rights over, the means of production. The workers must be expropriated. Control must pass to the owners, or their agents. Large-scale organization is only possible with centralized control; this cannot be achieved if the workers are not fully expropriated. This expropriation is the result of the rationality of capitalistic industry and organization, which requires the free use of large numbers of workers and the centralization of control – 'unified control', 'continuous supervision', coordination and 'stringent discipline'.

The expropriation of workers, being a result of the depersonalization of labour within capitalism, and its use purely for economic production is also required by the needs for centralized control, which results in the emergence of management, for this group takes over the control, monitoring and decision-making of the workers. This group assumes responsibility for the calculation and planning. The alienation of the employee is further increased by mechanization of work. This is a characteristic of modern industry, and it 'presupposes specialization of functions and the saving of human labour, and also a peculiar uniformity and calculability of performance, both in quality and quantity.' (Weber, 1964: 228.)

The process of expropriation of employees from control over their work, products and labour is not restricted only to shop-floor employees, however, although in this case it is most obvious, and exacerbated by more stringent supervision and control (see above). The process applies also to 'white-collar' workers and to management itself. Weber points to the split between owners and their managers, and notes that this implies the expropriation of such managers, who, like bureaucrats, are selected for their technical ability, rewarded by salaries, and do not own or have any rights over their jobs.

The development of capitalism itself also furthers the application and diffusion of rationality. Capitalism – like bureaucracy – requires the elimination of all non-rational elements. Calculation, impersonality, predictability are the necessary qualities of social relations. The rationality of capitalism is echoed in the rationality of bureaucracy. Both require the expropriation of the employee, the depersonalization of relationships, the supremacy of impersonal calculations. Weber was aware of the implication of the resultant spread of bureaucracy for the individual: 'the result will necessarily be a loss of substantive autonomy [self-determination and meaning] by the individual in the face of technically calculated production and consumption and impersonally formalized integration.' (Seidman and Gruber, 1977: 507.)

Finally, Weber clearly felt that the very essence of capitalism itself – 'rational conduct on the basis of the idea of the calling' – had given rise to institutionalized capitalism, to a dominating and oppressive way of life, which, in its relentless materialism, destroys traditional values and replaces them with the empty goal of meaningless consumerism. Capitalism as a form of economic order represents the triumph of rationality, with all its consequences:

The Puritan wanted to work in a calling; we are forced to do so. For when asceticism was carried out of monastic cells into everyday life, and began to dominate worldly morality, it did its part in building the tremendous cosmos of the modern economic order. This order is now bound to the technical and economic conditions of machine production which today determine the lives of all the individuals who are born into this mechanism, not only those directly concerned with economic acquisition, with irresistible force. Perhaps it will so determine them until the last ton of fossilized coal is burnt. In Baxter's view the care for external goods should only lie on the shoulders of the 'saint like a light cloak, which can be thrown aside at any moment.' But fate decreed that cloak should become an iron cage. Since asceticism undertook to remodel the world and to work out its ideals in the world, material goods have gained an increasing and finally inexorable power over the lives of men as at no previous period in history. Today the spirit of religious asceticism – whether finally, who knows? – has escaped from the cage. But victorious capitalism, since it rests on mechanical foundation, needs its supports no longer. (Weber, 1930: 181–2.)

Marx

Marx maintains that the nature and organization of work in modern large-scale work organizations reflect the essential nature of the employment relationship, which in turn determines all other aspects of society since it establishes the basic groupings (classes) and their relationships and is therefore regarded as the key feature of capitalism. Capitalism as a form of economy and society is revealed through the organization of work and the nature of work relationships. Under capitalism work relationships are characterized by the sale and purchase of labour power. Those with capital buy labour power to achieve profit, which they use to add to their capital and thus to strengthen their position as capitalists and employers. This relationship gives two classes which are in conflict with each other, at least potentially, if not always in practice.

At work this conflict relationship between expropriating employer/capitalist and expropriated employee gives rise to a number of necessary features of work under capitalism: the need for management to direct and organize the labour *power* that is purchased, and to control and discipline potentially recalcitrant employees whose commitment is always unreliable and who may at any moment demonstrate their hostility to their work, their product and their employer.

Since the search for profit from the use of purchased and exploited labour power creates conflict between employer and employee, greater efficiency at achieving profit is inevitably and irrevocably interconnected with greater control and discipline. Measures designed to achieve greater efficiency or productivity or profitability also entail (sometimes directly and explicitly) tighter control over employees, or reduction in the costs (to the employer) of employee recalcitrance or hostility. How could it be otherwise, Marx writes, when:

The directing motive, the end and aim of capitalist production, is to extract the greatest possible amount of surplus-value, and consequently to exploit labour-power to the fullest possible extent. As the number of cooperating labourers increases, so too does their resistance to the domination of capital, and with it the necessity for capital to overcome this resistance by counterpressure. The control exercised by the capitalist is not only a special function, due to the nature of the social labour-process, and peculiar to that process, but it is, at the same time, a function of the exploitation of a social labour-process, and is consequently rooted in the unavoidable antagonism between the exploiter and the living and labouring raw material he exploits. (Marx, 1954: 313.)

This basic overlapping of the search for profit with the need for greater control results in the politicization of all aspects of work organization. In the first place the design of work, the distribution of work rewards, the level of wages, the state of work conditions etc. reveal the primacy of profit over all other considerations, and demonstrate class-based assumptions about the value and moral worth of the 'hands'. Secondly, the design of work, the use of technology, mechanization, bureaucratization, the development of supervision and management, the emergence of specialist groups within the enterprise are all part and parcel of capital's efforts to increase profitability, cheapen labour, reduce the impact of employees' antipathies and resistance, and increase discipline and control. The division of labour at work is a way to achieve greater control and profitability. Marx writes: 'Division of labour within the workshop implies the undisputed authority of the capitalist over men, that are but parts of a mechanism that belongs to him.' (Marx, 1954: 336.)

Technology is used to cheapen labour, and to de-skill it, and thus make it easier to obtain and transfer workers. By converting the worker into 'a crippled monstrosity, by forcing his detail dexterity at the expense of a world of productive capabilities and instincts' (Marx, 1954: 340), the employer is able to concentrate skill in the hands of reliable agents – managers. 'Intelligence in production expands in one direction, because it vanishes in many others. What is lost by the detail labourers, is concentrated in the capital that employs them.' (Marx, 1954: 341.)

The same analysis applies to management itself. While

Marx admits that all large-scale enterprises require some coordination, management in the capitalist enterprise is necessitated by the attempt to achieve profit from the employment of alienated labour-power. Capitalism, he writes, requires managers as an army requires officers, to command in the name of the capitalist. The functions of management and the hierarchic structure of capitalist enterprises with their bureaucratic features reflect the attempt to increase labour's profitability, and acquiescence.

These features of work in capitalism have two major consequences: conflict relations between employer and employee, or capitalist and proletariat, and the alienation of the worker.

Work relationships between employer and employee are, according to Marx, unavoidably exploitative and, therefore, contentious. All aspects of the design of work, and work arrangements in general, plus the fact and design of organization, reflect this basic antipathy. But this potential conflict is not necessarily explicit, or realized. The organization of work under capitalism establishes the basic class groupings. But these classes are by no means necessarily self-conscious groups. Rather they are often either collections of disparate groups, or mere aggregates of people who occupy the same social and economic position but who are – as yet – unaware of their similarities and of their shared conflict of interest with their employers.

Certain essential aspects of capitalism assist the development of *class consciousness* among the proletariat. The nature of work itself – mechanization, degrading activities, de-skilling; the low wages allocated to labour, and the tendency for these to decrease; the increasing pressure of work – the exhaustion of long hours, or of intensively organized work regimes, add to the deprivations of the employees, and encourage the development of hostility.

Certain aspects of the organization of work assist the

development of class consciousness among the proletariat by revealing the real nature of the relationship between capitalist and proletariat, and by facilitating the growth of solidarity. Marx stresses the importance of work deprivations, both in the nature of work itself and in the conditions and rewards of work. He stresses the significance of mechanization, by which the worker becomes 'an appendage of the machine', and of the tendency to degraded and de-skilled work which means that ' . . . it is only the simplest, most monotonous and most easily acquired knack that is required of him.' (Marx and Engels, 1970: 41.) He argues that the decreasing skill of manual work is directly allied to the tendency for wages to decrease: 'as the repulsiveness of the work increases, the wages decrease.' (Marx and Engels, 1970: 41.)

The concentration of workers into factories assists their awareness of their common circumstances, Marx argues, as does their shared exposure to often brutal and demanding work discipline. As a result, and slowly, the proletariat begins to resist the capitalist. Initially as individuals, then as groups and then as the work people of a factory or a locality, the workers struggle against their employers. Initially such struggles mistake the nature of their oppressor, and turn on machinery, or the factory itself. But gradually, as mechanization and market pressures force the growing homogeneity of the proletariat, struggles between the two classes become more common, and more explicitly *class* conflicts. The proletariat becomes organized, through the formation of unions, and, overcoming internal divisions, increasingly engages the bourgeoisie in struggles which culminate in the victory of the proletariat. In a striking passage Marx and Engels write: 'What the bourgeoisie, therefore, produces above all, is its own gravediggers. Its fall and the victory of the proletariat are equally inevitable.' (Marx and Engels, 1970: 46.)

Work under capitalism, then, not only reveals the very

essence of this form of society; it exposes those who sell their labour power to such deprivation and indignity that collectively they realize their shared predicament and begin to oppose the system, in order to change it. This is the social consequence of such work circumstance. On the individual level, Marx argues that, under capitalism, the worker is *alienated*. This concept requires some explanation. The theme of man's alienation under capitalism is an important one in Marx's early writings. The concept itself is somewhat diffuse: Marx uses it to refer to a number of features of capitalist society, and various personal circumstances. The main idea behind the assertion that capitalist society is alienating is that within such a society individuals become separated from various of their attributes, activities, aptitudes and relationships, in the sense that they lose control over, lose any involvement in, become estranged from, their own activities and products, even, indeed, their own potential creativity, and sensuousness.

The most important and obvious area of alienation in capitalist society is in work, for example the worker's loss of ownership (expropriation) of his product, of his tools, even of his labour itself. As Marx puts it:

What constitutes the alienation of labour? First, that the work is *external* to the worker, that it is not part of his nature; and that, consequently, he does not fulfill himself in his work but denies himself, has a feeling of misery rather than well-being, does not develop freely his mental and physical energies but is physically exhausted and mentally debased. The worker, therefore, feels himself at home only during his leisure time, whereas at work he feels homeless. His work is not voluntary, but imposed, *forced labour*. It is not satisfaction of a need, but only a means for satisfying other needs. Its alien character is clearly shown by the fact that as soon as there is no physical or other compulsion it is avoided like the plague . . .

We arrive at the result that man (the worker) feels himself to be freely active only in his animal function – eating, drinking and procreating, or at most also in his dwelling and in personal adornment – while in his human functions he is reduced to an animal. (Marx, 1963: 124–5.)

By selling his labour power to the capitalist, by, consequently, being dominated and directed by design of work, technology, supervision, organization in the production of a product he will not own, and which will be sold in order to achieve more expropriated profit, the worker, according to Marx, not only becomes separated from his activities, his creativity, his products. He also supports his own domination and exploitation by creating profit which will be used to finance more employment of the same sort, or more machinery, which itself exacerbates alienation. The workers' products become their master (Avineri, 1968: 121), since past labour is used to finance new machinery, whereby the workers' faculties will be increasingly suppressd. It is in this sense that Marx says capital dominates labour, and the past dominates the present.

As Avineri notes, the implication of this line is that:

. . . the abolition of capital is a necessary prerequisite for the abolition of alienation. Since to Marx capital by definition engenders alienation, no amelioration in the conditions of labour can basically change the position of the worker so long as capital survives . . . Marx's concern is not the standard of living of the worker *per se* but the quality of life of the human being epitomized in the worker. (Avineri, 1968: 121.)

Under capitalism, then, the worker finds that his product 'ceases to be the objective embodiment of the individual's own personality and the distinctive expression of his creative powers and interests' (Schacht, 1970: 85). His work is oppressive, his rewards partial. These are the elements of alienation: that the worker not only loses control, and becomes dominated, loses possibility for expression, as his activity becomes directed and designed in the pursuit of profit, but also that these products, and the profit they generate, increase the power of the capitalist and finance more oppressive work arrangements. In this sense work and work products are not only separated from the worker, they are *hostile* to him.

Summary

Chapter 1 outlined the major features of the new industrial organizations of the industrial period, i.e. for the first time on such a scale, work was organized around employed labour; it was concentrated in large-scale manufactories, with new technologies and principles of work organization; the division of labour was specialized and developed to an extent, and in directions, which were entirely new; the new organizations faced very serious problems of recruitment, discipline and control, which in turn reflected a change in attitudes towards work and employment, from traditional to modern rational attitudes. Furthermore these developments within the factory were accompanied by the development of new specialisms and skills, notably that of management, for as work was subdivided, management must take on the functions of integration and coordination. These managers gradually initiated new, direct forms of control, and, in time, they themselves were faced with increasingly bureaucratic forms of control. Finally it was noted that throughout the industrial period, loose, indirect forms of control and employment were increasingly replaced by more direct forms of control and of employment, as managers replaced extensive use of labour by intensive forms: sub-contract and long hours were replaced by direct employment, shorter hours, fastidiously designed work, and the explicit emergence of the cash-nexus as the organizing principle of employment.

In this chapter the reactions of three major seminal

theorists to these developments were briefly described. Certain similarities and differences emerged. If, in general terms, the theorists agreed in what was occurring, they differed sharply on the origins and implications of the changes. There was agreement, for example, on the personal deprivations and indignities suffered by workers in the new work organizations. There was agreement that these were occasioned by technology, work organization, the division of labour, de-skilling etc. There was agreement that these developments could – or, in the case of Marx, would – result in societal instability through the emergence of classes and class conflict. There was agreement that the new work organizations represented entirely new principles of organization – rationality, the market, individualism and anti-traditionalism, and new forms of organization which articulated these principles. There was agreement that the new organizational forms not only constituted a major threat to societal stability; they also represented a major risk to personal freedom and autonomy. Modern work forms are seen by all three theorists to result in the domination of the individual, so that he has lost control over aspects of his work, his activity, his nature.

There is also basic disagreement, however; most importantly, about the *origins* of these 'pathologies', classes and organizations. Crudely, it is possible to see a major distinction between Marx and Durkheim, with Weber occupying a centre position. For Marx, these various developments in the organization of work, with their attendant consequences for society and the individual, are nothing less than the direct expression of a new, emergent form of economy – capitalism. These are no incidental problems, no results of the process of *industrialization*. They are, quite unequivocally, the direct statement of capitalist priorities and values. For Durkheim, however, the key development is that of industrialization. The personal costs, the pathologies of work and work conflicts, are deviations, unhealthy consequences of a too rapid process of industrialization. While their consequences for personal freedom and well-being, and for social integration, are noted (and regretted), Durkheim is quite clear that they are curable, abnormal forms of institutions and activities which should, normally, be assisting the integration and stability of society. Their elimination requires reform, argues Durkheim, not revolution. 'Anomie' and class conflict follow the lack of regulation of industrial relations, and the unsynchronized developments of the division of labour. These circumstances could be altered by the development of the regulatory role of the state and the setting up of occupational associations operating as intermediate centres of regulation and solidarity. They are the result of the unconditional development of the division of labour, not of *capitalism*.

This position does not however stop Durkheim from mounting a vigorous critique of the personal costs of industrialization, costs which follow the breakdown of control and moral regulation. While the assumptions and prescriptions inherent in the concept of anomie differ radically from those inherent in Marx's concept of alienation (see Horton, 1964; Lukes, 1967), it can be said that both are 'Critical concepts . . . [which] imply the judgement of society in terms of ideal, or at least future and unrealized standards.' (Horton, 1964: 286.)

Weber occupies an intermediate position. The key determinant variable is the spread of rationality in bureaucracy and capitalism. Although he is aware of the distinguishing features of capitalism, and notes the close connections between capitalism – and capitalist rationality – and the development of bureaucracy, he also, crucially, notes that bureaucracy, with the modes of appropriation or 'alienation' that accompany it, together with the development of rational institutions (accountancy etc.) would be a necessary feature of a socialist society. He argues, as we have noted:

... the capitalist system has undeniably played a major role in the development of bureaucracy ... Its development, largely under capitalistic auspices, has created an urgent need for stable, strict, intensive, and calculable administration ... [and] capitalism in its modern stages of development strongly tends to foster the development of bureaucracy ... Conversely, capitalism is the most rational economic basis for bureaucratic administration and enables it to develop in the most rational form. (Weber, 1964: 338.)

But, at the same time, capitalism is by no means alone in this close relationship with bureaucracy and rationality. Indeed, the only alternative to bureaucracy is 'reversion in every field to small-scale organization or administrative dilettantism, for "socialism" would . . . require a still higher degree of formal bureaucratization than capitalism.' (Weber, 1964:339.)

Inevitably associated with bureaucracy is the widespread expropriation of the employee – of all grades and sorts – and their exposure to the values and criteria of rationality. All grades of worker or employee are expropriated from ownership of the means of production under rational bureaucracy, not just shop-floor workers, as in Marx. For Weber, the most significant features of modern work organizations – and their personal consequences – are not restricted to capitalist societies, although he argues for a close link between the development of capitalism and bureaucracy. Thus the increase in the degree and form of the division of labour derives not simply from capitalism *per se*, but from the emergence of rationality in modern Western societies; a development which relates closely to the development of capitalism, but is not synonymous with it.

There is a complicated relationship between the

approaches and preoccupations of the theorists discussed above and more recent organizational theory. Some of the early themes have continued to excite interest and concern; but often in a rather muted form. Others have almost disappeared. At the same time conventional organization theory has developed its own interests. Often these relate closely to managerial problems of morale and organizational design. All in all, there has been a shift from interest in the societal level – the relationship between organizations and the societies within which they exist; the societal implications of organizational structures etc. – to the organizational level. As Mouzelis observes: 'Taking as their starting point Weber's ideal type of bureaucracy (which was used by Weber for broad cross-cultural and historic comparisons) they (more recent writers) tried to modify it and build a more empirical model of bureaucracy, more suitable for an analysis of the internal structure of bureaucratic organizations.' (Mouzelis, 1967: 167.) In so doing they move away from the 'broad scope', 'historical perspective' and 'humanistic orientation' of the early theorists, and give their attention to more narrow questions of internal organizational structure, or to problems of work design and productivity (Salaman, 1978).

Nevertheless, it is plain that the three theoretical traditions outlined by Durkheim, Weber and Marx still exercise an enormous influence over more recent organization theory, most of which can be seen to articulate some version of the concepts, assumptions and problematics developed in the early theorists' reactions to the startling organizational developments of the early industrial period. This is not to say, however, that all modern organization theory can be regarded in this way; for much of it takes its problematics from what are seen as more practical considerations. Nor is it to claim that the ancestry of all modern organization theory in classic concerns is always clear, or that modern organization theory always does justice to the theory from which it springs. But it is being asserted that both the perspectives of analysis clearly delineated in the works of the early theorists, and the characteristic foci of those traditions (the pathologies of organizational work; a theory of organizational structure; and a theory of class or stratification within organizations) continue to dominate the sociology of organizations. The remainder of this book is given over to a presentation and critique of the ways in which current research on organization deals with these questions, and how, in so doing, it articulates versions of these origins.

3 Alienation and the Meaning of Work

The theorists whose various sociologies of work were discussed in the previous chapter shared an interest in the personal deprivations of work – what might be called a concern for the personal pathology of work – in modern industrial society which, although diverse in its details, had a number of features in common: a vigorous humanitarianism; an attempt to evaluate work conditions against some moral standard; and an attempt to relate work deprivations to the form of society within which they occur. The concepts of alienation and anomie are integral parts of distinctive social theories. As such they not only reveal these theoretical contexts, they also develop a thorough critique of outstanding forms of deprivation and injustice current within modern societies.

However the concepts which originally were used as part of a radical and moral critique of modern industrial/capitalist society have, in some hands at least, become part of an effort to support and defend such social structures. The history of the progressive employment of the concepts in question reveals much about recent trends within sociology, the relationship between sociology and dominant social institutions, and the ideological nature of much so-called 'value-free' sociology which is advanced at the expense of the overtly committed theorizing of these early writers.

This chapter is concerned with a number of questions:

how far have the conceptualizations of the deprivation of modern work as advanced by Durkheim, Weber and Marx been employed and developed by more recent organizational or industrial sociologists? How far have the issues that preoccupied the early theorists continued to interest sociologists? And how far have new conceptualizations replaced the original ones? Answers to these questions reveal much about the sociology of work and organizations.

The basic problem and distinction are clear. On the one hand are writers who insist that no thorough or illuminating analysis of the meaning (deprivation, costs, frustrations) of work is possible without some clearly considered conception of what work could/should be like, and without some critical analysis of modern society, the forms of work which are absolutely integral to it, and the overall structures of domination and culture. On the other hand are those writers who regard the concepts of alienation and anomie simply as descriptions of possible empirical relationships between specific work arrangements and workers' attitudes and psychologies. For these writers the concepts are useful only when stripped of their unfortunate critical and ideological embellishments.

So, for example, articulating a version of the first position, Horton remarks that:

In the works of Marx and Durkheim, there are no simple operational definitions of alienation and anomie on either a psychological or sociological level. The concepts imply complete social theories explaining relationships between a social condition and behaviour. Critical concepts, they also imply the judgment of society in terms of ideal, or at least future and unrealized standards . . . alienation and anomie . . . represent radical criticisms of specific historical situations. (Horton, 1964: 286.)

On the other hand, Faunce, after briefly summarizing Marx's definition of alienation, writes that:

These [Marx's] meanings of alienation have an anachronistic ring in the middle of the twentieth century. Laying aside for the moment metaphysical concerns with 'human essence' and polemics regarding who *should* own the products of labour and the means of productions it is doubtful that many workers today *experience* these forms of alienation. To the extent that a sense of deprivation is the subjective counterpart of alienation, it seems unlikely that automobile workers feel alienated because they do not own either the assembly line or the completed automobiles that few even see leaving the assembly line. (Faunce, 1968: 86.)

For Horton and others such 'value-free', empiricist and operationalized conceptions of work in modern society are examples of the ideological, indeed alienated, status of sociology. He writes: 'Alienated thinking is especially apparent when the sociologist thinks about alienation . . . dehumanization has set in, the concepts have become transmogrified into things instead of evaluations about things, and it is no longer clear what alienated men are alienated from.' (Horton, 1964: 284.)

As was made clear in Chapter 2, Marx, Weber and Durkheim developed their own distinctive approaches to the pathologies of work in modern society, each articulating an approach which reflected the larger theory of modern society. For Weber, the alienation of modern society results from the parallel development of capitalism and bureaucracy, each based upon, and expressing, rationality and rationalization. Market behaviour is, ideal-typically, governed only by rationally calculated interests and exchanges. 'There are no obligations of brotherliness or reverence, and none of those spontaneous human relations that are sustained by personal unions.' (Weber, 1968: 636.)

This rationality is echoed in the organizing principles of the enterprise and the bureaucracy, both of which expropriate the employee from any vestigial rights in, or control over, his work or employment and subject him to ever increasing regulation and domination. It is in this expropriation, domination and rationalization – processes which Weber also recognizes as characteristic of the development of bureaucracy within *socialist* societies, that the alienation of modern man resides.

For Marx, alienation refers in all its work-based forms to the separation of man the worker from his tools, activities, creativity, fellow man, product of his labour, as a result of his position within a structure of hostile organization and domination. At work, men become 'means' for the pursuit of others' ends – profit. As a necessary result of the capitalist organization of labour, workers lose control over their work and ownership of their products. The alienation of the modern workers in capitalism stems from the commodity-like status of his labour, with all its ramifications.

Anomie, on the other hand, refers to the extent, or state of moral regulation applying to work. The pathologies of modern work stem not from the economic context, but from the disjuncture between work activities, aspirations and organizations, and regulation by values and tradition. Work is characterized by anomie to the extent that it has lost its moral character, its cultural significance.

The question of the personal significance of working-class – or, increasingly, white-collar – work has attracted an enormous amount of attention, for reasons which are discussed below. For some of this research the concepts and approaches of the early theorists have been a source of inspiration – although as we shall see these concepts have frequently been employed in highly idiosyncratic and partial ways. But much of this research appears entirely indifferent to, possibly even ignorant of, the notions of alienation and anomie, preferring to replace such 'loaded' concepts with what are seen as more useful and detailed measurement. In this preference, such research reveals its origins in issues of practical, governmental and managerial significance.

Most of this work is overtly empiricist – attempting to measure attitudes towards, or responses to, various aspects of work, and assessing the features of work which are of prime importance. It is not hard to see the appeal of such research: aggressively atheoretical in the main it seeks to supply answers to what are seen as urgent managerial, political and social problems. For example, the Director of the Institute of Human Relations, Yale, introducing Walker and Guest's classic, *Man on the Assembly Line*, speaks of the 'practical suggestions concerning changes in the management of assembly lines that may accrue from this and similar studies', and later adds, as an example of such a useful finding, the fact that 'the authors found in this plant a few workers who reported that they were quite happy doing simple repetitive and paced jobs. What are the personality characteristics of such persons?' It is however possible that this concern for practical answers to the problems experienced by those who run or own organizations, or who fund research, has, ironically, stood in the way of any genuine understanding of the meaning employees attach to their work.

The origins of much of this search for accurate assessment of the impact of modern forms of work on employees in practical managerial problems is well established. Scientific management, for example, while it did not require happy workers, nor ask anything of employees but a concern for financial rewards, certainly depended on a continuously high level of employee emphasis on maximizing money rewards. Although this 'instrumentality' as it was later called may have seemed mere common sense to Taylor (who saw it as the orientation which reflected the explicitly market-oriented employment relationship), in practice it turned out to be less pervasive and stable than Taylor hoped. Despite its claims to having isolated the basic ingredients of the employment situation and to have integrated these into a system of work design which simultaneously maximized benefits for employee and employer alike, Taylorism, like more recent work ideologies, can be seen to depend on the workers developing a narrow, and by no means reliable attitude towards work. Such an attitude could not, however, be assumed. In this country, much early influential work by the National Institute of Industrial Psychology, which was established in 1921 (see Rose, 1975, for a useful discussion of the role of the NIIP), was supported, as Friedmann notes, by a government panel on 'Human Factors', which had been set up because of governmental concern about the practical consequences of modern types of work. The impetus behind such research (into 'fatigue' and monotony) was the same as that which inspired the earlier research by the Health of Munitions Workers' Committee in the First World War into the relationship between hours and levels of productivity: the search for greater output. As Friedmann puts it, this sort of research is not the result of sentimentality, rather it reflects a growing disquiet about the possibly damaging effects of modern forms of work – damaging not least, to levels of production (Friedmann, 1961).

Early research during the First World War demonstrated, at least in this country, that production was not simply a function of the total number of hours worked, and that indeed, a reduction in hours could result in increased levels of output, with all the obvious implications of the key significance of the workers' psychological and sociological orientations. The Hawthorne research further confirmed the importance of attitudinal factors. Whatever else these researches demonstrated they suggested to the alert manager that the happy worker was a more productive worker.[1]

The Human Relations movement, with its emphasis on communications, participative management and supervision, and concern for 'artificial' restriction of output took the relationship between workers' attitudes and feelings and levels of output very seriously. Later approaches to, or ideologies of, industrial work, such as those whom Rose calls the organizational psycho-technologists (Maslow, Herzberg, McGregor etc.) also shared the conviction that achieving greater personal satisfaction (or, in their terms, fulfillment) at work was synonymous with increased efficiency. Rose remarks of these writers, 'Clearly men of goodwill, they are genuinely concerned with the well-being of all groups in the organization, and eager to remove destructive stresses. But equally obviously they are very concerned about efficiency and profitability . . . their whole analysis . . . tends to show . . . a fortuitous concurrence . . . between individual and organizational needs.' (Rose, 1975: 193.)

Managerial interest in the personal meaning of working-class work is not a result merely of the salience attached to workers' attitudes by changing managerial ideologies of work, important though these may be. Management concern with discovering the nature of workers' attitudes – or, as it used to be called, morale – is a direct response to the increasing pressure on management to employ labour even more thoroughly, rationally and efficiently. Rapidly changing technologies, market pressures, the increasing organization and strength of unionized labour and the (relative) rise in the costs of labour have resulted in management efforts to intensify the exploitation of labour by increasing, through technology, organization and integration, the productivity of each employee. The modern corporation, despite its apparent differences from the individual entrepreneur constitutes, as Baran and Sweezy have argued, only an *institutionalization* of the capitalist function. And, 'The heart and core of the capitalist function is accumulation: accumulation has always been the prime mover of the system, the locus of its conflicts, the source of both is triumphs and its disaster.'

(Baran and Sweezy, 1968: 55.)

The efficiency and success of the modern large-scale corporation depends on thorough and elaborate planning. The problem is no longer simply one of finding the best way to reduce the costs of commodities, it is the larger question of what commodities to produce. In making decisions, the senior members of the organization must have available information on materials, performances, markets, costs etc. 'The modern business organization,' writes Galbraith, ' . . . consists of numerous individuals who are engaged, at any given time, in obtaining, digesting or exchanging and testing information.' (Galbraith, 1969: 72.) One important type of information concerns employees' commitment and reliability. In an increasingly planned and organized world, the continuing recalcitrance and unreliability of labour not only constitute a source of managerial uncertainty, it is also, with advanced technology, and the increasing cost of product development, a critical and aggravating area of inherent instability and unpredictability.

For the manager of the large corporation 'the fact that the economy of large corporations is more, not less, dominated by the logic of profit-making than the economy of small entrepreneurs ever was' (Baran and Sweezy, 1968: 40), occasions considerable difficulties. Under modern conditions – market, technological, organizational etc. – such profit increasingly depends upon the efficient use, detailed regulation and thorough monitoring of employees. Yet such efficiency frequently depends upon control and work systems which are likely negatively to influence employees' work commitment. Under such circumstances workers' work attitudes become of more than mere academic interest and importance: they become of very considerable practical importance to management.

Parallel with these managerial priorities, there is evidence that workers themselves are decreasingly prepared to tolerate conventional work arrangements and subordinations. (See, e.g. Shepard and Herrick, 1972.) It is in the context of this situation that the search for 'humanized' work takes on its true significance.

What then of these attempts to discover the work attitude of today's workers? What, if anything do they tell us? If the established concepts and approaches of the early sociologists have been ignored in favour of 'practical' empiricism, what benefits can be seen to accrue?

Obviously this is not the place to attempt a thorough survey of the work satisfaction literature, should such a task be either desirable or possible. Besides, other authors have usefully reviewed this literature elsewhere (Parker, 1964; Davis, 1971; Blauner, 1960). What is required in the present context however, is an overview of the major conclusions reached by such studies, for it is only in the light of such findings that any analysis of the overall utility of this empiricist approach can be attempted.

First, a remarkably large number of studies apparently demonstrate high general levels of work satisfaction. Blauner, in his useful review of this literature, agrees with the conclusion of a British researcher that: 'Even under the existing conditions, which are far from satisfactory, most workers like their jobs. Every survey of workers' attitudes which has been carried out, no matter in what industry, indicates that this is so.' (Brown, 1954: 190–1.) Indeed, Blauner concludes that by 1958, analysis of the numerous available work satisfaction studies (406 studies in 1958!) showed that on average only thirteen per cent were dissatisfied. As we shall see, Blauner and many others have raised a number of methodological and other criticisms of these figures. Nevertheless, in the face of the earlier conceptualizations of the meaning of industrial work developed by Marx, Weber and Durkheim, such findings appear remarkable. They have been confirmed more recently. A review of job satisfaction surveys suggests that most workers are satisfied with their work. And a Gallup poll of 1973 shows that three out of four workers are satisfied with their work.

Secondly, however, most studies show that extent of satisfaction varies with certain features of the work. When questioned about their willingness or preparedness to take the same job if they could start their working lives anew, workers' responses varied with their occupation. Professional, management groups were much more likely to choose the same job again than were unskilled or semi-skilled workers. The findings suggest that the general impression of large-scale satisfaction with work should be viewed sceptically: even within the context of the strange world of work satisfaction questionnaires, it is clear that workers are able to differentiate and evaluate various work conditions and circumstances. Precisely which work features are of most importance in establishing levels of satisfaction is not clear, but certain broad patterns emerge. The literature on work satisfaction contains a number of attempts to isolate and evaluate the discrete elements of jobs which workers find satisfying or dissatisfying. Despite the variety of these conclusions certain generalizations are possible. For one thing, 'they are all likely to include, in one way or another, such variables as the income attached to a job, supervision, working conditions, social relations and the variety and skill intrinsic in the work itself.' (Blauner, 1960: 476.) Clearly these factors vary with class position or with the status of the occupation. It is one of the most persistent and obvious features of inequality in general and work-based inequalities in particular, that privilege or deprivation on one dimension (for example, financial rewards,) tends to be closely related to levels of privilege, or deprivation, on others (for example, the nature of the work itself, exposure to risk of accident, unemployment etc.).

Thirdly, these surveys show the continuing and persuasive significance of the process of organizational control as a

major factor in determining levels of satisfaction. (See
Blauner, 1960: 478–81.) As Chinoy points out in his
analysis of assembly-line work, for example, control in
assembly-line work is transmitted mechanically through
the speed of the line. The result? 'The unrelieved and
characteristically unchanging tempo of the moving conveyor . . . tends to generate an unusual amount of tension
and an urgent, almost explosive, desire for some break in
the day's routine.' (Chinoy, 1964: 61.)

Most workers do not work on assembly lines; nevertheless the evidence suggests that whatever the manner in
which work regulation and organizational subordination
are organized the very experience of being controlled,
regulated and monitored gives rise to feelings of dissatisfaction. (See, for example, Parker *et al.*, 1977: 161–2.)
Similarly, Blumberg, on the basis of an exhaustive survey
of the literature concludes that 'there is hardly a study in
the entire literature which fails to demonstrate that
satisfaction in work is enhanced or that other generally
acknowledged beneficial consequences accrue from a
genuine increase in workers' decision-making power.'
(Blumberg, 1968: 123.)

Fourthly, it is clear that workers' attitudes towards
their work are more complex than the crude satis-
faction/dissatisfaction axis suggests: workers' attitudes are
multi-faceted and variable; they vary not only in *direction*
(i.e. positive or negative) but in *intensity*: people can be
dissatisfied with aspects of their work precisely because
they are highly involved in it, such that certain dis-
advantages (as they see it) matter to them. Indeed Crozier's
analysis of white-collar work finds just this: 'the more one
rises in the professional hierarchy, the greater the tendency
to be interested in one's work and to complain about one's
position.' (Crozier, 1971: 97.)

Etzioni has suggested conceptualizing the emotional
significance of work in terms of the concept of involve

ment, defined as the emotional orientation of a person towards an object, in this case towards an aspect of work, or job. Other writers, notably Dubin, have suggested that workers vary in (a) the aspects of work which they consider important, or to which they are attached; and (b) in the intensity of their involvement in these objects. Various lists of such relevant features of work have been suggested. Etzioni emphasizes aspects of the organizational power system, including such things as: organizational regulations, rewards and senior personnel (Etzioni, 1961: 11). Dubin separates various rewards – money, power, status – from aspects of the work and the work place technology and the work itself and what is called 'systems of the Work environment' which includes various possible categorizations or memberships associated with work – i.e. union, work group, occupation (Dubin, 1976: 290). Additional writers have suggested their own lists. Walker and Guest, similarly, separate seven aspects of the total job situation which generate satisfaction or dissatisfaction: (1) the worker's immediate job; (2) his relations with his fellows; (3) pay and security; (4) his relations with his supervisor; (5) general working conditions; (6) promotion and transfer; (7) his relations with the union (Walker and Guest, 1952).

Dubin argues that increasingly, for many workers, work is no longer what he calls a 'central life interest'. Increasingly, workers seek emotional gratification and significance not in work activities, but outside, in leisure. Indeed some writers have even gone so far as to argue that leisure may compensate for the deprivations of work: though others, for example Friedmann, have insisted that fragmented and meaningless work may result in passive or pathological, leisure habits. The most important implication of the argument about the emotional salience of work to the modern worker lies in the common argument that workers who do not have a 'central life interest' in their work will define their work in 'instrumental' terms, i.e. as a *means* of achieving satisfaction elsewhere. This view sees the workers' withdrawal from work as related to the meaninglessness of the work itself, and as resulting in an emphasis on the rewards the work does offer – money – which is required in order to 'live outside'. Chinoy expresses this view thus: 'work . . . has become, in the workers' eyes, primarily instrumental. Its only value lies in what it makes possible off the job.' (Chinoy, 1964: 75.) The work of Goldthorpe *et al.* confirms the existence and nature of this orientation to work. (Goldthorpe *et al.*, 1968. See also Walker and Guest, 1952: 90; and Aronowitz, 1973.)

Such 'instrumental' orientations to work are most common among workers who are deprived of other sources of meaning in their work: whose work lacks any 'intrinsic' satisfaction or creativity.

This brief summary of the major conclusions of the prolific literature of work satisfaction highlights certain obvious difficulties. The most immediate of these is what Fox (1980) has called the meaning of meaning: that is to say, what do these findings mean? There are serious methodological difficulties, for example, as numerous writers have remarked. Blauner notes that respondents may find it hard to ignore the general cultural value placed on the importance of work; they may regard a rejection of their own work as reflecting a personal failure or deficiency (Blauner, 1964: 474). Parker *et al.* (1977) note that these general findings tell us very little since we do not know what the questions are actually measuring: they may, for example, be describing levels of *resignation*, rather than satisfaction. Fox (1971) makes a similar point when he notes that people asked about their work can respond on one of two levels: those which experience suggests may be realized, and those which however unrealistic are retained as offering some more radical improvement. In these terms, of course, the happy worker may indeed be a myth (Swados, 1957), since his satisfaction, as measured by the studies dicussed above, is merely a consequence of acquiescence and resignation. And as such it is unstable and superficial. Similarly the worker who, ostensibly, does not regard his work as a central life interest but is prepared to sacrifice work challenges in order to achieve a desired life-style out of work, may be revealing a deprivation which he is unable to overcome but which he is unlikely to accept entirely and vigorously. Certainly it seems ill-advised to regard such acquiescence, in the face of massive societal and economic pressures, as satisfaction in the same sense that a craftsman or professional can be satisfied with his work.

The recent *Work in America* Report supplies a good illustration of these deficiencies of the numerous work satisfaction studies which reveal high levels of worker satisfaction. The authors note the inadequacy of many of the conventional questions used in such surveys, which simply tap surface responses, or levels of acquiescence. They note that little probing is required to reach the deep despair which an increasing proportion of the work force feel about their work. This report concluded:

Simplified tasks for those who are not simple-minded, close supervision by those whose legitimacy rests only on an hierarchical structure, and jobs that have nothing but money to offer in an affluent age are simply rejected. For many of the new workers, the monotony of work and scale of organization and their inability to control the pace and style of work are a cause for *a resentment which they, unlike older workers, do not repress.* (Work in America, 1973: 18; my emphasis.)

The authors of this report note that no efforts to improve the nature of work experience can have any serious effect unless and until it challenges 'much of what passes as efficiency in our industrial society' (ibid: 19).

The problem of the meaning of many of these analyses of work satisfaction is not simply a methodological one, in the technical sense. It also raises questions of the nature of the attitude being measured (i.e. what is its significance to the person?) and, most critically, the question of the origin of these attitudes, or of the expectations which people have of their work. By regarding workers' attitudes as responses to aspects of their work arrangements, these studies, with some notable exceptions, ignore the role of out-of-work factors in establishing certain patterns of work expectation, self-image, work cultures etc. As we shall see, it is this process of work culturation within the larger society, as well as the plant, that alienation theorists emphasize. The studies by Goldthorpe *et al.* and others – see below – which point to the existence and significance of out-of-work factors in developing certain distinctive work orientations support such emphasis.

The findings discussed above raise certain problems, furthermore; for one thing, most of them seem remarkably unrealistic and naïve in asserting the generally high level of work satisfaction in societies where work is characterized by numerous indices of withdrawal, hostility, frustration etc. Secondly, the findings seem contradictory: workers are satisfied, but they would not choose the same job if they could start their work lives anew, and so on. A revealing instance of this ambiguity is contained in Walker and Guest's study. When analysing assembly-line workers' attitudes towards the various relevant aspects of their work they reported: 'the attitude of a majority of our sample towards each of the elements was favourable.' (Walker and Guest, 1952: 139.) But when they asked the workers if they thought the company did much/a little/nothing for the men, the were faced with a surprising finding: over half thought the company did nothing for the men; and what's more, the responses were loaded wih 'emotional impact'; there was 'angry criticism in words charged with emotion'. This finding clearly troubled and surprised the researchers who go to some lengths to explain it in terms of the particular characteristics of the question itself. But they are forced to admit that this hostility reveals a 'psychological process of frustration passing into aggression . . . and focusing upon the company as the agent responsible for what they did not like.' (Walker and Guest, 1952: 140.)

Chinoy reports of assembly-line work that it is so demanding that one worker, echoing others, complained: 'You get the feeling, everybody gets the feeling, whenever the line jerks everybody is wishing, "break down, baby!"' (Chinoy, 1965: 71.)

Similar findings can be found elsewhere in the literature: apparently high levels of general satisfaction allied with dramatic outbursts of resentment and hostility, or acceptance of working arrangements and colleagues allied with withdrawal and apathy (Crozier, 1971). The general inference would seem undeniable. The empirical analysis or measurement of levels of work satisfaction is frequently methodologically suspect. Very often the lack of any proper theoretical conception of the nature of work in modern society, or of the interests that determine the design of work and organization, or of the forces in society at large which encourage the development of appropriate and realistic expectations, entirely invalidates these exercises in a-theoretical, management-biased, empiricism. This type of industrial sociology must be criticized not only because it is, in the event, hopelessly out of touch with work events and conflicts, but also because frequently it represents, in its apparent value-freedom, the very alienation of sociology which Horton remarked.

This sort of analysis must be seen in the same terms that Baran and Sweezy have used to castigate much current work in micro-economics; that it 'aims at exploring the conditions for raising the efficiency and improving the performance of the capitalist enterprise. Its specific content is therefore determined by the needs of the capitalist enterprise and by the standards of efficiency and performance under which it operates.' (Baran and Sweezy, 1968: 295.)

The empirical and practical shortcomings of many of these surveys follows from the authors' systematic rejection of a conception of work which is actually shared by many of those they study: that work is a waste of life; that work experiences, activities and subordinations represent in acute form the oppression of the individual. Rather than consider how it is that men and women are coerced and indoctrinated into wasting their lives in meaningless toil (and, apparently, into finding the experience a source of 'satisfaction'); rather than consider by what means individuals put up with experiences of work-based inequality and subordination, or analyse the 'rationality' and origins of work design, those who measure levels of work satisfaction prefer to emphasize and reify the *outcomes* of these processes of coercion and enculturation. The nature, dynamics and justice of the system itself is disregarded. All this constitutes a remarkable contrast to the analyses of the early sociologists. To quote Marx: 'More than any other mode of production, [capitalism] squanders human lives, or living labour, and not only blood and flesh, but also nerve and brain. Indeed it is only through the most enormous waste of the individual development that the development of mankind is at all preserved and maintained in the epoch of history immediately preceeding the conscious reorganization of society.' (Marx, 1959.)

However, there are some studies of the meaning of work which explicitly employ the conceptualization – alienation and anomie – of the early theorists, and which therefore might be expected to avoid some of the problems outlined above. It is to these studies that we now turn.

There have been occasions when sociological interest in the quality of working experience has explicitly centred on the concepts of alienation and anomie. Frequently, in modern definitions attempts are made to integrate these concepts so that when operationalized, alienation contains a dimension of 'anomic' origin, such as 'social alienation' which, in Blauner's influential utilization of the concept alienation, is used to refer to the situation when 'the worker feels no sense of belonging in the work situation and is unable to identify or uninterested in identifying with the organization and its goals.' (Blauner, 1967: 24.) This collapsing of anomie into modern definitions of alienation, whereby it becomes merely another element in the various dimensions of the concept, was precedented in the work of Seeman (1959).

Blauner's study deserves attention. Briefly, Blauner claims to be concerned with the extent of alienation in modern society. He aspires to steer a middle course between the 'simplistic', 'politically inspired propaganda' of Marxist assertions of the fact and pervasiveness of alienation, and the bland empiricism of those who assert that the majority of workers are happy with their jobs and uninterested in resistance or militancy. Blauner accepts that there are 'powerful alienating tendencies in modern factory technology and industrial organization'. But he seeks to recast 'a politically loaded controversy into a manageable scientific question'. The focus of his enquiry, then, is 'to determine under what conditions these tendencies are intensified in modern industry, what situations give rise to different forms of alienation and what consequences develop for workers and for productive systems.' (Blauner, 1967: 4.)

This enquiry results in Blauner isolating three major elements of industrial organization which determine levels of alienation: technology, the division of labour (social organization) and economic structure. The most important of these (the most 'fateful', in Blauner's terms) is technology. This is important not only because it is the major determinant of levels of alienation, but because technology strongly influences the other elements of industrial organization. Blauner separates four types of technology – four characteristic forms of production, each with 'distinctive technological arrangements': craft technology, with little mechanization or standardization; machine-tending, with high mechanization, where workers 'mind' machines; assembly line, based around the conveyor belt; and continuous process, where the processes are carried out automatically.[2]

Alienation is defined by Blauner as 'a general syndrome made up of a number of different objective conditions and subjective feeling states which emerge from certain relationships between workers and the sociotechnical settings of employment.' (Blauner, 1967: 15.) Four distinct dimensions of alienation are isolated: powerlessness, which is broken down into four modes – '(1) separation from ownership of the means of production and the finished products; (2) the inability to influence general managerial policies; (3) the lack of control over the conditions of employment; and (4) the lack of control over the immediate work process' (Blauner, 1967: 16); meaninglessness, social alienation (isolation or social integration) and self-estrangement. Self-estrangement refers to the fact that 'the worker may become alienated from his inner self in the activity of work.' (Blauner, 1967: 26.)

The main thrust of Blauner's argument is that there is a relationship between the four dimensions of alienation and the four types of technology. These relationships have been well summarized by Eldridge (1971).

The interesting feature of this analysis is the conclusion that, viewed historically, the four types of technology can be regarded as characteristic of succeeding periods of capitalism. We are now in the epoch of automation, represented by continuous process work. In historical terms, Blauner argues that alienation has varied in ways that can be described on a graph by an inverted U-curve. In the early period alienation was relatively low. During industrialization, mechanization and rationalization, there is simultaneous intensification of all the dimensions of alienation. 'But,' he continues, 'with automated industry there is a counter-trend, one that we can fortunately expect to become even more important in the future . . . the chemical industry, shows that automation increases the worker's control over his work process and checks the further division of labour growth of large factories. The result is meaningful work in a more cohesive, integrated industrial climate.' (Blauner, 1967: 182.)

And so alienation and anomie are avoided by new, characteristically modern forms of technology and organization. Work is more meaningful, control is reallocated; the worker is 'integrated' into the enterprise; the 'innate' hostility between workers and management is replaced by understanding of the necessary functional differentiation and interdependence of the organization. Integration (i.e. non-anomie) is achieved by a number of factors including: the balanced skill distribution, the differentiated occupational structure which permits opportunity for mobility and achievement; the size and organization of continuous process plants (which permit the development of cohesive pro-management, work groups); the work itself, and economic factors which promote security and prosperity.

Blauner's analysis can be questioned on a variety of points. The most basic concerns his definition and use of the concept alienation itself, and of his attempt to subsume anomie within it. This is no mere academic quibble, as we shall see: by defining alienation in terms of 'subjective feeling states' which vary in response to different work circumstances, he ignores the role of out-of-plant factors in generating distinctive forms and levels of orientation to work. And by inserting an isolation-integration dimension into a bowdlerized version of alienation he focuses attention on some forms of integration (pro-management cohesion, of the sort ascribed to continuous process workers) but not on others which might be *hostile* to the employing organization. Blauner's employment of alienation owes more to Durkheim than it does to Marx, both in its conceptualization of the origin of work pathologies and its view of the dynamics of organizational development.

Secondly, Blauner's analysis of the nature and implications of continuous process work is empirically contentious (Cotgrove and Vamplew, 1972).

Other writers have developed markedly different conceptions of the implications of this sort of work for political conflicts and class confrontations. Mallet (1963), for example, accepts that jobs in advanced industries usually involve more autonomy and involvement. But he argues that such circumstances do not lead to greater satisfaction. On the contrary, the worker in advanced industries is likely to find his relative lack of autonomy in other areas than his work all the more frustrating, by virtue of his responsibility and status at work. Although, for example, the technician is qualified, he lacks any control over the policies he executes. His is a limited autonomy. Essentially he is still powerless. The discrepancy between the technicians' relatively privileged position on some aspects of work and their subordinate, powerless situation on others, results in a feeling of relative deprivation and *increased* militancy. Low-Beer (1978) notes that such an analysis also raises the significance of technicians' experience of a discrepancy between the 'rationality' of the pursuit of profit, and the 'rationality' of science. Furthermore, Nichols and Beynon (1977), for example, argue that the reality of automated work is very different from Blauner's rosy picture: the majority of workers at the chemical plant they studied were still doing 'donkey' work – unskilled, dirty and arduous. They note that fifty per cent of work in chemical production is officially classified as demanding virtually no skill. Similarly, Gallie argues that Blauner exaggerates the satisfactions of automated work: 'highly advanced forms of

automation [do] not make work a source of deep satisfaction.' (Gallie, 1978: 87.) Furthermore, Blauner
neglected the serious deprivations caused by the shift-work
necessarily associated with automation.

Thirdly, Blauner's analysis lacks any explicit consideration of the *origins* of work and organizational structures.
Touraine (1971), for example, and Braverman (1974) argue
that the development of automation must be seen in the
context of the process of differentiation of functions within
modern, large-scale industry, whereby manual and non-
manual execution of tasks, and the design of tasks are
entirely separated. Under these conditions integration,
coordination and control become separate and critical
tasks. The computer is able to take on many of these
separated tasks. But in so doing, it establishes new
requirements for skilled and unskilled computer workers.
Blauner's analysis focuses on workers' responses to work
and technology, and possibilities of manipulating these,
but pays scant attention to the *forces* lying behind choice of
technology. Nor does he consider the possibility of a
determinant connection the other way: workers' attitudes
influencing management's choice of technology (see
Braverman, 1974).

Under capitalism, firms must not only strive to make
profits, but constantly explore new ways of increasing
profitability because of the persistent threat of the market,
of competition. No enterprise can afford to cease its efforts
to accumulate capital, for such relaxation leads to a lack of
competitiveness, a loss of existing levels of profit and
eventual bankruptcy or take-over. It is these market forces,
particularly at the international level, with the consequent
constant need to accumulate capital (to install new process
technologies and procedures, obtain new skills, gain
greater market 'penetration', greater market dominance)
which establish the need for the ever increasing intensification of the exploitation of labour. This means using every

possible method to increase the efficiency (in the context of capitalism) of labour, by the division of work, the organization of the flow of work, the management of fragmented procedures, and the design and installation of technology.

We shall return to these points later. First we must consider another utilization of alienation and anomie in analysis of modern work forms. Faunce's analysis, *Problems of an Industrial Society*, advances the thesis that 'conditions inherent in the social structure of industrial society result in the alienation of industrial man.' (Faunce, 1968: 2.) The book firmly adopts a structural-functionalist approach, employing the concept of role as its 'basic part', and regarding the differentiation of the societal structure as determined by three attributes of social units: division of labour, the distribution of status, and of power. Together these compose forms of structural differentiation. Social integration refers to the way the divided parts 'fit together'. It is one of Faunce's central arguments that processes of structural differentiation within industrial societies have occasioned severe problems of social integration. This latter concept is also defined in terms of roles: 'Degree of social integration then, refers to the extent to which *role definitions* either isolate people from each other and bring them into conflict with each other or link them together in conflict-free interaction. People who are isolated from each other tend to develop different attitudes, values, and patterns of behaviour.' (Faunce, 1968: 9.)

The inherent social problems of industrial society result from the coincidence of high levels of differentiation with low levels of social integration. And one aspect of industrial society which, more than any other, is directly and indirectly responsible for this disjuncture is the development and employment of modern production technology, which is best displayed in the process of automation.

Faunce argues that as a result of the disjuncture of

structural differentiation and social integration, the individual in modern society is alienated. His definition of alienation, however, differs markedly from that of Marx. For Faunce,

> . . . it seems clear that the complex differentiated division of labour generated by industrial technology would produce alienation from work irrespective of the type of economic system in which it is embedded. Large-scale production and bureaucratization, along with the functionally specialized nature of jobs, have made it impossible for workers to feel that they have an active and important role in the production process or that their work is an end in itself. (Faunce, 1968: 87.)

This passage contains some key ideas: that alienation is a function of industrialism not capitalism; that the division of labour is caused by technology; that alienation consists of workers' reactions to, or feelings about, divided and differentiated work within large-scale, bureaucratized settings. We shall return to these suggestions later in this chapter.

One of the most surprising features of Faunce's analysis is the way in which Marx's concept of alienation is systematically pruned of its 'anachronistic', 'metaphysical' and 'polemical' ingredients and redefined in terms of individuals' self-esteem. Faunce insists that originally alienation was used as 'a shorthand expression for all the socially-based psychological maladies of modern man' (Faunce, 1968: 88). Having thus muddled the origins and meaning of the expression he proceeds to offer clarification, but a clarification of a very peculiar sort.

For as Faunce sees alienation in terms of psychological maladies, his improved version constitutes an effort to isolate the basic features of such maladies which would cause people to withdraw themselves from, or minimize their personal investment in, an activity. According to Faunce a person's self – his view of himself – varies with his roles. Each role can offer a system of criteria for self-evaluation. These criteria may or may not be the same that are used by others to accord social status. An individual is alienated from his employing organization when the criteria used to evaluate him are different from those used by others to evaluate him. The obvious example of this condition is when workers define themselves in terms of their out-of-work roles and activities, but are defined by their employers in terms of their unskilled organizational role. Clearly this definition of alienation means that the condition can be seen as representing, on the personal level, the problem of lack of integration which Faunce regards as characteristic of industrial societies. The conditions which represent the manifestations of alienation – apathy, indifference – are seen as 'products of a lack of identification with, or commitment to, *shared* goals and beliefs' (Faunce, 1968: 101). This in turn is the result of the low status levels of many organizational positions, and the lack of integration of the work role with other out-of-work roles, and other factors (Faunce, 1968: 132).

Faunce and Blauner are by no means the only writers to seek to operationalize and de-politicize the concepts of alienation but there is no need in the present context to supply an exhaustive review of all such attempts. The two studies discussed above are sufficient to illustrate some general points about the applications of this concept.

The first point concerns the way in which the concept of alienation is defined and operationalized in these two studies. Marx was not the only theorist to offer a way of describing and conceptualizing the personal pathologies of work; both Weber and Durkheim also developed approaches to the understanding of the personal significance of modern types of work. Each of these approaches, despite their wide disparity, have some features in common. Each attempts to relate a humanitarian concern at the costs of modern work experiences to an analysis of the nature of modern society. In other words their analyses of work were couched in terms of their societal analyses. However, we find with the studies discussed above that little, if any, attention is paid to the social context of the processes and reactions under consideration. Work arrangements are seen to emerge automatically in response to other inexorable developments. They are seen, if they are accorded any attention at all, simply as cruel but unavoidable realities. Similarly, people's work attitudes are seen simply as *responses* to various isolated features of work arrangements.

The point is, however, not that these studies have no theory of society, no view of the determinants of organizational and work forms, no conception of the nature and origin of work attitudes, *but that these elements are held implicitly*. In seeking to depoliticize the concept of alienation and to establish a value-free approach to the measurement of the pathologies of work, Blauner and Dubin and others in fact articulate a covert version of one of the classic approaches. Their functionalism stems from, and represents, the Durkheimian tradition, but a Durkheimian approach which is masked (but not radically altered) by Marxist language – the language of alienation. This confusion between the language of Marxism, suitably emasculated, and the essence of functionalism characterizes and weakens these approaches.[3]

The two studies considered above raise two related questions: how thoroughly do they describe and explain workers' work attitudes; and how do they explain the nature and origins of work and organizational arrangements? It is in the context of these two issues that the basic dilemma, described at the beginning of this chapter, becomes central: is it possible and desirable to describe work attitudes simply as measurable responses to discrete work attributes, or should any thorough analysis of work attitudes seek to locate these in terms of an explicit theory of the interconnections between work-place arrangements, work attitudes and behaviour and the societal structure of interests and domination?

The next two chapters are devoted to a consideration of the two questions posed above: the nature and origins of work attitudes, and of the work arrangements towards which they are directed. We shall see that to consider these two issues takes us immediately to basic differences between what can broadly be described as Durkheimian (functionalist) and Marxist approaches to the pathologies of work.

4 Orientations to Work

Any discussion of the nature and origins of work attitudes is faced immediately by a central paradox: how is it that those who fill the monotonous, subordinate and (relatively) disadvantaged positions within the divisions of labour accept, or at least tolerate, their position? Worsley has remarked of inequality in this country: 'The uninterrupted albeit modified, dominance of the property-owning classes, in a society which has long been the most highly 'proletarianized' in the world, is surely one of the most striking phenomena of modern times.' (Worsley, 1964: 22.) The question can also be asked of work-based inequalities: how is it that they are tolerated, year after year?

For many writers on the meaning of work, different attitudes towards work are simply a response to various features of the work experienced. There are two implications of this one-sided, determinist approach: by focusing on technical aspects of work organization and design, the overall nature and goals of the system are ignored. This omission is, of course, all the more likely if technology and organization are themselves viewed as neutral elements of industrialization. In this way alienation, for example, can be seen, as Faunce regards it, as an inevitable result of the application of technology and rationality to the pursuit of economic growth in industrial societies. Alienation here has nothing to do with the *purposes* of the enterprise, everything to do with its organization and design.

Secondly, the emphasis on the determinant role of aspects of work or organization in generating attitudinal responses from the workers concerned means that the possibility of any process of preparation or socialization for the deprivations of work is ignored. Insufficient attention is devoted to the processes whereby people develop the remarkable aspirations which permit them to accept, however grudgingly, their work experiences.

The first of these implications has been vigorously denied by authors writing within a Marxist framework. For Braverman, Beynon, Sennett and Cobb, Nichols, Fox and others, the meaning of work, or the existence of alienation, is a result not simply of technology but of the purpose for which the technology is devised and installed – the control and exploitation of potentially recalcitrant labour. In this view, alienation results from the role of the market, antagonistic relations between managers and workers, and the overall organizational goal; the pursuit of profit, and the forms of work these generate: scientific management and the minute division of labour. Braverman, for example, argues, as did Marx (see Chapter 2), that alienation has nothing to do with job satisfaction. Alienation is a result of selling one's labour to another, of losing control and ownership of one's labour, product, tools and the work process itself (Braverman, 1975; see also, e.g., Foster, 1974). Thus, within capitalism, work is carried out by workers who, because they have no control over, or rights in, the outcome (a state of affairs which is reflected in all aspects of the design of work and control), are likely to be indifferent to their employers, if not hostile. By the same token, capitalism gives rise to characteristic forms of work design (Braverman, 1974).

Under such circumstances, workers learn to regard their job, in many cases quite accurately, as little more than a source of income. Since the major feature of work in capitalism is the purchase of labour power, and the predominance of the cash nexus, the employees learn the 'rules of the game' and develop instrumental orientations to work. But they never entirely learn to restrict their work aspirations to the financial. The prevalence of dissatisfaction with lack of control at work in the studies discussed earlier, and the occasional bursts of aggression and hostility described by Walker and Guest, Beynon, Chinoy and others, testify to the survival of some conception, albeit possibly at a 'low priority' level, of what work could be like, of the pain of missed opportunities (see Aronowitz, 1973). Capitalism and the ideology of instrumentalism denies the working-class majority intrinsic work satisfaction and aspirations for meaning and creativity. In this view, the prevalence of instrumentality not only accounts for much of the apparent work satisfaction (since this limits workers' aspirations to just one dimension, and permits satisfaction to be based upon relative comparisons and differentials), it also reflects workers' alienation. Thus Cotgrove remarks:

. . . an instrumental orientation to work stems primarily not from technology, but from the market situation; from the overriding need of men whose market situation is weak and vulnerable for a job which offers pay and security . . . it is the weakness of the contractual situation of the wage worker which leads him to attach such overriding importance to work as a source of secure income. (Cotgrove, 1972: 445, 448.)

It is in these terms that the high levels of work satisfaction recorded by some industrial sociologists are defined not as evidence of low levels of alienation, but of alienation itself. For workers to be satisfied with their work reflects their impoverished work expectations, or their concern only with financial rewards from work. Alienation is revealed in the aspirations towards work which workers in a capitalist society are pressured to develop, as well as in the economic, legal and organizational context of the

enterprise. As C. W. Mills has remarked, modern workers
do not compare themselves against some historical reality
of craftsmanship two hundred years ago: they make small-
scale, local comparisons, emphasize the only rewards they
are likely to receive – extrinsic ones. Mills writes: 'the
historical destruction of craftsmanship and of the old office
does not enter the consciousness of the modern wage-
worker or white-collar employee; much less is their absence
felt by him as a crisis, as it might have been if, in the course
of the last generation, his father or mother had been in the
craft condition.' (Mills, 1956: 228.) Later he writes that
modern workers must accept their work as inherently
meaningless, perform it with disgruntlement and seek
meaning elsewhere. But how and where do workers learn
these lessons? How are these minimal and self-destructive,
self conceptions and expectations developed? To understand their origin and development it is necessary to
appreciate the objective facts of many people's work
situations (for these exert a considerable socializing
pressure in themselves) and the cultural significance of
work in modern industrial society. Within capitalism work
must be designed to achieve competitive advantage, to
maximize profit and to control labour. In general, these
result in work forms designed around the principles of
scientific management. Few subjects attract as much
cultural attention as work. Work itself, as an activity, is the
subject of elaborate and strongly-held beliefs concerning
its necessity, its moral value, its therapeutic value, its
ability to supply meaning for life and so on. But these
cultural meanings of work which are available within
modern society do not exhaust the cultural significance of
the activity as a whole. There are also available ideas which
stress the relationship between work achievement and
personal worth, which ascribe different degrees of social
honour to different positions within the division of labour,
which define and evaluate the relationships between sub-

ordinates, and which exhort subordinates to commit themselves to their work and their enterprise. As Anthony
remarks: 'many historical, and more to the point, contemporary views about work which have been regarded as
axiomatic are ideological in that they are intended to influence the behaviour of subordinates.' (Anthony, 1977: 2.)

The work attitudes and behaviour of modern workers in
large-scale enterprises are a result of their exposure to the
conflicting and often damaging implications of low-status,
repetitive, subordinate work and current philosophies of
work urging its importance for creativity and development,
and evaluating people by their jobs. It is in this central
contradiction that we find what Sennett and Cobb (1973)
describe as the 'hidden injuries of class'. These authors
note that the damage of working-class work is not restricted
to the obvious facts of such things as conditions, danger,
disease, job design and pay levels. The damages of work
within class society have a psychological dimension. One
important aspect of the problem is this: in class society
different jobs are not only evaluated and rewarded differently, but they are allocated or seen in terms of merit,
moral character, intelligence and ability. The implications
of this, for the mass of the population, are very clear:
workers deserve to be workers; their repetitive, low-skilled
work reflects their personal ability and worth. It might
seem that this distribution of people to positions within the
division of labour, and indeed the distribution of rewards
among the positions themselves, owes something to factors
other than merit, intelligence or achievement. It might
seem, for example, particularly from below, to owe
something to the ability of classes to reproduce themselves
and transmit advantage generationally. But such possibilities are denied in the dominant ideology. This results in
a serious dilemma for workers. 'The badges of inner ability
people wear seem . . . unfairly awarded – yet hard to
repudiate. That is the injury of class, in day-to-day

existence, that the people we encountered face; it is a tangled relationship of denied freedom and dignity infinitely more complex than a resentment of "what other people are doing to me".' (Sennett and Cobb, 1973: 171.) (See also Aronowitz, 1973, for a perceptive analysis of the ambivalences experienced by modern workers.)

Other writers, too, have attempted to understand work attitudes, and especially instrumentality, in terms of the dynamics of class position and class cultures. Willis, for example, in his analysis of a school counter-culture notes that 'the lads'' rejection of school, discipline and qualifications prepares them for the realities which lie behind the rhetoric of working-class work. Ironically, by their assertive counter-culture they assure for themselves a subordinate position within the division of labour. But that is precisely where most working-class youths end up anyway. The occasional achievement of middle-class jobs by working-class youths does not alter the fact that, as a class, the working class does not, cannot, achieve such successes. It is because working-class people attempt (understandably) to achieve the qualifications which will enable them to obtain more privileged positions within the division of labour (and few succeed in the attempt) that the system as a whole, with its claimed reliance on merit and achievement, is legitimated. 'The refusal to compete, implicit in the school counter-culture, is therefore in this sense a radical act: it refuses to collude in its own educational suppression.' (Willis, 1977: 128.) For Willis, the reflection of the realities of the working-class predicament – at school and at work – within the lads' counter-culture constitutes a form of class consciousness. It is in this sense that he regards the instrumental worker as representing 'one of the most advanced and potentially radical working-class types, rather than the most incorporated' (Willis, 1977: 137). The accurate reflection of the priorities of work values in workers' culture is seen as a form of class consciousness.[1]

For others, the connection between work attitudes and class is more direct. Capitalist society represents a striking development of the cult of consumerism and materialism. Within such societies, the majority of the population are prepared – schooled – to learn to accept their final position within the division of labour as just and, as it were, merited. In fact the process of schooling serves to legitimate inequality, and to support it, not to alter it. The working-class pupil must overcome his ownership of low-status forms of knowledge and language. That most fail to do so further fuels the legitimacy of the system. For those who are condemned to subordinate, working-class work, the major source of gratification, therefore, is the financial one. Of particular salience within a materialist order, such instrumentality is enormously supported by the organization of work itself. For at work, the cash nexus is explicitly and vigorously institutionalized:

For a large number of people, therefore, and particularly those in the lower ranks of the occupational hierarchy, the lesson taught by the experience of work is that it must be expected to offer mainly extrinsic satisfactions. Intrinsically, it must be expected to be burdensome, restrictive, and often irksome, involving subjection to the control of others and often proving monotonous and stultifying into the bargain . . . a common [reaction] is to lower aspirations or rationalize skin-deep levels of satisfaction into major justifications of one's work.
(Fox, 1971: 14.)

As we shall see, the design and organization of work constitutes a massive socialization force. It is this above all which communicates to the employee what work means, and how he – and his labour – are valued. But the impact of these work experiences varies with the critical and evaluative equipment employees bring with them: the final meaning of work is the result of a process of interaction between the objective features of work and the expectations brought to bear on them. This has two major implications: for the sociologist it has complicated the analysis of the meaning of work because it is quite impossible to assume the significance of work to those concerned without some analysis of the workers' expectations. (See, for example, Goldthorpe *et al.*, 1968.) Who, for example, would ever have guessed that so many employees of modern large-scale organizations could be satisfied with their work? Secondly, it has important implications for management: if workers vary in their work attitudes, then management would be made much easier if only compliant and deferential workers who were likely to support the legitimacy of management hierarchies, were recruited. So we find a constant managerial/personnel search for suitable workers, a search which very often is accompanied by changes in the organization and design of work to make it more appropriate for the desired work force. Very often this results in the de-skilling of work, since the lower the skill requirements of work, the more transferable the work force and the less the organizational importance of any particular employee. Furthermore, there is often a connection between unskilled work and less militant, or less demanding workers, because unskilled workers may to some extent internalize management's assessment of their importance, or constitute to some degree a disadvantaged labour market, and be anxious for any sort of employment.

There is firm evidence that people's work attitudes vary with certain extra-work identities and characteristics. Lockwood (1966) suggests that work attitudes vary with certain work/community factors. Goldthorpe *et al.* (1969) argue for the importance of differing and distinctive orientations to work. This study focuses in particular on an instrumental orientation to work which was found to be characteristic of the relatively 'affluent' workers studied. Such an orientation was distinctive; it marked these workers off from others who were less prepared to sacrifice the possibility of intrinsic work rewards in order to maximize the financial rewards. Yet as Westergaard (1970) and Daniel (1969 and 1971) have remarked, the existence of an instrumental orientation to work should not be regarded as constituting any sort of *stable* commitment to forms of work which supply no rewards other than money. Nor should the apparent congruence of workers' orientations and organizational reward systems disguise the extent to which the design of work and the subordinate position of shop-floor employees constitute continuing (if, occasionally, covert) foci of frustration and resistance. On the contrary, an instrumental orientation to work simply demonstrates the extent to which those concerned have learnt the rules of the game and are attempting to improve their position within such rules. But there is no evidence that such groups will consequently increase their commitment to their subordinate position, or to the system itself.

Work attitudes vary with age, sex and race.[2] These attributes are the subject of considerable social significance, for the possession of certain social identities or conditions has implications for work opportunities and restrictions. Because, for example, in our society the role of woman is defined in certain ways, and these definitions are backed up by cultural, economic, familial and legal resources, women in this society find it hard to reject the notion that their prime role is in the home, 'servicing' male breadwinners. Such cultural values are backed up by discrimination against women at work. When, as is increasingly the case, women go out to work, they find themselves restricted to particular sorts and levels of work – 'women's work' – and are expected to regard their work not as a central feature of their lives, or as a source of personal and family income, but as a source of comradeship, and as a way of supplementing the family income: work as a source of pin money, not of a career. True to the old sociological adage that when a situation is defined as real it is real in its consequences, many of these discriminatory notions of women's place and women's work and their attitudes towards it, become true, at least in the short term. Beynon and Blackburn, for example, on the basis of their research into work attitudes, report that despite basic similarities in the workers' employment situation, they nevertheless 'found considerable variation in the ways in which different workers had come to understand the work situation and their position in it . . . The demands made upon women by marriage and childbirth in our society have meant that women have tended to develop a much lower commitment to employment than have men.' (Beynon and Blackburn, 1972: 146.)

These authors make the important point that deprivation at work, the nature of work attitudes, and the out-of-work situation or identity tend to interrelate and support each other. Thus, given the nature of most working-class women's work, it is not surprising that they accept the general emphasis on their role as housewives and see their work as somehow less than *real* work – man's work. Other writers have seen the interconnection between out-of-work identities and discriminated-against identities and work attitudes and restrictions as an integral part of the process, within capitalism, of the creation of a subservient and differentiated working class. According to this argument, the deprivations and discriminations suffered by, say, non-whites and women, are highly advantageous for capitalism since they serve to force these people to accept types of work, levels of pay or working conditions which other people would not accept.

Undeniably, members of these discriminated-against groups are attractive to employers. Often they are a source of cheap labour, of labour that can be dealt with in an authoritative way, of labour that can be hired and dismissed as demand fluctuates. Beechey, for example, discussing female wage labour in capitalist production, notes that 'the introduction of women and children may be advantageous to capital, both because they can be paid lower wages and because their introduction may be used to foster competition.' (Beechey, 1977: 55.) The immigration from the West Indies to the UK, for example, was in direct response to labour shortages in this country (see Peach, 1968). And within the Common Market as a whole, the EEC Commission remarked that 'the presence of a large migrant population will, in any event, always be required because of the unwillingness of community workers to perform certain dirty, difficult or dangerous jobs.' (*Guardian*, 30 July 1974, quoted in Braham, 1975.) The attractiveness of foreign labour at a time of labour shortage is obvious. Furthermore, the situation of the immigrants caused them, from the employment point of view, to seem like that rare creature: the economist's idea of economic man – 'The majority of immigrants are single adult males less constrained than the English worker by non-economic factors such as socially awkward hours of work and are willing to work as long hours as possible to earn as much as possible.' (Cohen and Jenner, 1968: 55.) The Italian and Polish peasants who found work in the USA earlier this century were also attractive for their cultural acceptance of subordination; their subservience, as well as their capacity for hard work.

It is useful to see the work force as so drastically differentiated as to constitute two or more labour markets. One market for labour is open to males and whites. It recruits for skilled, clerical and managerial/professional jobs. The secondary labour market is made up of women, non-whites, the old and others who might find it difficult to get work. These groups discover that they are only eligible for jobs which 'tend to be low-paying, with poorer working conditions, little chance of advancement, a highly personalized relationship between workers and supervisors which leaves wide latitude for favouritism and is conducive to harsh and capricious work discipline; and with considerable instability in jobs and a high turnover among the labour force.' (Piore, 1972: 3.) This suggestion of a dual structure of labour markets focuses attention on the extent to which occupations and jobs are differentiated on sex and colour bases. Even when one finds an occupation with both male and female members, it transpires that there is internal, hierarchical differentiation along gender lines.[3]

The relationship between various underprivileged groups and work situations is a two-way one: not only can management deliberately seek to recruit women, or non-white immigrant workers, for jobs which members of the primary labour market would not be prepared to accept (and thus take advantage of their necessarily restricted work aspirations), but management can use the employment of members of these groups to reduce the status and skill levels of existing jobs. It is for this reason that conflict often occurs between white, male incumbents of jobs, and the newly recruited women, or non-whites, for the newcomers are seen to represent a decline in relative status and market situation. De-skilling and the use of labour from the secondary labour groups go together. Crozier, for example, in discussing changes in the situation of clerical workers, notes: 'The loss of economic privilege of white-collar employees can be explained in large measure by the progressive invasion of white-collar occupations by women, whose level of compensation is distinctly lower across the board in all industries.' (Crozier, 1971: 15.) What is hapening to clerical work, writes Crozier, is not only that it is being *proletarianized*, it is being *feminized*, with all the consequent advantages, to the employer, of a relatively unskilled, compliant and cheap work force. Changes in the content and rewards of jobs, and feminization interact and support each other.

The interplay of the factors responsible for cheapening

and feminizing work has been described by a number of writers. The ideology that women are 'natural' office workers is connected to the feminization of the clerical labour force. With women employed in large numbers in offices, an ideology developed which justified their presence there. Women were employed in offices because they were cheaper than the male labour force. As organizations expanded they were forced to draw on the pool of educated female labour to meet the rapidly increasing demand for clerical workers. The new office structure meant an increase in low-level, dead-end jobs. It was primarily women who filled these jobs. The sexual division of labour is one of the major bases on which the labour market is segmented. It has proved to be an effective base. (See Warner and Low, 1947.)

In conclusion: chapter 3 noted the importance for sociology and for management, of understanding the personal meaning of work, particularly working-class work. That chapter showed how sociological analyses and conceptualizations of the personal meaning of work, while often employing the language of sociology – alienation and anomie, for example – in fact demonstrated a commitment to managerial conceptions of workers' work attitudes. Such a conception was presented as sociologically inadequate on two grounds: that it paid no attention to the out-of-work factors which encouraged acquiescence and resignation, and limited the development of 'unrealistic' aspiration, and that it was insufficiently curious about the values and interests which lay behind, and were articulated within, the design of work, and of organizational hierarchy. It was argued that no useful understanding of workers' attitudes could stop with a description of the attitudes themselves; a consideration of the cultural, economic, social, technological and organizational contexts was necessary.

Chapter 4 has been concerned with the first of these questions: the role of out-of-work factors in encouraging limited work aspiration, reducing alternative conceptions of work, establishing the normality of boredom, deprivation and injustice at work. The chapter has briefly noted some of the major factors that are relevant: the structure and context of the education system, the societal emphasis on materialism, consumerism, the emphasis on work as achievement – and, therefore, on incumbency of low-grade work as personal failure – the sheer fact of the prevailing principles of work design, in all their apparent 'rationality' and inevitability, the differentiation of the work force along gender and racial grounds. All these factors operate to predispose workers to limit their aspirations to available options. It is this process – which many sociologists would regard as evidence of alienation – which lies behind the surface acquiescence recorded by so many work-satisfaction surveys.[4]

5   Alienation and the Design of Work

We have seen that in order to understand the extent of workers' alienation it is necessary to attend to the meaning which people bring to work, and to the factors which encourage people to develop alienated work orientations. It is now time to consider the work situations which people find at work. What aspects of the organization and design of work in large-scale organizations are responsible for workers' alienation? Behind the variety of factors adduced by writers, two basic tendencies are operative, tendencies which have been explained by writers using theories directly derived from the work of Marx, Weber and Durkheim.

1 The division of labour and technology

The most important source of alienation at work is the way in which work itself is designed and controlled. As far as possible, for most workers within capitalism work is designed in accordance with the precepts of Taylorism (see Chapter 1). Numerous writers have recently noted the continuing pervasiveness of Taylor's work-design principles, which, essentially, involve the 'decomposition' of work in accordance with certain criteria: maximum fragmentation; the divorce of planning and doing; and the divorce of direct and indirect labour, i.e. separating the worker's task from the preparation and organization of the job; minimization of skill requirements; reduction of material handling (see, for example, Braverman, 1974; Littler, 1978). It is important to stress that Taylorism also has consequences for the organization of control. Taylorism separates design and execution, establishes 'expert' departments and standardizes procedures. Finally, Taylorism advocates a definite conception of the employment relationship – one where the organization seeks to reduce the skill levels and training needs of personnel, to maximize flexibility.

To repeat, these principles remain prevalent in the present design of work some seventy years after the publication of *Principles of Scientific Management* (1911). 'Taylorism continues to be . . . almost invariably present in American firms.' (Leavitt, 1973: 339.) Indeed, Fox (1974) argues that a distinction between high- and low-trust jobs, the latter being characterized by strict and persuasive control, established routines and procedures, strict supervision, the assumption of low commitment, or hostility, permeates current work organizations.

Furthermore, fragmented, divided and minutely specialized de-skilled jobs are very frequently allied to the use of modern technology. Mechanization and job fragmentation support and reinforce each other.

As we have seen in Chapter 3, for Blauner, an organization's technology is the single most important factor in determining other aspects of the organization's structure and the experience (alienation potential) of work itself. This conviction is supported by numerous writers, who see the modern organization of work – the extreme division of labour – and the increasing use of machines, and mechanical pacing of work, as major factors in generating alienation.

In a work context the advantages of the employment of technology in production is that it can result in mass production of standardized, hence interchangeable, parts. This results in higher levels of output and the downgrading – de-skilling – of the work. In assembly-line work, additional principles are apparent. Here the product proceeds through the factory in carefully-planned series of stages. Each job is broken down into its constituent parts so that each is performed by a different individual on the product as it is mechanically delivered to him, each job, of course, being standardized through the design and setting of machinery and materials or parts.

As Chinoy has remarked, from management's point of view the assembly line has numerous advantages: it eliminates time spent by labour in moving from job to job; it enables the extreme division and simplification of labour; and it places the control of the operation, through the speed of the line, firmly in management's hands. The time for each job is established by the speed with which the assembly appears in front of the worker (Chinoy, 1964). These managerial benefits, however, are experienced by the workers as costs – skill and creativity are reduced as tools, processes and operations are predetermined by engineers, work technology and work study; individual decision-making is supplanted by the mechanically paced line.[1] It is this development – the inability to control one's own work – which occasions most objections (see Beynon, 1973).

The assembly line represents an extreme case of mechanization, and of Taylorism, since here machines not only determine the nature of jobs, but the flow of materials and products between them. However we find that the alienating consequences of mechanization are by no means restricted to assembly-line work. Modern factory technology is allied to the imposition of Scientific Management principles: the extreme division of labour, whereby jobs are sub-divided and specialized, and responsibility for planning located in specialists' technical or professional departments. These elements are greatly assisted by the use of machinery, which can be designed rapidly to execute a predetermined operation which is part of a larger, overall design developed by specialists elsewhere. In this operation the worker/operator has few decisions left (whether or not to activate the machine, how often to do it); skill, creativity, variety, are replaced by repetition, frustration and anxiety. The work is depersonalized, meaningless, without interest (Friedmann, 1961).

The imposition of the principles of Scientific management – the extreme division of labour – is often regarded as directly related to alienation at work. These principles find support and expression through modern production technology. Clearly, however, technology can be applied to more than one aspect of the production process. For example, it can be used to replace the skilled worker. In this case the machine carries out the function previously executed by the worker on the basis of his judgement and skill. At this stage of mechanization the worker becomes a machine operative. One man's job is divided among numerous operators and machines. Technology can also be used to organize the flow of goods and products to workers, as in an assembly-line set-up. With mechanical pacing of work, technology is applied to the conveyance of materials as well as to the job task. Finally, with automation, technology is applied to the control and monitoring of the work itself. Whereas with the assembly line the speed of work is controlled by the speed of the line, and the nature of the work operation is, as far as possible, built into the machine or its setting, the operator still retains control over the activation of the process. This residual control is a problem for management, for workers can affect the level, and quality, of output. With automation, however, built-in feedback loops ensure that an automatic process is initiated appropriately and is regulated in the light of the overall condition of the system. Automation requires more than automatic feedback and control: it also requires that work processes be entirely mechanized and organized in an interconnected flow. This is most possible with the production of liquid or gaseous products; for example oil refining, which is why automation has reached its fullest expression in the chemical and petroleum industries.[2]

At one time the advent of automation was hailed as representing a possible escape from alienation. It was argued that in the factory of the future automation would eliminate dirty and boring work and transform workers into white-coated monitors of integrated and automatic production systems. Blauner advances this view of automation which is seen as increasing skill levels, breaking down old animosities between managers and labour, establishing meaningful and responsible work. Most important of all, 'continuous process technology leads to considerable freedom from pressure, control over the pace of work, responsibility of maintaining a high quality product, choice of how to do the job, and freedom of physical movement.' (Blauner, 1967: 141.)

These are the ingredients of the utopia of automation. But it is a utopia which has been seriously questioned. First, automation simply is not possible with the vast majority of jobs. Secondly, by pointing to the exaggerated possibility of automation, its apologists do a disservice by denying the empirical realities of much current work. As recent writers have argued (Levison, 1974; Braverman, 1974; Fox, 1974), the work of the majority of workers – male and female – remains characteristically working class, that is, it is manual work, highly controlled, and most of it is still unskilled or semi-skilled (see Davis *et al.*, 1972). Thirdly, the enthusiasts' descriptions of automated work and its meaning for workers has been questioned on empirical grounds. An early example is Bright's classic study of thirteen automated plants in the USA. He concludes his analysis with the conviction that automation did not, as widely thought, result in an upgrading of skill, but a downgrading. The increasing application of technology to more and more aspects of the work task and its control and integration – from the use of the simplest tool through powered tools, pre-programmed machines, machines that detect errors and correct them to machines that modify their own behaviour – involves a progressive decrease in skill levels from a high point in the early stages of mechanization, when the worker still retains control, to a low point with automation.[3]

Those who have argued that automation increases skill requirements are either assuming that complex and sophisticated jobs inevitably require complex and sophisticated skills (a relationship which in reality is reversed) or are assuming that the increased role of maintenance in automated factories will mean increased skill demands. In contrast Bright remarks: 'If we think carefully about the skill, education, and training required to become a suitable operator on the machinery around us it becomes clearer that we tend to confuse the maintenance and design problems of exceptional operator jobs with the most common situation: namely, that *growing automation tends to simplify operator duties.*' (Bright, 1958: 183.) Furthermore, while conceding that some increase in skill or numbers of maintenance work occurred with automation, he argues that this did not make up for the much greater overall *reduction* in skill levels.[4]

Debate about the impact of automation on skill levels has been particularly vociferous in discussions about the automated office, for 'automation may have its biggest initial human impact in the office . . . the white-collar worker . . . is now confronted with the demand to relate to a machine environment.' (Mann, 1962: 55.)

During the course of this century clerical work has undergone a number of radical developments. Offices have increased in size; relations between clerks and management have become more impersonal; mobility opportunities have reduced. But the most devastating change has been in the work itself. Clerical work, once a job which required rare skills and educational qualifications, which was concerned with what would nowadays be regarded as managerial functions, and which was well-rewarded financially and highly esteemed, has changed so drastically that some commentators insist that 'this working population has lost all former superiorities over workers in industry, and in its scale of pay it has sunk almost to the very bottom.' (Braverman, 1974: 355.) Central to the fragmentation of office jobs and the imposition of Scientific Management criteria of job design has been the mechanization and automation of the office, which has resulted from the application of technology to the expanding functions of clerical work in modern large-scale organizations.[5]

Office work has been exposed to the same work-design principles as the shop-floor – those of Scientific Management, of work study and measurement and rationalization. As on the shop floor, the process has been accompanied and assisted by modern technology. Indeed, in a sense, in the most extreme cases, mechanization, integration and automation have been installed to such a degree that work processes are readily recognizable as continuous flow processes. This is the outcome of deliberate planning by work-design specialists. Thus Braverman sees the application of technology in the office as reflecting the same general directions described by Bright in his categorization of types of technology: the early forms of technology – typewriters, for example – reduced mental labour to a series of repetitive operations. In the next step, thought processes of any sort are removed. Now the machine dominates – a computer is simply 'fed' information which it processes. At this stage clerical work becomes manual work.

The computer automates the office. Information-processing operations, which were discrete and which required human interventions, are, with the computer, centralized and integrated into one operation which requires only manual operations from those who service it. The use of computers has a number of implications for the division of labour in the office: it de-skills and routinizes jobs which previously required some judgement and skill – book-keeping, or higher grade clerical, for example – and creates new jobs, most notable of which is that of punch card operator. It has repercussions throughout the office, however, since even those jobs not directly related to the computer must now prepare information in ways which can readily be processed by the computer, and the installation of a computer encourages a centralization of management control.[6]

What implications do these developments have for the meaning of work in modern offices? First, they have resulted in the 'feminization' of office work, as discussed above. The application of Scientific Management principles, the rationalization of work and the automation of office procedures results in the enormous expansion of unskilled, repetitive, fragmented jobs. That over time these jobs are seen to require 'typically' female characteristics – dexterity, quickness etc., and are now allocated to women – is highly convenient since it not only ensures a flow of labour into jobs which might otherwise have been difficult to fill, it also makes it possible to de-skill the work even further, should this be necessary.

The implications of these developments in office work are obvious: 'As office machinery is introduced, the number of routine jobs is increased, and consequently the proportion of "positions requiring initiative" is decreased.' (Mills, 1956: 205.) This view is supported by other writers – Crozier (1971), Shepard (1971), Hoos (1961). Hoos presents empirical evidence on the consequences of the installation of computers in offices. She notes that the introduction of electronic data processing changes jobs both quantitatively and qualitatively. Furthermore, she suggests that for every five jobs lost through EDP, only one is gained, and while the lost jobs are skilled ones, the new job is usually that of punch card operator. Of this work she remarks: 'key-punching is universally regarded as a dead-end occupation with no promotional opportunities. The work is simple, monotonous, and repetitive, but requires a high degree of accuracy and speed.' (Hoos, 1961: 75.) Other writers have noted the stress and anxiety this work occasions. The impact of automation as described by Hoos confirms the generalizations of Mills, Braverman and others: there is greater sub-division of jobs, less meaningful work, more pressure, more boredom. Once again, technology and the minute, fragmented division of labour are seen as supporting each other and as generating alienation among workers.

2   Bureaucratization

The other major source of alienation is the increasing bureaucratization of the enterprise. This process has a number of elements. First, the term bureaucratization is sometimes used to refer to the process of rationalization, that is, the systematic ordering and design of jobs, processes and organization in order to increase the efficient flow of goods and materials, in order to reduce waste of time, labour and materials and to maximize the return of stock, labour and capital. The rationalization of work and organization refers to the explicit, systematic and deliberate analysis of work from the point of view of efficiency and profit. It is revealed, for example, in the reorganization of clerical offices described above, but similar processes are carried out in all areas of the organization, reflecting the increasing need for thorough, intensive and competitive utilization of the enterprise's resources.

Rationalization not only reflects the basic principles

upon which bureaucracy is centred, it also facilitates the centralization of power within the organization, which is one of the major features of bureaucracy. Bureaucracy is both a *form* of control and a way of describing the *location* of control. The classic bureaucracy, as described by Weber (and redescribed very frequently since), entails a formal and rigid specification of duties and procedures, with explicit demarcations of responsibilities and authority, and, as a result, the centralization of power in the hands of those who design rules and supervise and monitor subordinates. A bureaucracy is a structure of control. As such it has been seen to constitute a major source of alienation – both by the manner and the fact of bureaucratic domination.

To deal first with the characteristic bureaucratic form of control, many writers have regarded this as a primary source of work alienation. Writers on changes in the nature of clerical work, for example, lay stress on the increasing impersonality and formality of office relations, with previously personal relationships transformed by formal procedures and regulations (see Mills, 1956). Of particular importance in causing an increase in bureaucratic forms of control has been the increase in size of most employing organizations. Numerous writers have postulated a relationship between size and degree of bureaucratization. Ingham, for example, on the basis of a review of the literature, writes that 'large organizations inhibit . . . vertical interaction and therefore favour the use of bureaucratic rules in the problem of the administration of the labour force and its work.' (Ingham, 1967: 244.) Furthermore, he stresses that bureaucratization has been used in two ways – to refer to the development of the formal structures of management, or to the '*method of administration of the labour force* and the work process – that is, to the use of unversalistic, effectively neutral rules in the regulation of specific tasks and relationships.' (Ingham,

1967: 242.) It is bureaucratization in the latter sense, he continues, 'which has the greater consequences for worker attachment and behaviour.' (Ingham, 1967: 243.) This conclusion about the relationship between size and degree of bureaucratization has frequently been supported elsewhere. Similarly, the alienating consequences of bureaucratic forms of control have often been reported (see, for example, Gouldner, 1954).

It is, however, in the case of professionals that most objection and resistance to bureaucratic forms of control have been commonest. A striking feature of the occupational structure of advanced capitalist societies is the dramatic increase in the proportion of the working population engaged in professional work (see Bell, 1974: Chapter 3). Most of these professionals are employed in large-scale organizations either to supply expert assistance in the achievement of profit, or, when employed within professional organizations such as hospitals or law firms, to supply a form and extent of service which the individual practitioner would be unable to supply. It has been noted that there are conflicts between the professional model and the bureaucratic model in abstract – that is, the professional form of occupational organization differs significantly from the bureaucratic form of organization (Hall, 1972), mostly with respect to the way in which control is exercised. Within the profession, control is exercised by the professional on the basis of his/her expert judgement. Within the bureaucracy, control is exercised through rules and precedents. While the latter form of control permits centralization, the former does not.

Empirically, it has been found that 'a generally inverse relationship exists between the levels of bureaucratization and professionalization.' (Hall, 1972: 160.) Furthermore, professionals within bureaucracies are apt to find the characteristic bureaucratic forms of control inhibiting or counter-productive. A study by Miller (1970), for example, argued that professionals within bureaucracies found bureaucratic control and restriction a source of alienation from work. These findings are supported by Aiken and Hage, who report that 'highly centralized and highly formalized organizational structures are characterized by greater work alienation.' (Aiken and Hage, 1970: 525.) This alienation was the result of the professionals' inability to participate in decision-making, and their exposure to strict regulation.[7]

Bureaucracy does not just refer to a particular form of impersonal, formalized control; it also is used to describe the location of control – control that is vested, by numerous means, in the hands of those who own or run the organization. This sense of bureaucracy, as centralized, expropriated control, is a major source of alienated work attitudes (see above, Chapter 3). More than any other single factor, lack of control at work – over the pace or nature of work – is voiced by workers as a source of dissatisfaction and stress, of alienation. Bureaucracy represents a major source of the expropriation of employees' control.

The conventional analysis of bureaucratic control stresses two major factors: centralization of decision-making and control, and formalized procedures. Blau and Schoenherr remark: 'The prototype of bureaucratic control is the authority exercised through a chain of command in which superiors give orders subordinates are obliged to obey . . . A second mechanism of control . . . is the establishment of explicit regulations and procedures that govern decisions and operations.' (Blau and Schoenherr, 1971: 348.) Bureaucracy in either of these forms is a likely source of alienation at work.

But Blau and Schoenherr argue that increasingly, within large-scale organizations, power is exercised in less obvious and explicit ways. For example, technology itself is a method of achieving and exercising control, since it can be used to remove control over work from the workers and to vest it in the person who designs and oversees the work system. Similarly, according to Blau and Schoenherr, professionals can be used to control, although in subtle and insidious ways, the work of others (see also Perrow, 1972). These authors also point to the control implications of such bureaucratic features as payment systems, personnel practices or selection systems.

In short, 'if we want our material civilization to continue as it is, we will have to have large-scale bureaucratic enterprises in the economic, social and governmental areas.' (Perrow, 1972, 58.) But such structures, in both the manner in which they control their employees and the fact that they by various means, some of them elusive and insidious, expropriate control from those who work in them – worker and professional – represent a major source of alienation.

We are left with one final question: what factors determine the emergence of these alienating forms of technology and bureaucracy? We shall find that answers to this question can be related to the early analyses of Marx, Weber and Durkheim.

Theories of organization

As much for practical managerial as for academic reasons, organizations have been the subject of a great deal of research. What is known, rather charitably, as organization *theory* contains a variety of different approaches, some of which reflect this concern for practical problems. This is not the place to attempt another classification of varieties of organization theory – for that has been attempted elsewhere (see, for example, Perrow, 1972, and Mouzelis, 1967). Much of this organization theory falls outside the scope of this book, because it is directly concerned with management priorities and problems.[8]

What will be done here is simply to show that recent efforts to explain the nature and origins of the features of organizational structure discussed above – the minute division of labour and bureaucracy – involve reference to the theories and insights of the theorists discussed in Chapter 2. This is not to say that the writers whose works are discussed below would necessarily acknowledge their shared precedents or even that they are aware of the traditions within which they work. It is to argue that in facing the question of the origins of organizational structure a substantial proportion of writers employ the assumptions and insights of the classic theorists – explicitly or implicitly.

Each of the three types of theory discussed below advances a general theory of modern society and of its relationship to organizational forms.

The logic of industrialism

There is a widely prevalent view of modern society and the nature of employing organizations which can readily be seen to derive from Durkheim. This is the view which stresses the industrial nature of modern society and which ascribes to the process of industrialism itself a logic which causes all industrial societies to show a convergent pattern of development with respect to their major elements and institutions regardless of their ostensible differences of ideology and politics. According to such a view, industrial societies will show similar features regardless of whether they are seen as (or claim to be) socialist or capitalist. The fact of industrialization itself creates requirements and imperatives which override the significance of such factors.

So, for example, within industrial societies, class structures and relationships are transformed. Class structures are modified by the development of a large, expert middle class and the growth of new skilled working-class occupations – both occasioned by the requirements of the new industrial order. Relations between these new, differentiated classes may still be conflictful, but such conflicts stem not from polarized class positions: 'manager and managed do not form any separate and clear-cut classes . . . there is a hierarchy of managerial relations far too complex to compress into simple class relations.' (Kerr *et al.*, 1973: 259.) And they are within the terms of the existing order, not about the nature of that order itself: they are structured by 'the distinctive consensus which relates individuals and groups to each other and provides an integrated body of ideas, beliefs, and value judgements.' (Kerr *et al.*, 1973: 53.)

The industrial society is, overwhelmingly, a society of integration and consensus. The differentiation of occupational structure, and the separation of previously coincident bases of power and conflict, result in a qualitative change in the nature of conflicts which is accompanied by an increase in the degree of ideological consensus around such core values as the importance of science and technology, the value of progress, materialism, the work ethic (Kerr *et al.*), or rationality, achievement and equality (Dahrendorf, 1959). This consensus serves to integrate individuals and groups and supports the 'web of rules' which, increasingly, governs the actions of organizations and institutions and which are enforced by an ever more active state apparatus.

Within the industrial society organizations play a crucial role. In the industrial state, writes Galbraith, the industrial system, composed of a few hundred technically dynamic, highly organized and massively capitalized organizations, is *the* dominant feature: the feature which, by its efficient use of long-term planning and modern technology, makes advanced industrial society possible and gives it its characteristic elements.

Since industrial societies have superseded capitalism, and since they are characterized by consensus and integration, organizations can only serve the society's interests, not class ones. And organizations within the industrial society are characterized by the same elements as the society itself – integration, functional differentiation and consensus. Organizations are *systems* which satisfy the society's various needs by their own internal organization into sub-systems: production, supportive systems, maintenance systems, adaptive systems and managerial systems (Katz and Kahn, 1967). Parsons, for example, defines organizations as 'a social system which is organized for the attainment of a particular type of goal: the attainment of that goal is at the same time the performance of a type of function on behalf of a more inclusive system, the society.' (Parsons, 1970: 81.)[9]

The internal structure of organizations – the division of labour, the organization of work and the forms of control – are determined by the goals that the organization is consensually striving to achieve, and by the means which this requires. Organizational structure is a means for the achievement of socially necessary goals. Of particular significance in mediating between goals and structure is the technology which is employed (see Woodward, 1970; Davis, *et al.*, 1973; Perrow, 1972). Technologies are employed in order to cut costs and raise productivity, to standardize raw materials and minimize non-routine cases (Perrow, 1972). The application of modern technology, and the minute division of labour go hand in hand. Both are necessary in order systematically to apply modern scientific technical knowledge to organizational production.

The application of modern, scientific, technical knowledge to organizational structure, production, planning and performance, and the resultant high levels of productivity, are the hallmarks of the industrial society. The internal structuring of organizations – the division of labour, the design of work and the forms and degree of control – are the result of the application of science and technology to societally necessary goals. The expansion of management and expert professional groups within the organization is simply a necessary part of the developing managerial function, a result of the application of new techniques of control and planning: 'the "control" of the great corporations should develop into a purely neutral technocracy, balancing a variety of claims by various groups in the community and assigning to each a portion of the income stream on the basis of public policy rather than private cupidity.' (Berle and Means, 1933: 356, quoted in Baran and Sweezy, 1968: 33.)[10]

Any inequalities and deprivations – any alienation or variations in the distribution of organizational rewards and frustrations – are attributed not to sectional interests or values, not to conflicts between organizational groups, not to struggles for control and legitimacy, but to neutral and undeniable technology and science harnessed to society's requirements.[11] This apolitical conception of organization and technology is allied to a view of alienation which bears little connection to the work of Marx (see below) but much to Durkheim, a view which regards alienation in terms of dimensions of workers' attitudes and as consequences of the technological and organizational aspects of the work. This view has little interest in the *origins* of work forms, or the *origins* of work attitudes. Alienation is defined here in terms of measurable, work-related variations in workers' attitudes, or in the congruence between expectations and reality. The causes of these conditions, if they are considered at all, are either ascribed to the necessary, but unfortunate technological rationality of the industrial society, or to what Eldridge, in discussing Durkheim's critique of 'abnormal' forms of the division of labour, describes as a lack of congruence between system integration and the social integration of the individual – i.e., between the involvement of the individual in the society and the inter-relationships between the parts of the society (Eldridge, 1971).[12]

If alienation (anomie) results from the unregulated, amoral character of the modern enterprise in industrial society, the solution to these conditions is obvious: industry, organization and work must be reorganized so as to resuscitate workers' commitment, to re-establish the meaning of work, without, of course, departing from the constraints of efficiency and output imposed by the industrial order. Hence the frequency of calls for the humanization of work, or for 'human relations' schemes, designed to engage the involvement of the worker.

Rationality and efficiency

While much organization theory can be seen to bear some relationship to the writings of Weber on bureaucracy and the enterprise, and even more claims such a connection, much of it manifests a distorted version of Weber's work. This distortion takes a number of forms. First, while Weber was concerned with the question of individual freedom in a modern, rationalized, bureaucratized world, much modern organization theory appears indifferent to such evaluative considerations, or, by making them the focus of a value-free, empiricist sociology, seriously misunderstands them. Secondly, while Weber's writings show a broad historical and societal perspective, an attempt to relate organizational developments to broad societal tendencies and to historical movement, many of his successors have shifted their level of analysis to the organizational and replaced his humanism with empiricism. Weber's societal analysis has frequently been rejected, and replaced by a search for the most 'rational' form of organization under various internal and external circumstances. In this way, Weber's concept of rationality has been seriously misinterpreted by some writers who regard it as synonymous with efficiency. This crude confusion has been identified by Albrow (1970).

Characteristically, much organization theory has sought to legitimize its practical, managerial concerns by adopting the language, but not the content, of Weber. This is particularly noticeable in the numerous attempts to break down, operationalize and measure the Weberian concept of bureaucracy and so to correct or improve it. Misunderstanding the concept of the ideal type, numerous writers have attempted to measure the existence of, and interrelationships between, the various dimensions of Weber's analysis of bureaucracy. Many of these studies have argued that Weber's description of bureaucratic forms of control in fact masks an empirical distinction between a number of different control systems.

For example, Stinchcombe (1970), distinguishes between what he calls 'bureaucratic' and 'craft' principles of administration; Udy separates 'bureaucratic' and 'rational' (Udy, 1959). Basically, they and many others are noting an empirical tendency for organizations to employ more than one form of control system. Weber's model itself can be seen to contain more than one such principle. For example, empirically, control can be achieved by centralizing decisions, or by delegating decisions within a structure of tightly established and monitored rules. Centralization and formalization, then, are probably functional alternatives. Similarly, either of these systems may be compared to a system where control is exercised by careful selection and career management of appropriately trained and programmed professionals (Blau and Schoenherr, 1971). Scientific Management, bureaucracy, the employment of professionals, are seen then as functional alternatives.

Unquestionably, much of this work is interesting and useful. But it is equally clear that while it is related to the work of Weber, it simplifies that body of writings, and in fact demonstrates, through its naïve conception of the concept of rationality, a prime interest in matters of current, managerial interest – i.e., variations in organizational structure of control under varying conditions. Much of current work in organization theory which claims links with Weber seeks to discover the organizational forms which are most suitable for varying circumstances, i.e., in its terms, most 'rational'. In this category are such thorough-going studies as those by the 'Aston School' (Pugh and Hickson, 1976; Pugh and Payne, 1977; Pugh and Hinings, 1976). The basic intention of these and other analyses of inter-organizational variations along a number of dimensions in the face of various internal or external conditions is to discover 'the predictive impact of a range of contextual variables on a range of structural situations' (Pugh and Hinings, 1976: vii).

Such analyses regard the characteristically bureaucratic pattern as one possibility among many.

Rationality, then, has become defined in terms of efficiency, and bureaucracy as a form of organization which is most rational/efficient simply in terms of the nature of the raw material, the task, or other variables. The legacy of Weber, as revealed in these studies, is the effort to discover the range of organizational structures that are most efficient under different circumstances. A purpose which is valuable enough, but does not do full justice to Weber's complex notion of rationality, nor to his analysis of the interconnections between bureaucratic organizational forms and the cultural and class structures of modern societies. What is most obviously lacking in modern, neo-Weberian studies is any consideration that the origin of different forms of organizational control might lie anywhere else than in the working out of some neutral, apolitical structure of ideas. By confusing rationality with efficiency, and adopting an incurious conception of efficiency itself, the correlations between organizational structure and other variables are given the status of organizational laws, owing nothing to interests, ideologies or conflicts. Relations of super- and sub-ordination, the existence of rigid control systems, of formalized procedures, and the design of fragmented work, are all seen as reflections of necessary laws of organization, as *things* beyond human choice or control, a conclusion which is in marked contrast to Weber's explicit concern for the social origins of bureaucratic forms which he realized entailed severe restrictions on individuals' freedom.

Within such a tradition, alienation is regarded as the result of exposure to modern, rational forms of organizational control. Particular emphasis is placed on the alienation of the professional who finds himself caught in a conflict between organizational and occupational control principles. Such analyses of alienation lay particular stress on the relationship between bureaucracy as one common and rational organizational form, and personal freedom in a bureaucratic context.

Profit, contradiction and control

Although Marx's writings have been of enormous significance within sociological theory and although, as we saw in Chapter 2, he established an analysis of modern large-scale organizations, there has not been, until recently, much work within conventional organization theory which took much serious notice of the Marxist tradition. This is probably because of the pro-managerial leanings of much of organization analysis, and its preoccupation with what those who initiate and fund research regard as practical problems (Salaman, 1978).

Recently this situation has changed. Following the publication of Braverman's *Labor and Monopoly Capital*

(1974), a Marxist oriented approach to organizations has emerged. Its elements are as follows.

First, the notion that capitalism has been superseded in the West by industrial society is vigorously denied. Certainly alterations have taken place in the *form* of capitalism: these include the developments of a welfare system, the increasing intrusion of the state, a significant proportion of public ownership and until recently, some genuine improvement in standard of living. But these do not constitute any alteration of the basic nature of capitalism. Modern forms of capitalism are still dominated by the priorities, mechanisms and structures of the search for profit. In this country the mass of the population still depend for their livelihood upon the sale of their labour to an employer who will buy it only so long as he can use and direct it to achieve a profit. This in turn will depend upon the employer's ability to reduce costs (including labour), increase efficiency, discipline the work force, satisfy investors, all within an unstable market. This basic feature – the sale and purchase of labour power in order to achieve profit – is reflected in drastic differences in the distribution of incomes, work benefits and deprivations, and wealth. (See Chapter 7 for a discussion of the impact of large-scale organizations on class structure.)

Secondly, despite the recent variations in the form of capitalism, which may be seen as attempts either to avoid class opposition, to 'buy off' resistance, or to deal, in suitably-disguised forms, with the inevitable contradictions and victims of capitalism – redundancies, unemployment, subsidies etc. – work organizations within capitalism are seen as experiencing a crisis. It takes a variety of forms – declining profit margins, market instability, the growing recalcitrance of organized labour, increasing personal withdrawal and 'desubordination' on the part of individual workers. These problems are inter-related: the need to increase profit rates in current conditions of organized labour can no longer be satisfied by 'extensive' utilization of the work force (i.e., lengthening of the working day); it now requires that the labour force be used more efficiently, more intensively. This can be achieved through forms of organization, technology, the design of work – through the '. . . rational, systematic division of labour and the fragmentation of the work process' (Crompton and Gubbay, 1977: 72). These raise efficiency as they cheapen labour and fragment and divide the labour force. However, these work and organizational developments encounter resistance, sometimes incoherent and unorganized, occasionally orchestrated, organized and articulate. The manner in which labour is divided and organized under capitalism is a prime source of worker resistance and hostility to the enterprise. Management meets this recalcitrance by installing tighter controls, more surveillance, less unreliable work systems (see Fox, 1974). So the organization of work and the achievement of control become inextricably intertwined.

Bureaucracy is necessary to control and monitor the labour of alienated and recalcitrant employees. The development of bureaucracy entails the centralization of control, the dehumanization and systematization of procedures. It involves the dominance of rationality, of instrumentality, and the differentiation of the work force.

The design of work within capitalism is seen to take a number of forms: bureaucracy, classical Scientific Management, human relations and others. But always the underlying priorities are the same: the achievement of profit, and, relatedly, of control. Within capitalism, those who own work organizations are faced with two major problems: the need to be, and to remain, profitable, to be able to compete, nationally and internationally, to attract investment, to accumulate sufficient capital to finance further expansion and the installation of new technologies. Secondly, since management within capitalism must seek

the ever more profitable utilization of labour, it is
constantly faced with the problems of employee recalcitrance and resistance. These reactions stem from the
experience of workers within capitalism. They take place in
a context of capitalist rationality, where opposition to work
design, redundancies, wage levels, technologies and so on is
defined not as opposition to a form of economic order
which deprives the many as it enriches the few, but as
opposition to modern technology, to the development and
distribution of consumer goods, or to modern, industrial
forms of social life.

The major thrust of work design within capitalism,
which serves at the same time the twin aims of intensive
exploitation and control, is towards de-skilling work and
making it increasingly subject to mechanical control. This
cheapens labour both directly, by making it unskilled, and
indirectly by making it easily transferable, and flexible
(jobs can be learnt in a very short time). It reduces the
decision-making discretion of the potentially unreliable,
and permits the intensive organization and systematic
rationalization of the labour process, without interference
from craft pride. This de-skilling of manual – and,
increasingly, clerical – work is accompanied by the
expansion of expert functions. The separation of *execution*
from *design*, of the application of rules from the creation of
policies, encourages a major feature of capitalist work
forms: the development of management and expert
functions. Management, Marglin argues, did not develop
as a result of technical superiority or efficiency. Both the
fragmentation of tasks, and the development of management, he claims, developed because they enabled the
manager to achieve greater control over the process of
accumulation. 'By mediating between producer and
consumer, the capitalist organization sets aside much more
for expanding and improving plant and equipment than
individuals would voluntarily if they could control the pace

of capital accumulation.' (Marglin, 1976: 14.) The development of management is an integral part of the fragmentation of tasks. Control stripped from manual jobs, now fragmented, is located in, and results in the expansion of, those whose job it is to integrate and coordinate disintegrated tasks. The manager now takes control of decisions which were originally the province of the worker – how much to produce, what to produce, how long to work – which, with employed labour, cannot be left to the employee, since the employee might resolve these issues in ways which reflected his antipathy to forms of work and employment relationships under capitalism.

Marglin carefully disputes Adam Smith's arguments for the greater efficiency of the division of labour (that it permits the increase of individuals' dexterity, that it saves time and that it encourages technical innovation) by showing that they either apply to pre-capitalist forms of the division of labour, or that they may apply to *separation* of tasks, but not to *specialization*, whereby individuals are allocated solely to fragmented and specialized jobs. This latter feature of work in capitalism – the restriction of the worker to the same fragmented operation – was the result, claims Marglin, of the capitalist's need to regulate and to dominate the employee, of his need to interpose between production and consumption. The development of technology did not cause the fragmentation of work. Rather it was a result of factory organization and work design. The aims of this tendency are described by Braverman: 'It was to ensure that as craft declined, the worker would sink to the level of general and undifferentiated labour power, adaptable to a large range of simple tasks, while, as science grew, it would be concentrated in the minds of management.' (Braverman, 1974: 121.) Modern technology is of great use in this ambition. It permits the centralization of control, it establishes a constant regulation, it assists the integration (by mechanical pacing) of work. The design, development, installation and utilization of modern technology are regarded as integral parts of the priorities and contradictions of *capitalism*, not *industrialization* (see Gorz, 1972; Braverman, 1974; Marglin, 1976; Stone, 1974).

A major implication of the Marxist approach to employing organizations is to repoliticize all aspects of organizational structure and functioning. If technology, the division of labour and the expansion of expert functions assume political significance as attempts to maximize profit and control, so conflicts within the organization are seen as directly concerned with these efforts, in some form or another, whether they be conflicts between victims who mistake the symptom for the cause of their problems (male skilled workers who oppose the entry of female workers, for example) or groups which seek to oppose the actions and logics of rationalization. Similarly, movements within management thinking and organizational design take on a political significance, especially with respect to ideologies of control, however transformed by current vocabularies of job enrichment or responsibility.

Within this tradition, the frequent work satisfaction surveys described in Chapter 3 represent an alienated, or pro-management sociology, and, to the extent that the findings reflect anything about the respondents (it is accepted that they reveal much about the researchers), they are themselves regarded as evidence of alienated work attitudes: they demonstrate the extent to which working people are indoctrinated and coerced into developing resigned and unambitious work attitudes which reflect the depriving undemanding realities of work life.

These processes are achieved outside of work – through the mass media, education, organized religion, through the differentiation of the working class by the encouragement of racist or sexist attitudes and practices, by consumerism, by nationalism, by the search for cheap compliant labour.

But they are massively supported inside the factory by the everyday experience of modern forms of work.

It is, of course, in this tradition of analysis that the concept of alienation has its origins, although most recent usages of the concept owe more to Durkheim than to Marx. A Marxist employment of the concept would not only insist on considering the origins of the alienative work forms, and the nature and origins of the widely prevalent instrumental and extrinsic orientations which permit workers to acquiesce in their deprivation, but would insist on viewing alienation not simply as states of feeling, as workers' attitudes, but as a way of describing their condition within capitalism: exposed to intensive exploitation and rationalization; filling fragmented jobs; the subjects of constant discipline and exhortation. In short, expropriated and exploited in every aspect of their work, and, indeed, in their reactions to their work which are orchestrated by the considerable machinery of state, of party politics, mass media and education.

The alienation of the worker under capitalism, as revealed in his or her acquiescence in a form of work which is denying and depriving and, ultimately, exploiting, demonstrates the hegemony of capitalism to which the worker is exposed. Hegemony (a concept developed by the Italian Marxist, Gramsci) refers to the coincidence of capitalist activity – characteristic forms of organization and of work, the unequal distribution of work rewards, the private ownership of capital, competition and the mobility of capital and labour – and bodies of thought in which a definite notion of reality is presented. Under capitalism, this form of thought, which pervades education and mass communications, is also implicit in the decision-making criteria and rationality of large corporations. The important point about hegemonic consciousness is that it becomes part of everyday life – of 'common sense'. Hegemony operates so as to mystify and confuse; it encourages adaptation, passivity and acquiescence in the face of the 'natural' order. It presents as necessary and inevitable what is contingent and alterable. It regards inequalities and deprivations as merely 'relative', and as costs required by consumerism. It celebrates the status quo, denies the possibility of change.

Thus the alienation of workers in capitalism prevents them from developing a true understanding of that society and their role in it. Certainly workers develop hostility; certainly they are acutely aware of the deprivations they experience. But the inability of workers to grasp the true facts of their exploitation lies in the role and nature of ideology within capitalism and in the organization and design of work. Within capitalism, relations between managers and workers, in the determination of workers' wages, the nature and development of the market, take on the appearance and reality of things, external to the individual, beyond his control, subject to 'natural' not social laws. Sociology itself, at least in some of its forms, encourages this conception of social and economic processes. Conventional organizational sociology, with its preoccupation with establishing connections between various 'determinant' organizational variables and other key features of organizational structure is regarded as confusing correlation with cause. By assisting the 'normalization' of characteristically capitalist work forms, and presenting them as necessary and the result of sociological laws, such forms of sociology represent an aspect of hegemony. By confusing description with causation they obstruct the possibility of change and transformation. Furthermore, as we have seen, the alienation of the worker cannot be seen solely in the context of the workers' *reactions* to unquestioned work arrangements. It is encouraged by the penetration into all aspects of social, family, work and personal life of the primacy of the commodity. It reveals hegemony. People, activities, personalities, skills, are valuable only in terms of their financial, exchange value. And alienation reflects the values and interests lying behind work design and organizational structure and the total work experience and societal enculturation (or indoctrination) of the worker.

Chapter 4 began with an attempt to understand the *origins* of work attitudes. This required reference to two considerations: theories of organizational structure and work design (for these constitute the objective aspects of work experience), and factors which structure work expectations, or encourage certain fatalistic or limited aspirations. We have noted that any understanding of work attitudes which attempts any more than a partial and inadequate measurement of workers' responses to researchers' questions must seek to locate these responses within a theory of organizational structure and an analysis of work cultures, education etc. This chapter has considered three such theories. It will be clear that these theories of organizational structure also carry clear implications for analyses of work cultures. A theory of organization which explains the unequal distribution of organizational rewards and the division of labour and organizational hierarchy in terms of the exigencies of modern technologies, or of the requirements of efficient performance, also asserts the inevitability of these structures. Worker attitudes and responses, then, are only problematic in the practical, managerial sense, since the only question to be explained is why do workers fail to understand the inevitability and fairness of the existing forms of work organization and their position within them? A functionalist theory of organization raises the issue: what factors stop workers seeing organizational hierarchy and design of work in terms of functionalist theory?

For the Marxist, or certain forms of radical Weberian theory, the question is a very different one. Here again we find that a theory of organizational structure has direct implications for a theory of work cultures and attitudes. But here the question is reversed. Instead of focusing on why it is that workers persist in misunderstanding the origin and nature of work structures, Marxist theory asks what factors, at work and outside, structure workers' expectations and attitudes such that, to a considerable degree, they acquiesce in their own deprivation. In view of the evident inequality of work arrangements, and of the distribution of work rewards, deprivations and delights, this seems a more sensible question. It has another advantage. The functionalist approach insists on explaining work organizations and employee attitudes in terms of depoliticized concepts and assumptions (value-free science and technology, the industrial society, the supersession of class, consensus) which are evidently inappropriate, and in dealing with deviations from the model (constant class conflict, the persistence of class structures, the capitalist nature and priorities of employing organizations) in terms of misunderstandings, confusions. The Marxist account, on the other hand, takes the inequalities and deprivations of work, the issues of conflict and control, as the starting point for its analysis. This not only relates it firmly to a well-developed and plausible theory of class (see Chapter 7), it also asserts an important feature of any adequate theory of organization: that it establishes the relationship between organizational structures and management theories and societal cultures, and the forces within society which assert the reasonableness of organizational control and inequality, and the unreasonableness of employee resistance or recalcitrance. The strength of the Marxist theory of organization is that it regards organizational relationships in class terms, and involves explicit reference to societal and ideological processes which encourage acquiescence among employees, but which reveal further aspects of class domination.

6 Organization and Control

Organizations are structures of control. The persistence which defines an organization is the result of individual members adjusting their work behaviour in certain predictable ways. By whatever ways such predictability is achieved (whether it emerges as the result of negotiations and struggles or blind obedience), it still constitutes the major – indeed, defining – feature of employing organizations. Organizations are structured: functions persist beyond the incumbency of particular individuals; individuals' behaviours reflect organizational directives and constraints, not just idiosyncratic personal preferences. Furthermore, the persistence of predictable patterns of behaviour takes various forms so that we can speak not only of the structure of an organization, but also differentiate *types* of structure – various organizational profiles, or configurations. Furthermore, these structural variations consist, in the main, in different types and structures of control. This chapter will describe and analyse some of these control mechanisms, and consider how they have been interpreted by different types of sociological theory.

Control of members' behaviour – and their attitudes – is central to organizational existence. Katz and Kahn remark: 'organizational structure is created and maintained only as the members of the organization interact in an ordered way ... the organization lives only so long as people are induced to be members and to perform as such.' (Katz and Kahn,

1967: 454.) The fact of organizational membership exposes members to the dual nature of their membership: that it is both an economic and a political relationship. This duality is undeniable. By joining an employing organization a person exposes him or herself to the organization's direction and control in exchange for payment or other reward. The wage-effort bargain consists of the organization buying workers' effort, and through a variety of control methods regulating and directing that effort. The political dimension of organization employment is revealed in another obvious feature of organizations: the unequal nature of organizational life and the constant possibility of subordinates resisting or avoiding the efforts of their seniors (however mediated and obscured) to control them. Within employing organizations a number of highly-valued resources and highly-depriving – possibly dangerous – experiences are unequally distributed. The majority of the members not only receive significantly lower wages than middle and senior management, their conditions of work and employment are far inferior, and their work experiences are vastly more damaging and depriving. It is precisely these least advantaged members of the organization who find themselves being controlled by senior (and more privileged) members. Workers who experience the reality of insecurity, deprivation, dehumanized work and subordination are likely to demonstrate some resistance to the oppressive controls to which they are subject. Herein lies the second sense in which the employment relationship can be said to be political – it not only contains built-in relationships of super- and sub-ordination, but these relationships (which carry their own implications for deprivation or delight) occur between groups of people which differ greatly in their share of the organization's resources – and deprivations – and between whom conflict frequently occurs. In short, inequalities of power correlate with inequalities of other organizational resources. Why should this be so? We shall see that theories of organization vary in their interpretation of this connection.

The undeniable fact of conflict between controllers and controlled, privileged and deprived, has been interpreted in numerous ways by sociologists, most of whom employ variants of the theories of the three theorists discussed in Chapter 2. We will discuss these varying views later. These conflicts attract much managerial attention and activity, with a view to establishing within the organization the legitimacy of the organization's structure, or personnel selection, or the distribution of organization rewards. For example, concerning the distribution of financial rewards, Hyman and Brough remark that 'The dominant cultural perspective, persistently inculcated by the various agencies of social indoctrination, is that high material advantages are the rewards for personal ability, effort or initiative, a prize potentially open to all.' (Hyman and Brough, 1975: 201.)

Processes of organizational control involve numerous elements: work-based regulations (of various sorts, technical, bureaucratic, professional); controls aimed at reducing or making unimportant, employees' resistance; controls which attempt to discipline the potentially recalcitrant, and efforts to establish and disseminate the legitimacy of the enterprise with all its inequalities and deprivations. These efforts are easier to separate conceptually than they are in reality. Nevertheless, the distinctions are important since theorists differ as to the importance – indeed, existence – of these various imperatives.

Within the enterprise, employers and controllers are able to exercise control over subordinate members of the organization by virtue of their control over desired resources – money, careers, promotion, conditions, the conferring of status, approval, and so on – and their control over sanctions – unfavourable treatment, the withdrawal of rewards, dismissal. These are the obvious realities of organizational power from the point of view of the employees. But where does this power come from? What is the origin of this capacity to dominate and structure the lives of subordinates? To answer these questions forces us to address the question of the relationship between organizational structure and hierarchies (and the power that resides in them) and the structure of the larger society. We shall find that, once again, sociologists differ in their analysis of the nature and origins of organizational power. Whatever the preferred interpretation (and this writer's will be made plain in Chapter 8,) it is clear that it is important to analyse the relationship between organizational structures of dominance and subordination, and societal hierarchies, or classes, particularly since the organizations of which we speak are not merely organizations, they are also private property, which is owned by a very small proportion of the society. It is, of course, the owners of the organization, or their representatives, who have the 'right' and the resources to control and direct the labour of the propertyless. And it is the propertyless subordinates who are the least advantaged members of the organization. Internal organizational allocations and relationships reflect external societal ones.

We shall now turn to a consideration of some influential analyses of organizational processes of control. These will be related to the approaches of our three founding fathers. It must be stressed that although links can be seen to exist between the current analysis discussed below and the theorist concerned, this is not to say that the current sociologists acknowledge or even accept such a connection. Nor is it to argue that each writer would accept wholesale the theories which echo in their work. But it is to claim that their analyses show clear traces of the ideas and problems of at least some aspects of the classic theorist.

Moral regulation and systems theory

Durkheim's work on the division of labour contains much reference to the importance of moral regulation of the world of industry. In his discussion of the various forms of the 'anomic' division of labour, he describes those conditions under which it fails to generate the expected degree of integration. One major source of such pathology occurs when specialization and differentiation are pushed too far and so rapidly that they generate a 'dissolving influence, which would be particularly obvious where functions are very specialized'. This is a result of lack of moral regulation – 'We know ... that wherever organic solidarity is found, we come upon an *adequately developed regulation* determining the mutual relations of functions.' (Durkheim, 1964: 365; my emphasis.) The obverse is a lack of regulation concerning the relations between capital and labour and the individual employee's conception of, and involvement in, his work. Durkheim describes the meaninglessness of modern, fragmented, mechanized work (Durkheim, 1964: 371) but sees the solution to these serious problems not in altering the division of labour itself, but in the worker seeing the meaning and purpose of his actions. Under 'normal' conditions of the division of labour, the worker 'keeps himself in constant relations with neighbouring functions, takes conscience of their needs, of the changes which they undergo etc. The division of labour presumes that the worker, far from being hemmed in by his task, does not lose sight of his collaborators, that he acts upon them and reacts to them.' (Durkheim, 1964: 372.)

How is this state of affairs to be achieved? As Eldridge points out (1971), Durkheim's view of the anomic character of some forms of the division of labour must be seen in the context of his treatment of anomie in his other works – notably *Suicide*, and of his efforts elsewhere, notably in *Socialism* and *Professional Ethics*, to devise solutions to the widespread problem of anomie in modern society. A central feature of these solutions is that they involve the rediscovery of the moral character of society and social life. This can only be through the re-emergence of the power, the moral pressure, of collective forces which will attract the commitment of citizens and workers to their collective (but differentiated) existence. In practical terms, this can only be expressed through various work – or occupationally based secondary associations (see his *Professional Ethics and Civic Morals*).[1]

These arguments of Durkheim concerning the importance of the moral regulation of industry, of workers' understanding of their role in a differentiated work process, and of the role of various forms of memberships to re-establish this commitment, have been influential in recent work in industrial sociology, i.e., in that tradition which is known as the Human Relations movement.

The Human Relations approach to organizations owes its origins to the researches of Roethlisberger and Dickson at the Hawthorne plant of Western Electric, a subsidiary of AT and T. These researches have been thoroughly described and criticized elsewhere (see, for example, Argyle, 1953; Carey, 1967; Perrow, 1972; Rose, 1975). The important point about the Human Relations movement (but not necessarily the original researches which were used as a source of inspiration by many later interpreters) is the emphasis placed on the work group as a source of meaning, culture and discipline for the worker; within these work groups, workers were exposed to, and soon internalized, sentiments which stressed certain patterns of group-supportive behaviour (restriction of output) and conceptions of the management which legitimized these activities and values.

These interpretations of the Hawthorne studies have been influential. As Perrow notes, 'After the Hawthorne studies were published, a small-scale social movement got under way – financed by government agencies, business organizations, universities and business-supported foundations – which sought to find ways to increase productivity by manipulating social factors.' (Perrow, 1972: 104.)

Such a response was due to the attractive (to management) proposition that workers' attitudes towards their employers, and their work, were highly influenced by 'social' factors, that is, the groups of which they were members and the ideas which circulated within these groups and which were enforced on and by group members. If only these loyalties could be widened, to take in the company as a whole . . . And if only these irrational sentiments urging and justifying work restrictions could be replaced with more wholesome and positive notions of the relationship between worker and employer . . . The managerial appeal of such 'discoveries' is obvious.

But if the Human Relations movement has always been attractive to managers, and those who share their commitments, it has never been without its critics. Most criticisms point to the excessive concern of the authors with consensus and cooperation and the negative place allocated to conflict. Conflict is given little attention, such instances as are noted being attributed to worker irrationality. Management, on the other hand, is seen as representing rationality. Furthermore, the importance attached to the work group distracts attention from the larger society, and from the economic and social context of employment: the rationalization, mechanization, unemployment, union management-conflicts, and so on. As Perrow nicely puts it, 'That such conflicts of interests and inequalities of power might be solved by better face-to-face relations between workers and management, or by the famous counselling system, seemed doubtful.' (Perrow, 1972: 103.) Finally, critics have pointed out that the Human Relations movement is not only vulnerable on conceptual and theoretical grounds. It is also weak empirically. The much advertised connection between social factors and productivity does not always stand up. (See Argyle, 1953; Sykes, 1965; Perrow, 1972.)

There should be no need to stress the close relations between the Human Relations model and Durkheim's conception of the division of labour and its pathologies, although it must be noted that, for example, Mayo showed a selective interest in Durkheim's analysis of the various causes of pathological forms of the division of labour. For Mayo, a leading interpreter of the Hawthorne studies, and a major influence in the movement, social *problems*, including those of work, can be resolved by social *skills*, most importantly leadership and counselling, i.e., skills of communications (see Rose, 1975: Ch. 12). The Human Relations emphasis on the work group as a source of belongingness and meaning to the worker which compensates for the anonymity and enormity of modern society, parallels Durkheim's advocacy of professional associations. And the Human Relations insistence on communication and social skills engaging the worker's commitment, establishing involvement and meaning, and eliminating irrational sentiments, makes use of, if it does not do justice to, Durkheim's view that the pathologies of the division of labour are not the fault of the organization of work itself, but of the lack of moral regulation – anomie – that can exceptionally occur.

Durkheim's emphasis on the essential nature of modern society – the division of labour and the new form of integration it creates, at least under normal circumstances – can be seen to be closely related to another important trend within sociological analysis of work organizations: that tradition which ascribes the nature of modern organizations, and indeed of the societies within which they occur, to the fact of industrialism itself. Such a view is in direct opposition to that which asserts the primacy of the form industrialism takes – e.g., capitalism. The relationship between this form of analysis and Durkheim's work have been discussed already, in Chapter 2. Certainly Durkheim, as Giddens notes, did not advance an explicit theory of industrial society, nor did he use the term frequently. But in Durkheim's insistence that the determinant feature of the new society was the division of labour, and the changes it was undergoing. And in his attributing the personal pathologies of work and the conflicts between developing groups within the new order to the strains of tradition, the incomplete synchronization of the various elements, Durkheim in general terms fits into the tradition established by Saint-Simon, and continued more recently by such writers as Kerr, Bell and Galbraith.

This tradition, which seeks to understand and describe the imperatives of the process of industrialism, and which stresses the common features of all industrial societies, regardless of claimed differences in political philosophy or economic principle, was discussed in Chapter 5. It contains an explicit theory of organizational control. Essentially, Kerr *et al.* claim that the process of industrialization itself requires large-scale employing organizations of a hierarchical and differentiated sort. Within these organizations control is organized through hierarchy and 'an elaborate web of rules that is made the more intricate and complex by technology, specialization, and the large scale of operations.' (Kerr *et al.*, 1973: 51.) These rules cover personnel practices, work organization and integration, and performance etc. This control is necessitated by the goals of the organization, and by the application of modern technology and science. Both these features are the subjects of a distinctive consensus: both ends and means are agreed and accepted by all groups. Furthermore, the ever-influential process of modernization and rationalization is accorded high value. Of course, conflicts occur but these are not against the system of industrialization but are over

questions of distribution. 'Workers now protest more in
favour of industrialization than against it. "Machine
breakers" are no longer heroes.' (Kerr *et al.*, 1973: 224.)

These views are echoed by Galbraith (1969) and Daniel
Bell (1974), both of whom stress the role of planning and
knowledge in modern 'post-industrial' societies. These
writers see organizational control as based on the functional significance of science and information in achieving
the efficient production of modern goods and services.
Control, then, is neutral; it is demanded by the task in
hand, which in turn is for the benefit of society at large,
indeed for the workers themselves as citizens and consumers, and is achieved through the application of science
and technology. The 'post-industrial' society, 'by making
decisions more technical . . . brings the scientist or
economist more directly into the political process.' (Bell,
1974: 43.)

These views of the nature and origin of control and
hierarchy within employing organizations have obvious
ramifications for analyses of conflicts and classes. These are
discussed in Chapter 7.

The suggestion that organizational control is simply a
response to the (shared and consensual) organizational
goals, which themselves reflect societal requirements, is
most developed in the work of systems writers. Parsons, for
example, defines organizations as social systems which are
organized to achieve a goal for the larger society, to perform
societal functions. Within this model, organizational power
is defined in consensual and legitimate terms: ' . . . we may
speak of power as a generalized societal resource which is
allocated to the attainment of a wide range of subgoals and
to organizations as the agents of the attainment of such
subgoals.' (Parsons, 1970: 79.)

The problems with this view of power (and, consequently, of the control which it supports) have been
well rehearsed elsewhere: Giddens, for example, notes

Parsons's preoccupation with authority at the expense of power and coercion, and criticizes the claim that power rests upon value consensus rather than on conflicts of interest, which may of course give rise to more or less successful legitimating ideologies. Giddens points to the obvious and important point, glossed over by Parsons, that power differences reflect differences of interest and resource, and he notes that supporting values may, if they actually exist, be (deliberately) constructed ideologies, i.e., *reflections* of power differences, not *determinants* of power allocation (Giddens, 1968: 264). (For an excellent analysis of power in organizations, see Clegg, 1979.)

Finally, the influence of Durkheim on current theories of organizational power and control can be seen in recent developments within a form of theory which owes much to Durkheim's functional sociology and the organic analogy which underlies it: socio-technical systems. The relevant argument of this approach is contained in the work of Woodward and Perrow: that given a commitment to a specific organizational goal, organizations develop and install appropriate technologies to get the work done, and that these in turn have a major impact on the structure of the organization and, most pertinently, for the organization of control. Woodward, for example, in exploring the relationship between technology and other organizational variables, notes that with unit batch production and continuous flow production the connection between technology and the appropriate form of control is tight. In the case of unit batch production, control is relatively simple and based mainly on the personal hierarchy. Work is mostly unprogrammed. In continuous flow production, the equipment and the organization of work contain built-in controls. Decisions about products, mixes and quantities are made through established mechanical or computer systems. However, with the intermediate type of tech-nology, the link between technology and particular control types was less close; here, possibly, management could exercise some choice. The interesting thing about Woodward's analysis of the relationship between technology and control is that she argues for a conceptual separation of design and programming on the one hand, and execution on the other. The various types of technology simply represent different locations of these two processes. In unit batch technology they overlap; with continuous flow technology there is total separation (Woodward, 1970: Ch. 3).

In other words, technology itself represents, among other things, a form of control, or at least a possibility of control, such that when technology is designed which contains built-in controls and direction, other forms of hierarchical control are not necessary. This immediately raises the question: what, then, determines the choice of technology? The answer, within this tradition, is that technology is determined by: the overall state of technical and scientific knowledge; the economic and engineering resources of firms; and the nature of the thing that is being manufactured or assembled. This last mentioned will, of course, have reference to the firm's marketing position and aspirations. To this list Perrow would add another factor: the characteristics of the raw material, and the extent to which it permits standardization. Perrow sees organizations as constantly attempting to achieve regularity and predictability, except when they are forestalled by the characteristics of the raw material, or the work tasks: 'Organizations uniformly seek to standardize their raw material in order to minimize exceptional stituations.' (Perrow, 1972: 51.) Perrow, and Davis *et al.*, (1973) see this attempt to achieve predictability limited by the goals the organization seeks, for organizational goals establish organizational tasks, and these in turn ' . . . allow different amounts of freedom to various people to seek their own goals.' (Davis *et al.*, 1973: 159.)

This analysis of the relationship between technology and organizational control, and the role of organizational goals in establishing technologies, will be discussed and criticized later in this chapter.

These approaches to control within organizations share certain characteristic Durkheimian features: control itself is defined in terms of moral regulation, and relationships between controllers and controlled are defined in terms not of any systematic conflict of interests, but in terms of the requirement of the system of organization and the technology employed. Such conflicts and problems as undeniably occur are attributed not to the system itself but to various pathologies not yet removed, or to an excess of system success, whereby contributors to the division of labour within industrialization compete for resources and so demonstrate their commitment to the society's goals and values. The organization, and the state which buttresses it, reveals – in its hierarchy and power – the societal function it performs. Power itself stems from the consensus surrounding the organization's function, just as the need for control stems from the means employed to achieve these consensual goals. These organizational analyses share with Durkheim the conviction that organizations, and their internal structure and process, represent the technical inevitabilities of agreed goals. They do not consider that organizations exist to preserve existing patterns of exploitation and subordination.

Rationality, bureaucracy and control

Weber's analyses of bureaucracy takes the issue of organizational control as its central element. In Weber's model, as noted in Chapter 2, bureaucracy is seen as representing an institutionalization of a distinctive form of authority – one based on 'rational' authority, and rational control. Weber's ideal type bureaucracy attempts to describe in exaggerated and partial ways the various characteristics which exemplify, in coherent fashion, the basic tendencies of bureaucracies of various sorts. Underpinning Weber's analysis is his emphasis on the 'rationality' of bureaucracy; and the implications of this for organizational structure and control are: impersonality, formality, hierarchy, strict and exact demarcation of duties and responsibilities, and recruitment on the basis of ability and experience. These prevalent (but, in Weber, exaggerated) qualities of bureaucracy, reflect the value, widely diffused in modern (for Weber, capitalist) societies, of rationality. But two points must be reiterated about Weber's view of bureaucracy as articulating rationality: (1) he does not argue that rationality is synonymous with efficiency, though later writers have understood him to mean this. For Weber, rationality was a highly widespread and influential cultural value, apparent in an increasing number of societal institutions especially those of capitalism; (2) he was not interested in using his concept of bureaucracy to analyse particular organizations, or to advance theories of internal organization structures. His analysis of bureaucracy was part of a wider interest in classifying forms of societal development and, in particular, different forms of legitimate domination and administration (see Mouzelis, 1967).

Not surprisingly, therefore, given this interest in societal and organizational structures of domination and control, Weber's work has been highly influential in the development of Organizational Theory. However, this influence has been one-sided, revealing, in many cases, an almost systematic misunderstanding of Weber's intentions. Weber's language is often used, but not his analysis. Only recently have we seen a revival of interest in Weber's use of the concept rationality to mount a critical – not celebratory – analysis of modern society, and the organizational forms which proliferate.

The influence of Weber's writings on bureaucracy is most apparent in two recent preoccupations: the analysis of the negative effects of bureaucracy, and research which regards the bureaucratic type – or the various 'dimensions' which are seen to constitute this type, as one of a number of organizational forms. This latter tradition analyses the relationship between a variety of environmental or internal factors – size, market conditions, and so on – and different types of organization.

The analysis of bureaucratic dysfunctions assumes that when Weber described bureaucracy as the most rational type of organization he was evaluating the efficiency of the characteristics listed. Within this interpretation it is therefore appropriate to note the divergence between Weber's model and modern empirical arrangements. A number of writers have argued that, empirically, organizations develop many patterns of behaviour which are not specified by Weber, indeed are obviously directly contrary to the principles he adumbrates. Furthermore, these 'informal' patterns and relationships can directly assist the achievement of formal organizational purposes. This point is also made by Blau's study of an employment exchange in his *Dynamics of Bureaucracy* (1972). Similarly, Gouldner, in *Patterns of Industrial Bureaucracy* (1954) argues not only that informal, unregulated, personal relationships can be, under certain circumstances, 'functional' (i.e., efficient) for the achievement of formal organizational goals, but also – echoing Merton – that formal, rule-bound impersonal procedures can obstruct such efficiency. Gouldner's analysis makes a further important point – that the process of bureaucratization itself can be seen as part of power relationships between controllers and controlled. Bureaucracy, argues Gouldner, is a method of control which senior organizational members attempt to impose on subordinates when they find previous control mechanisms inadequate.

As Mouzelis remarks, for all three writers, bureaucracy is seen as a system of tension and change, a dialectic between formal and informal processes, between order and disorder, between control and resistance (Mouzelis, 1967). The same view of bureaucracy is advanced by Roy (1973) in his analysis of 'informal' organizational groups. Banana Time

Ironically, these writers, by stressing the dialectic nature of bureaucracy, by emphasizing the role of bureaucratic measures as control mechanisms, by revealing the complex relationship between characteristically bureaucratic procedures and bureaucratic efficiency – indeed in asking the question, 'efficient for whom and for what?', most of all perhaps in demystifying the concept of rationality, these writers are not, as they themselves seem, occasionally, to think, criticizing Weber. They are actually using and supporting Weber's analysis of bureaucracy, since his model also at least implicitly makes the same broad argument. Weber regards bureaucracy as demonstrating certain features which reflect a widespread cultural value. These characteristics constitute a form of organizational domination, the articulation of certain values (calculability, measurement, regulation by formal rules) not simply the reflection of efficiency. It is only by misunderstanding Weber that one can see the important studies of Merton, Gouldner, Blau, Crozier, and others, all of which regard bureaucratic control as part of the efforts of senior members to control the recalcitrance of subordinates as modifications of Weber. Besides, these revealing studies require no such claims in order to establish their own interest.

Rather, they are important for their view of organizations as arenas of conflict between competing groups, with senior, dominant groups striving to maintain their dominance through the imposition of bureaucratic controls, and subordinate groups trying to avoid such control, and to achieve some area of autonomy, often through informal group organizations. They are useful in questioning the naïve interpretation of Weber's notion of rationality, whereby formal organizational structure and process are seen as reflecting the search for efficiency, with any deviations from managerial dictates regarded as hopelessly reactionary or obstructive. In these analyses, rationality in the Weberian sense is seen as a form of managerial – or organizational – philosophy, employed by senior members in their efforts to manage and structure the organization so as to achieve their conception of organizational goals. This concept of rationality, of course, has many echoes in the surrounding society, where the criteria of organizational rationality are highly influential. To this extent, a serious and informed neo-Weberianism – although it usually adopts a less ambitious level of analysis, nevertheless, if it regards the concept of rationality as a highly prevalent mode of thought and analysis, and not as pure reason, and if it considers such a mode of thought as proving useful to senior organizational members in both legitimizing and disguising their dominance, and in structuring the organizations they control (through rational, i.e., bureaucratic means) – can be seen to continue Weber's analysis of the characteristic organizational forms of modern society, and the relationships between internal organizational structures, and larger societal patterns. We shall return to this view of rationality later.

But one point remains. While much of the recent work by Gouldner, Blau etc. points to the facts of organizational struggle, and of the role of bureaucratic controls in these struggles, there is little analysis of the *origins* of highly unequal distribution of power and resources within organizations. If organizations contain constant (although frequently implicit and disguised) conflicts, how can we understand the differential resources and capacities of the various organizational combatants? One answer focuses attention on the organizational position of the various groups: organizational power follows from organizational position and, most significantly, from the group's capacity to retain (or achieve) some control over work processes or activities, which constitute a potential source of uncertainty for senior members, thus interrupting their efforts to standardize and regulate organizational activity. Such regulation permits prediction, planning; it reflects senior members' control. This view is most explicitly expressed in Crozier (1964) and Hickson *et al.* (1973). Such analyses are useful in understanding internal conflicts, but how far is it feasible to seek to explain such conflicts, and the distribution of resources which they articulate, and the divergences of interests which they reflect, *solely* in organizational terms? What are the connections between organizational struggles and societal ones? How do organizational groups relate to societal categories, to classes? Is the origin of internal organization struggles, demarcations and resources entirely a question of organizational history, of the slowly emerging power of certain groups, of the significance attaching to key organization jobs, or do these matters have something to do with the appearance, within the organization, of class differences, interests and resources?

It is on this issue that the new-Weberian and Marxist approaches to organizations diverge most obviously, the latter regarding many if not most of the conflicts described by the former as examples, in however mediated and distorted a form, of what are ultimately class-based conflicts of interest. To adopt such a position obviously requires a distinctive interpretation of the rationality of organizations. Now such rationality is regarded as directly supporting the domination of capital, and the exploitation of labour, although presenting this in forms which seek to evade the consciousness of those so exploited through the appearance of neutrality and impartiality, of abstract forces and reifications such as the Market, Modernization or Rationalization. Rationality is no longer simply a distinctive form of modern thought, but a direct consequence of capitalist exploitation: 'the pervasive character of capitalist commodity relations and of the technological rationality upon which they are based tends to reduce social relations and social consciousness to a single dimension: their instrumental value in terms of maintaining the structure of social domination.' (Aronowitz, 1973: 9.) We shall return to this interpretation later, in discussion of the Marxist approach to organizations.

Such a notion of rationality is, however, certainly not found in the other major neo-Weberian tradition which, in as far as it conceptualizes the values and criteria underlying the production of various organizational forms, regards them simply as mediating between various contextual or internal factors – size, market – and the organization's structure. Thus the relationship between size and the 'structuring of activities' (composed of specialization, standardization of procedures, formalization of roles and communications), once empirically discovered and verified, is seen as a law of organizational development – as organizations increase in size they will demonstrate greater structuring of activities. This is a general organizational characteristic apparent, it is claimed, in various societal contexts. The aim of the Aston studies – most famous of all exercises in this tradition – was based on the belief that it is 'feasible to explore comparatively how far there are *organizational characteristics in general* . . . an aim of the Aston research was to arrive at statements which would be applicable to as many organizations as possible.' (Pugh and Hickson, 1976: vii.)

The Aston research contains a mass of information on the empirical inter-relationships between various dimensions of organizational structure and selected contextual, size and technological variables. For purposes of this chapter, the most pertinent findings concern varieties of organizational control, and the relationship between these and work designs, and technology. Much of the Aston research concerns forms and origins of organizational control systems. Two arguments are of particular importance, and have general relevance. The Aston studies suggest that within organizations various strategies of control may be employed. Decision-making may be centralized, or control may be achieved through standardization and formalization. It seems that as employees are more and more hedged around with controls and limitations on their decision-making, so senior members can afford the risk of delegating formal responsibilities to them (see Pugh and Hickson, 1973). As Child points out, these findings, which have been supported by Blau and Schoenherr's study (1971), do not argue that decentralization and structuring of activities are unitary or identical; merely that 'these dimensions form two related elements in the strategy of administrative control.' (Child, 1976: 41.) The suggestion that senior members of organizations can choose between various control strategies, suggested by Child in another paper (Child, 1973), and that control may be achieved by unobtrusive, even (as Blau and Schoenherr put it) insidious, mechanisms is obviously important. Apart from anything else it raises the possibility that organizational structure as a whole might reflect senior management's need to maintain control, and to achieve some degree of legitimacy for their dominance, as much as any neutral rationality. It also suggests that the bureaucratic response, as described by Gouldner, Blau and others, might not be the only way in which senior organizational members attempt to cope with the potential recalcitrance of their subordinates. Pugh and Hickson, for example, classify three control strategies, three ways in which organizations can be structured: the work-flow structured kind of organization, where roles are specified tightly, and procedures clearly established; the employment structured organization, where personnel matters and selection are closely controlled; and latent structured organizations, where scores on the measures of control dimensions are relatively low but where control occurs in other ways – possibly by socialization into an implicit body of convention and procedures (Pugh and Hickson, 1973). Perrow, for example, has described a variety of ways in which organizations can dispense with overt, oppressive control without risking any real loss of control. He notes the advantages of leaving employees free to make their own decisions on the basis of their expertise and judgement, but so constraining them through rewards, careers, promotions, appraisals, organizational cultures, organizational loyalty and so on, that the resulting decision is 'safe'. To control employees, he remarks, it is not necessary to change the individuals, just to control the premises on which they make their decisions (Perrow 1972). Similarly, Blau and Schoenherr have noted the importance of personnel policies and controls in effecting the insidious control of which they warn (Blau and Schoenherr, 1971). Many of these arguments are discussed in Salaman (1979). One particularly important form of insidious control is described by Perrow. He argues that a common way to reduce formal bureaucratic specifications is to mechanize the work process: 'Any machine is a complex bundle of rules that are built into the machine itself. Machines ensure standardized products, thus eliminating rules regarding dimensional characteristics.' (Perrow, 1972: 24.)

This point is echoed by the Aston research. These researchers note that different sorts of work technologies are related to different control systems, since the work process itself may or may not contain built-in controls. This suggests that one control strategy might be to design work processes which by their very nature severely constrain the activities of those who operate them. The design of work is thus a strategy of control. The Aston researchers simply report this inter-relationship of technology, work design and control, as they report the various forms of structuring which, empirically, appear to represent separate methods of control. Other writers have interpreted these possibilities in very different ways, however, as we shall see.

Exploitation and the search for profit

In Chapter 2 it was established that a central element of Marx's theory of work organizations within capitalism was that all aspects of organizational functioning were irrevocably permeated with control implications. Technology, bureaucracy, the organization of work, organizational structure, all reflected capitalism's need to control and direct a potentially recalcitrant work force whose exploited labour was the basis of the system for the creation of profit and wealth. Capitalism, being based upon the *exploitation* of those who sell their labour, necessarily sets the capitalist, or his agents, problems of control, direction and legitimacy. Employees cannot be 'trusted' to identify with the goals of management, or to adhere to the spirit – or the letter – of their work instructions, for the goals of their organization, and the procedures and specifications which follows from them, are quite antithetical to their interests. The structure of the organization, and everything within it, reflects the employer's pursuit of profit at the expense of his employees, and the constant possibility and occasional reality, of their apprehending this over-riding fact, either as a source of personal withdrawal, 'instrumentality' or bloody-mindedness or as a cause for group, organized resistance. Within capitalism, then, employing organizations, being based upon the organization of exploitation of employees reveal the primacy of profit, and the conflict between employees and capitalism's agents that inevitably follows. Such conflict cannot be disregarded by reference to the 'satisficing' behaviour of managers, or by pointing to the separation of ownership (concerned with profit) and control (concerned with organizational and managerial survival or job security). First, the separations of ownership and control through public ownership of the majority of business corporations, and the diffusion of ownership through share ownership, does not represent any significant change in the function and interests of capital. Nor does it represent a significant alteration – or decomposition – of capital, since these changes have not seriously affected the concentration of share capital. Westergaard and Resler remark: 'Most shareholders are smallholders. But most share *capital* is tightly bunched in few hands. And it is capital that carries weight, not heads. People owning shares to the tune of £20,000 and more in 1970 were a small minority among a tiny minority – no more than eight per cent of all individual shareholders; about one half of one per cent of the entire adult population. But they disposed of nearly seventy per cent of all corporate capital in personal hands.' (Westergaard and Resler, 1975: 159.)

These authors also question the argument of a division of interest between owners (profit) and controllers (security, growth etc.) by noting, as many writers have done, that senior controllers and directors are, usually, themselves owners of share capital. They have a stake in the profitability of the company; they are unlikely to condone the pursuit of policies antithetical to their interests.

But the argument that modern enterprises are concerned with the achievement of profit, and that this has implications for internal organization or work design does not require analysis of ownership of the enterprise. Within capitalism companies must pursue profit. If they fail they risk collapse and bankruptcy. It is unlikely that the controllers of a company would deliberately choose to

reduce their profitability, although they may of course fail
to maximize their profit. This goal is also pursued by the
many experts who analyse trends, assess various business,
technological, organization or market options, advise on
financial, personnel, information and other systems. The
modern enterprise cannot rest assured of its continuing
profitability. To survive, it must seek to improve. Since its
competitors are operating on the same basis, this orientation is constantly justified. Crompton and Gubbay note:
'The best way to cope with these threats to profitability as
such is to plan, calculate and organize methodically to
maximize long-term profit; the controllers of the modern
corporation are characteristically devoted to that cause.'
(Crompton and Gubbay, 1977: 67.) The design of work
and the organization of control are both potential threats to
profitability – especially the attitudes and behaviour of
labour, wage demands etc. – and a consequence of
management's attempts to achieve increased profitability
by intensifying the efficiency of labour – i.e., the speed of
work, the reliability of labour, the flow of work.

Internal organizational arrangements, philosophies of
work design, the existence of ostensibly neutral, 'technical'
experts, various employment arrangements, all can be seen
to reflect (a) the search for profit and (b) efforts to control
those who are exploited, and to increase their efficiency.
Internal organizational arrangements and conflicts are
connected with extra-organizational circumstance. Within
capitalism, organizations, like the society itself, are riddled
with and only explicable in terms of, classes, class interests
and class conflicts. Similarly, various external organizational events and processes are regarded as directly related
to the organization's class basis, in that the external
organizations of power and resources have direct ramifications for the organization. For example, external
agencies, the law, the state, support internal domination;
employees' work expectations are systematically moulded,

and made 'realistic' by education, mass media and counselling agencies; external societal segregations and distinctions, such as gender, race and age, fuel internal discriminations. As such, organizations are seen not only as arenas of class exploitation and conflict, but all socially structured inequalities are viewed as ultimately supporting the persistence of capitalism and the accumulation of profit. These inequalities obviously have direct implications for employment practices and for the organization of control.

Organizational control is required by capitalism and the search for profit through exploitation, not by the task, or technology, except inasmuch as these themselves are designed in terms of the search for profit. It is therefore capitalism, not industrialism, which establishes the need for control. Furthermore, all aspects of the organization reflect, in one way or another, this constant and necessary preoccupation: profit and control. The achievement of control, however, depends as much on extra-organizational factors as on internal ones. It is only in the light of external preparation and experience that internal arrangements can appear 'normal' or rational, or succeed in their purpose of employee control and direction. Finally, the centrality and primacy of control within capitalist employing organizations requires, if it is to succeed, that it appear neutral, a requirement of neutrally-designed tasks, or a reflection of some natural ordering of individual qualities and achievements. Successful organizational control is regarded as legitimate and necessary. Hence the significance attached to such legitimacy.

For the remainder of this chapter, we shall consider some of the most important methods – or strategies – of organizational control employed by capitalist organizations. This discussion will require consideration of internal and external organizational processes. Once again, the inclusion of any particular writer in this section does not mean that he or she is necessarily regarded as a Marxist, though most are. The intention in these sections is to mount a description of an overall type of approach, which will occasionally require the use of arguments and material from various camps.

1 The design of work

The organization and design of work in capitalism represents its twin and inter-related needs: profit and control. It is one of the major virtues of a Marxist approach to organizations that it re-politicizes those aspects of organization which much organizational analysis regards as resulting from the working out of some neutral law of market, technology or organizational purposes – the design of work and organizational structure itself. A Marxist approach regards the design of work, the choice of technology, the structure of the organization as results of the capitalists' needs to establish control and to achieve efficiency, in terms, of course, of profit.

Since Marx, the most celebrated statement of these arguments is advanced by Braverman in his *Labor and Monopoly Capital*. Braverman argues that the principles – and practices – of Scientific Management – Taylorism – are fundamental to the requirements of capitalism. Taylorism is the realization of capitalism on the shop floor. Its advantages are clear. It cheapens labour, makes it more easily transferable, makes it more manageable, permits the separation of design and execution (brain and hand, in Marx's terms), fragments labour's solidarity, permits the intrusion of managerial control into aspects of the job previously unassailable. Obviously these developments in job design are very closely linked to developments in technology, and the application of technology to work tasks. First, the fragmentation of work takes place within a context of mechanization and automation. Secondly, the worker's loss of control is paralleled by the design of machines and processes where control is built-in. 'Machinery,' remarks Braverman, 'offers to management the opportunity to do by wholly mechanical means that which it has previously attempted to do by organizational and disciplinary means.' (Braverman, 1974: 195.)

This analysis has a number of important implications. A central theme is that the 'rationality' of organizational structure and, in particular, of science and technology, is a capitalist rationality – engaged in the aims of capitalism, reflecting (albeit in disguised, obscure ways) class interests, class conflicts. Similarly, the pervasive arguments of the Industrial Society school and elsewhere, that modern forms of work, technology, organizationality structures etc. are responses to the need efficiently to produce goods and services for all citizens as consumers, is overturned. According to Braverman, Marglin (1976) and others, modern technologies, and the work arrangements which are connected to them, owe more to the need for control, than to pure 'efficiency'; and efficiency itself is only in terms of the achievement of profit, not to the achievement of socially desirable and neutral goods. Efficiency within capitalism always means efficiency in terms of profit. Therefore no separation of the issues of control and efficiency is, ultimately, possible. Furthermore, Gordon (1976) argues a distinction between *quantitative* and *qualitative* definitions of efficiency within capitalism. The former describes conventional notions of efficiency, i.e., outputs against inputs. The latter describes processes which reproduce class relations and domination. Under capitalism, work is designed to maximize the latter within the constraints of the former. He writes that capitalist labour processes are efficient if they reproduce capitalist control over the production process and minimize proletarian resistance to that control. However it is possible that quantitative and qualitative efficiency may, on occasion, be in conflict. Gordon cites the case of job design and enlargement experiments which result in increased worker productivity, but risk the loss of control and discipline. Under capitalism, the employer is caught by the twin imperatives of quantitative efficiency by competitive pressures, and qualitative efficiency by the requirements of class conflict and worker recalcitrance. Any particular form of work organization represents a compromise position between these two imperatives.

Stone (1974), for example, records changes in job structures in the American steel industry. She argues that these changes must be seen as management's efforts to increase production without decreasing profits. This required them 'to break the workers' power over production and all institutions that had been part of it . . . They were successful, and the prize they won was the power to introduce labour-saving technology, to control the production process, and to become the sole beneficiary of the innovations.' (Stone, 1974: 27.) Stone argues that technology does not create work arrangements. At most it defines the range of possibilities. Other writers have argued for the wholly political nature of technological developments themselves, and of the ideas on which such developments are based. Braverman's analysis, for example, constitutes a decisive break with those Marxists (but not, of course, Marx himself) who had accepted the technology and organization of the modern work enterprise as largely beyond criticism or alteration, except in terms of the goals involved, i.e., profit instead of state planning. Braverman, like Marx, regards the emergence of differentiated work (Taylorism) and management as interrelated aspects of the expropriation of control. With these innovations, direct control over the work process is achieved. Braverman argues that Taylorism constitutes a basic requirement of capitalism. He criticizes those who have argued for the gradual supercession of Taylorist principles in capitalist work practice. The development of Taylorism accompanied the development of technology and science. As Coombs notes: 'these two processes together played integral parts in constituting monopoly capitalism as a distinct phase in the progress of the capitalist mode of production.' (Coombs, 1978: 85.)

This form of analysis has implications for more than just the design of shop-floor work. It also explains the nature and functions of managerial, technical work, since these exist only at the expense of the de-skilled shop-floor jobs, or are directly concerned with devising new forms of regulations and integration. We shall consider these developments under section (2), and in the next chapter.

Braverman's thesis requires some modification. It is likely that he exaggerates and romanticizes the autonomy of pre-Taylor work forms, in particular disregarding the prevalence of sub-contract in various forms (Littler, 1978 and 1980). More importantly, he overemphasizes the connections between one particular work design philosophy – Scientific Management – and capitalism. Undoubtedly his analysis of the relationship between Taylor's principles, and capitalist objectives and requirements is accurate. But he overlooks the possibility that Taylorism represents only one of a number of possible work strategies, albeit a highly successful one (see Friedman, 1977). In part this omission results from Braverman's decision not to deal with working-class consciousness and resistance, since it is precisely the occurrence of resistance to the de-skilling of work and to loss of work control, that constitutes one of the major grounds for the deployment of alternative strategies of work design in capitalism. As numerous writers post-Braverman have pointed out, the actual ways in which work is designed is a result of the *interaction* of capitalist interests and intentions (and the work forms which represent these) and worker resistance: 'it is the interplay of employer structures of control, forms of resistance and employee counter-pressure which primarily shapes the labour process.' (Littler, 1980: 179.)

But potential or actual resistance only partly explains the deployment of alternative employer strategies. Also significant is the functional importance of the employees concerned – their place within the capitalist division of labour, and the relative cost, in terms of disruption and loss of commitment, of employee resistance. Commitment is particularly important. Fox (1974) argues that it is possible to see the division of labour in terms of the amount of discretion employers permit their employees to exercise. Those granted discretion must be trustworthy, reliable. Such reliability can be achieved by permitting (or, alternatively, by not actively seeking to reduce) discretion. Some jobs are allowed to retain some discretion, some opportunities for creativity and decision-making. Elsewhere, Friedman describes what he calls the 'responsible autonomy' employer strategy, whereby employers grant discretion but surround this with various efforts to encourage the recipient to identify with the organization and with the goals of senior management. This can be done through privileged conditions, careers, some preparatory socialization into appropriate attitudes ideological exhortations and so on. This sort of strategy contrasts with its alternative – direct control – which conforms with the principles of Scientific Management. Friedman and Fox suggest that the (relatively) high-discretion strategy is most likely to be applied to those employees performing central, key functions, whose commitment is most important (Friedman, 1977).

2   Organizational differentiation

The differentiation of functions, and treatment within organizations, is both a method of achieving control and a result of such efforts. Within organizations, major work divisions reflect class divisions, and relations across these distinctions reveal class-based animosities. The existence of these class-based groups, which we will discuss in the next chapter, follows from the orientation of the organization towards profit, and the resulting potentiality for conflict. Major forms of organizational differentiation, in particular that between employees who design and employees who execute work systems, are a result of the employers' need for discipline over the exploited work force. Braverman, following Marx, is clear on this: the destruction and fragmentation of the pre-industrial craft takes the form of the differentiation of once-unified functions – execution and design – which constitutes the major axis of differentiation within modern organizations. While it is true, however, that the existence of managerial and technical specialisms of various sorts is only possible because of a basic split between design and execution, it is also clear that many of the new managerial specialisms were never part of the craftsman's role, and have emerged in response to the characteristic problems of large-scale organizations in advanced capitalism. Many of these are concerned with control issues such as the 'efficient' management of the organization's 'human resources': work study, personnel, computer services or Industrial Relations. (See Watson, 1977, for a useful discussion of the personnel function.)

The new organizational specialisms concerned with achieving organizational control, with designing new work systems, manpower planning, training, organizational development and so on, employ various forms of scientific, rational, technical knowledge which are themselves (despite their ostensible neutrality, their concern only with the *means* to achieve agreed goals) thoroughly permeated by class priorities and assumptions. Systems theory, industrial psychology, motivation theory, certain brands of organization theory, all reflect the employers' goals – profit – and the primacy of this over the interests of employees.[2] Such organizational developments, serving the needs for new forms of insidious, subtle control in the monopoly capitalist era (when the 'problem' of motivation and control is of particular importance) reflect an 'instrumental' reason – a pervasive form of reason which is concerned not with liberation and escape from constraint, but with domination of things and men. This form of reason is preoccupied with *technique*; the goals are assumed, regarded as beyond debate, forgotten. Yet this form of thought is itself a major support for patterns of domination and oppression, for it mystifies the realities of the situation – exploitation and oppression – by regarding them as the manifestations of consensual and neutral forms of thought (Marcuse, 1972). Just as the technology which assists the de-skilling of working-class work itself is based upon class interests, so the science and rationality employed by new managerial specialisms is predicated upon, and serves to support, existing class relations. The ideology of technology is oriented towards instrumental effectiveness and reflects precisely the forms of analyses characteristic of positivistic notions of science, which assert the homogeneity and neutrality of scientific thinking. Such analyses, which are reflected both in organizational technologies, and organizational decision-making and process, separate subject and object and present knowledge as neutral representations of reality. Thus alternative priorities, other than instrumental mastery, are rejected (or placed beyond reason), and decisions and structures deriving from expert (neutral, scientific) knowledge are placed beyond debate. Technology as a form of analysis and knowledge asserts the primacy of instrumental mastery and control, while denying validity to alternative notions of knowledge (or alternative social forms) and simultaneously claims unique truth status. Within forms of society which, as many commentators have noted, rely increasingly on scientific knowledge, and knowledge in general, the pervasiveness and ascendancy of particular forms of knowledge are assured. But such technocratic forms and the types of social arrangements which they justify, have been disputed by those who argue for forms of knowledge and analysis which take as their starting point the *variety* of forms of knowledge and analysis that are available and the importance of establishing a type of scientific analysis which is not concerned with technical control, but with people's active everyday consciousness of their social and symbolic world. Such forms of analysis of course assume that people establish their capacity to change their world, not just resignedly to experience it. Technocratic forms of thinking not only entail a distinctive type of societal and organization control; they also mystify such control by asserting its inevitability and neutrality.

Organizational differentiation, reflecting instrumental rationality, reflects the fragmentation of once unified functions, and reveals the growing importance of new control specialists. It is at the same time a mechanism of control. The differentiation of the organizational work force acts to divide employees, even to set them against each other. The existence of numerous subtle gradations, levels, offices, ranks, offers to some members of the organization the appearance of some sense of superiority over other members. It permits the impression that personal or group experiences and deprivations are the result of personal inadequacy, the inability to achieve, moral failure, or of hostile behaviour by 'rival' departments, other shifts, certain identifiable groups of workers and so on. Indeed, a number of writers have suggested that these divisive consequences should be seen as results of purposive employer strategies; that to a considerable degree the differentiation of the organization reflects the need for control through fragmenting potential solidarity, distracting attention from real sources of deprivation, individualizing structural processes.

For example, Aronowitz notes that it was ' . . . divisions within the working class that constituted the critical deterrent to the development of a unified working-class social and political movement.' (Aronowitz, 1973: 140.) But he attributes these divisions to extra-work factors: the formation of the American working class out of immigrant and native-born people, as well as the division of social and technical labour. Aronowitz stresses the divisive ethnic and religious distinctions within the American working class: black versus white; Irish versus Italians; Catholics versus Protestants; South versus North etc. Certainly out-of-work factors are important, but within the organization we can see that societal distinctions are deliberately echoed and supported. For example Warner and Low in their classic study, *The Social System of the Modern Factory*, note that as real skills are broken down by management, as management attempts to achieve greater control and 'integration' through technology and mechanical pacing of work, 'an effort is still made by management and workers to rank technological jobs in a status hierarchy. Management feels a need for such ranking in order to justify wage differentials in various technological jobs; and operatives cling to the ideology that theirs is a skilled craft. This traditional view of the latter is flattering to self-respect, giving the workers a sense of pseudo-security and prestige.' (Warner and Low, 1947: 83.) Such views are not simply erroneous, though reassuring, they are responsible for division and rivalry among the work force.

Modern organizations represent a remarkable proliferation of subtly differentiated offices and ranks. Indeed it is one of the defining characteristics of bureaucracy that it involves such finely graded distinctions based on technical, organizational, formal and status distinctions. These differentiations serve to reduce class consciousness: 'The dynamic response of capitalists to the quantitative growth of the working class and its increasing class consciousness has been to stratify labour. Consequently . . . monopoly capitalism appears to be accompanied by a fragmentation of the working class.' (Wachtel, 1975: 99.) This tendency has been reported by a number of writers – Edwards (1975), Stone (1974), Nichols and Armstrong (1976) – all of whom maintain that the process of de-skilling of industrial jobs – of homogenization – was accompanied by the (deliberate) development of elaborate, but largely meaningless, job hierarchies. One important feature of this stratification of labour is the existence of what Lenin called the aristocracy of labour: a group of manual workers experiencing distinctively privileged conditions. Foster (1974) has seen the emergence of such workers within the working class as part of a deliberate employers' strategy of dividing the working class and, at the same time, bribing its upper layers into political acquiescence, into identifying with the interests of the employers. Foster reveals how this 'creaming off' strategy effectively broke working-class solidarity, particularly when the labour aristocrats were those who occupied positions of authority within the enterprise, which were accompanied by relatively privileged conditions and rewards, and which encouraged the development of a new, more accommodating, working-class sub-culture: opposition replaced by identification.

A broadly similar argument is advanced by Edwards (1975) and his co-contributors. The development of monopoly capitalism, dominated by a few very large and enormously powerful international corporations, has resulted in the emergence of stratified bureaucracies which sought deliberately to divide labour markets. The internal stratification of jobs for control purposes is paralleled by a segmentation of labour markets which supports this fragmentation. Internally, large organizations established a variety of distinct internal labour markets. Particular jobs, or categories of jobs, could be approached only through specified recruitment routes, with formalized entry levels and requirements. Workers in some grades were absolutely barred (in effect) from entry to the jobs above them, since the requirements could only be achieved outside of work. Once launched on particular career routes, employees found it difficult to move 'sideways'. These differentiated labour markets are supported and often legitimated by educational differences. These, and the ideologies of intelligence and achievement which sustain them, maintain the distinction between management and office work, and between office work and shop-floor work.

As we have noted in Chapter 4, these internal labour markets are related to a more obvious, cruder difference between primary and secondary sectors in the overall labour market. External social inequalities and distinctions – sex, race – form the basis for a differentiation of the social labour market into 'primary' and 'secondary' sectors. These are related to a dualism *within* organizations concerning working arrangements, rewards, conditions, mobility opportunities. Both internal differentiations, and these larger, socially-based external distinctions, assist the division of workers whose real position varies very little.

Marxist writers tend to pay relatively little attention to formal control procedures, focusing their attention on ways in which control is built – into work differentiated hierarchies and so on. Nevertheless, there is a considerable literature within the sociology of organizations which can be seen as highly relevant to the Marxist perspective. The discussion earlier in this chapter of the Weberian approach, and the literature it has inspired, is a case in point. The main conclusions of this tradition is that organizations employ a variety of mechanisms of control for differing types of employees (though most analyses are of management levels), and under various internal and external circumstances numerous types of control have been identified. These can now be seen as different strategies of control. Indeed, Child's argument that senior members of management have some role to play in *choosing* organizational structures and control systems supports this interpretation.

A Marxist approach to formal control mechanisms within organizations would accept all the research described in the earlier Weberian section, but insist that the dynamic underlying control struggles was that of class struggle. Similarly, the search for unobtrusive, insidious, disguised control mechanisms only makes sense in the light of the functional significance of the groups concerned for capitalism, in supplying various services.

The origins of control procedures and traditions in the employers' search for profit and control is demonstrated, for example, in Edwards's analysis of bureaucracy. For this writer, bureaucracy is not merely a rational response to certain technical exigencies or increase in size. Bureaucracy itself was a response to the increasing problems of discipline and integration faced by the early employers as they attempted to replace personal control by institutional control – a form of control which can be so embedded in procedures, rules, established criteria, that its origin in class interest and class conflict would become increasingly hidden. The great advantage of bureaucracy as a form of control is not simply its thoroughness, covering many aspects of all employees' work through a series of levels of responsibility and monitoring, but it establishes *institutionalized* impersonal control. The control is now located 'out there'. It is the rules which are oppressive, not people. But, of course, 'The top-echelon management retained their control over the enterprise through their ability to determine the rules, set the criteria, establish the structure, and enforce compliance.' The result: 'The power relations of hierarchical authority are made invisible, submerged and embedded in the structure and organization of the firm rather than visible and openly manifest in personal, arbitrary power.' (Edwards, 1973: 9–10.) Furthermore, bureaucratic controls, by formalizing and making explicit career steps, recruitment criteria, reward systems, promotion procedures etc., serve to encourage stability of employment, commitment, acquiescence.

3 Employment relations

The employment relationship itself, involving the exchange of effort for financial reward, constitutes a form of control in that management can manipulate levels of reward in order to encourage employees to vary their input of effort, can threaten to terminate the relationship, or hold out the promise of careers, promotion. More than this, management frequently makes efforts to influence employees' perception of their place in the firm. If successful, these efforts constitute a form of control; if, for example, they persuade employees to commit themselves to management's goals, or to see the enterprise in terms of a functionally based division of labour, with each party playing his or her allotted function in the achievement of a *shared* organizational goal.

Despite the obvious centrality of the wage-effort exchange to organizational life and organizational control, few sociological analyses have paid much attention to this relationship, preferring, presumably, to regard this exchange as 'normal' and given. Yet as Baldamus, in his important work, *Efficiency and Effort*, shows, a thorough understanding of this relationship illuminates much of the organization. In particular it draws attention to the various aspects of effort control exercised by management, and the ways in which the whole exchange is based upon cultural notions of what constitutes a fair day's work. For Baldamus, employing organizations are firmly based upon an exchange of employees' *effort* – with all its implications for tedium, fatigue or danger – for money. From the employees' point of view, the salient question is their assessment of the 'reasonableness' of the rate of exchange, as measured against some implicit notion of fairness. Nevertheless, the relationship itself is only viable, from management's point of view, so long as the reward for employees' efforts is less than the value of these efforts on the market. The employer purchases effort, but in order to make it profitable and useful, this effort must be controlled in two major ways. It must be *stable*. There can be no wild fluctuations in levels of effort. If there are, the delicate integration and coordination of the enterprise is jeopardized. And they must be at a required level of *intensity*. The greater the (stable) level of intensity, the more productive the enterprise.

Baldamus emphasizes that the wage-effort bargain involves an integral conflict: there is a disparity between effort and reward. Management seeks to increase this disparity; employees seek to reduce it. On this reality of employment is built industrial conflict. However, as Hyman and Brough point out, this is not to deny that the employment relationship is also based upon a moral basis – on the whole most workers accept some degree of managerial legitimacy, hold to some agreed standards of effort. Indeed, these authors argue that: 'The very fact that contemporary economic organizations function at all is an indication that workers' orientations to their employment are not merely instrumental but contain important value-attachments . . . it would appear that employee norms of performance *do* in most (even if not all) cases prescribe a minimum as well as a maximum level of effort.' (Hyman and Brough, 1975: 26.)

Etzioni suggests that organizations employ three distinct types of reward – material (financial, fringe benefits etc.), symbolic (receiving superiors' or peers' approval, conforming with accepted and valued standards) and coercive (physical force and constraint, or the threat of these). Most work organizations use the first very widely; the second is used mostly by organizations with some strong and pervasive ideological basis – churches, political groups; the third is used in prisons, mental hospitals. Etzioni also suggests that organizational employees or members can vary in their orientation towards the power the organization exercises over them – and the form of reward used. Three sorts of orientation are distinguished: moral (which involves some strong commitment to the control and the reward); instrumental (when obedience is seen as a direct exchange for a satisfactory level of recompense, with little moral element); and alienative (when members will seek to avoid the controls, and will deny the justice of the control system entirely). These orientations vary in the amount of involvement shown by employees or members in the organization's control structure and the rewards utilized. Furthermore, Etzioni suggests that different forms of reward are directly associated with specific forms of orientation: coercive rewards generate alienated responses; symbolic rewards have little impact on employees with an instrumental orientation but relate to moral involvement. Instrumental orientations require material rewards.

However, though it is possible to isolate forms of organization in which these different reward/orientation combinations are fully demonstrated, it is also true that many organizations employ more than one form of reward, and are characterized by more than one form of involvement. Sometimes rewards vary over time with the same group of employees. More frequently one finds that different groups within the same organization are involved in different forms of control and rewards, and demonstrate different forms of involvement. Finally, of course, it is not unusual for employers to utilize material rewards; but they also attempt to generate some moral involvement through exhortation.

Many aspects of employees' definitions of work obligations demonstrate a commitment to work and employment as having a moral character of some minimal sort. Hyman and Brough also emphasize how workers' assessment of the *value* of their efforts are restricted and partial. Just as effort is constrained by work norms, so assessments of the worth of the effort are limited. The 'choice of pay comparisons is typically unambitious and powerfully shaped by custom: major inequalities which form an established part of the income hierarchy are rarely a focus of contention, the choice of comparative reference groups is structured by an acceptance of prevailing norms of the 'proper' rewards and status of different socio-economic groups; or at least by a belief that inequalities are "natural" and inevitable.' (Hyman and Brough, 1975: 61.)

These attitudes are formed by a number of factors: the experience of work itself and of subordination; managerial ideologies stressing the legitimacy of organizational structure, and of persons' positions within it; notions of individual differences in intelligence and ability; the realization of the limited power of disruptive groups; the inability to imagine an alternative social order. What is at issue here, ultimately, is the role and origins of the ideological assumptions which back up notions of fair pay, of a fair day's work. As Hyman and Brough emphasize, these crucial underpinnings of the employment relationship, without which it would hardly be viable, at least in its current, highly differentiated inegalitarian forms, must be understood in the light of an analysis of the nature and origin of work and class ideologies within capitalism.

Precisely because the employment exchange relies upon workers' unambitiousness, their acceptance of their position, and of the order within which they work and on their limited wage aspirations, management strives to structure workers' conceptions, to encourage their view of the wage-effort exchange as based on a harmony of interests. Such efforts have always characterized the employment relationship (see Bendix 1963). But there is evidence that increasing worker 'de-subordination' (Milliband, 1978) occasions management concern for the increasing problems of motivation. An important aspect of this problem in the UK is reflected in the almost continuous series of incomes policies since the Second World War. Incomes policies, as Tarling and Wilkinson (1978) point out, are used to lower 'real wages relative to productivity, as part of a total package aimed at attacking inflation' (Tarling and Wilkinson, 1978: 412). Yet these authors note that the actual operation of these policies has created an *impasse*: each wave of pay policy meets increasing resistance; each period of enforced restraint results in a catching-up process post-policy, but fails to achieve increased investment in the private sector. The result is the increasing resistance of the trade union movement to income control, and the increasing politicization of the relations between manager and worker. Questions of remuneration and control become, through the operation of incomes policy, irrevocably interconnected. Indeed, from the management point of view, incomes policies can *increase* the problem of worker motivation by restraining limits of remuneration.

One proposed solution to the problem of motivation is to alter (or appear to alter) the costs incurred by employees in the exchange. By enlarging jobs, enriching or humanizing work, it is hoped to reduce worker alienation and re-engage their commitment. Such efforts are described and analysed in Nichols and Beynon (1977). The contradiction at the heart of such efforts is obvious: if jobs are genuinely altered so as to allow incumbents some degree of control, of autonomy, then the employees must be likely to use this control to bring into question the overall organizational hierarchy of the enterprise. If they cannot, their discretion must be more apparent than real. This point is argued by Zimbalist (1975) who shows that work 'humanization' promotes labour's identification with management control – but only as long as the capitalist remains in control. Soon the workers demand more: at this stage the experiment must be curtailed. Capitalist organizational forms, argues Zimbalist, are ultimately incompatible with substantial worker input into the decision-making process in industry (Zimbalist, 1975).

There is a danger that such arguments ignore the room for manoeuvre which exists within capitalist forms of control. Of course, 'ultimately', Zimbalist's assertion holds. But before that point is reached, capitalism is capable of displaying a variety of control strategies, as we have seen. One common option for example, is to delegate responsibility and authority, but to guarantee the re-liability of the delegatee through various measures, many of which have been described in this chapter. (See Blau and Schoenherr, 1971; Perrow, 1972; Pugh and Hickson, 1973.) To argue that different forms of work organization – bureaucracy, Scientific Management, job-enlargement, professionalism – are strategies of control and regulation within the context of capitalism, and the pursuit of profit, requires analysis of the factors responsible for such dramatic variations in rewards and autonomy. The most obvious explanation is in terms of functions of different categories of employees within the capitalist system, and their class position. These arguments are presented and considered in the next chapter, and in the conclusion.

Certainly cross-cultural studies by Dore (1973), and Gallie (1978) lend support to the importance of different strategies of control and employment in achieving worker acquiescence and commitment. Dore, for example, after describing and comparing Japanese and British employment relations, argues that arrangements in the two countries are sufficiently different to justify being regarded as different *systems*: the Japanese is made up of life-time employment, a seniority plus merit wage system, an intra-organizational career system, a high-level of enterprise welfare, and of enterprise consciousness; the British system is composed of mobility of employment, market-based wages, self-designed careers, more state welfare, less enterprise consciousness, but greater professional, craft or class consciousness (Dore, 1973: 264). One major difference between the two systems is that the Japanese employment relationship accords to manual workers – at least those lucky enough to achieve full membership of large corporations – those employment privileges which in Britain are restricted to middle-class employees. Dore applies to this system the term 'welfare corporatism'. He notes that this system has definite advantages for the employer. It encourages identification with the enterprise and its goals, it permits the more ready management of industrial conflicts and while he agrees that the Japanese system could be seen simply as a manipulative strategy: 'To say that the Japanese system is manipulative and the British is not is presumably to suggest that while both Japanese and British managers would like to diminish distrustful antagonism among their workers, the Japanese do it better.' (Dore, 1973: 260.)

Of course, Dore does not argue that managers can choose any strategy they like. The emergence of different patterns in Japan and Britain is the result of cultural differences, and, most importantly, of the different timings of industrialization in the two countries. Japanese managers and politicians have, as it were, been able to avoid the pitfalls Britain, as an early developer, has experienced. Between

1850 and 1920 'the world had changed in significant ways...
the objective structure of opportunities and constraints,
and hence the means by which profits and growth can be
maximized can never be the same for the late developer, as
they were for the early developer.' (Dore, 1973: 403.)
History however applies an inertia to organizational
innovation, previous patterns of worker-manager relations
exert constraints. Nevertheless, Dore notes that some
tendency within British organizations to apply some
'Japanese' employment practices is evident. Gallie's study
of French and British organizational structures also reveals
contrast in managerial strategies, the French managers
regarding organizational structure as part of managerial
prerogative, the British managers seeking some measure of
consent to proposed changes. These two strategies were
related to markedly different levels of union militancy,
which are themselves the products of historical/cultural
differences in the two countries.

This chapter has been concerned with characteristic
theories of organizational control which derive directly
from the classic theories of Durkheim, Weber and Marx.
Each theorist can be seen to have initiated an approach to
organizational structure and control which still exerts
considerable influence.

The theories discussed here differ not so much in their
analyses of the mechanisms of organizational control –
bureaucracy, technology, forms of work design etc. – but in
their analysis of the *origins* of these mechanisms and
strategies. Within the Durkheimian tradition, organizational structure and mechanisms of control originate in
the organization's goals and the technology employed to
achieve these. The neo-Weberian approach, which often
involves a one-sided interpretation of Weber's theory,
emphasizes the variety of organizational forms, and seeks
to relate these to variations such as organizational environ-

ment, size or market. The significant variable determining these empirical relationships is efficiency. However, as discussed above, to regard Weber's analysis of bureaucracy, and his emphasis on bureaucracy as articulating in institutional form the increasingly pervasive value of rationality, as an emphasis on the determinant role of *efficiency* is naïvely to misunderstand Weber. What Weber attempts, in fact, is an analysis of bureaucracy as the 'institutional prototype for the emerging rationalized society' (Wilson, 1977: 146). In such a society, science, calculation, technology and measurement serve the achievement of ends. Such priorites and methods of analysis are reflected in rational-legal bureaucracies, established to achieve, by established, explicit, calculable impersonal principles, the goals of capitalist employers. As numerous commentators have noted, Weber saw a close relationship between capitalistic priorities and bureaucratic, i.e., rational, means. For Weber, then, the key variable is the increasing application of rationality.

In contrast for Marx, and later Marxists, the key variable is capitalism, with all that this implies for classes, class relations, and the pursuit of profit by the utilization of alienated labour. Within a capitalist economy enterprises are constantly subject to competitive pressures, and to pressures emanating from employees. These result in the limited number of very specific work design strategies, the most obvious of which is Taylorism. Marxist theorists regard the design of work within enterprises, and the choice of technology with which it is closely related, as reflections of the capitalists' efforts to maintain profitability and control. Externally, these arrangements are supported by the differentiation of the work force into primary and secondary labour markets, and by the pervasiveness of a technocratic ideology which upholds and mystifies organizational structure and decision-making. Furthermore the design of work and organizations is supported by various efforts to incorporate the working class into the objectives and forms of thinking characteristic of, and conducive to, capitalism. Partly this is achieved by a considerable degree of agreement over objectives – profits – associated, of course, with continuing disagreement over distribution. Partly it results from the fact that the capitalist economic system and its detailed elements and exchanges appears to the worker as relations between things. Value is determined by exchange. Employment relations become depersonalized. The system as a whole which so depersonalizes work activities, employment relations and individual value, itself appears as beyond human agency, or prospect of alteration.

7 Organizations, Class and Conflict

The analysis presented so far has frequently referred to, or made use of, notions of the class nature of organizations. The account of recent studies of the personal costs of industrial work, and their origins in the works of Marx, Weber and Durkheim, the analysis of theories of the origins of organizational structure, and of processes of organizational control have all constantly referred to a number of available and competing theories of class. Now is the time to consider such theories and their implications for organizational investigation.

The centrality of class to analyses of organizations is no surprise. Class is a major sociological tool of analysis. And if, as we shall see, sociologists differ radically in their theories of class, and, consequently, in their conceptualization of the phenomena and processes in question, in very general terms there are some areas of common interest – namely, that class describes economically based differences in the distribution of life chances, that it explains such structured differences usually by reference to ownership of property, and advances an analysis of the nature of the relationship between those differently located within economic/distributive order. We shall find, however, that the theories vary drastically in their definitions of class, their explanations of classes, and their analyses of the relationship between classes or strata.

In view of such common concerns, it is to be expected

that class analyses will have considerable relevance for the study of organizations, for the analysis of different roles or positions within the enterprise – and the different rewards associated with them – for the analysis of relationships between levels or types of organizational member, and their origin. More precisely we expect to find that class theories would have answers to the questions: how can we understand the relationships between managers and the managed, or, what determines the distribution of rewards within organizations, or the design of jobs, or how do we account for the fact of conflict between organizational levels? Most of all, perhaps, since theories of class inevitably involve theories of society, we would expect such theories to offer interpretations of the relationship between organizations, their structure, goals and process, and the wider society.

Once again, we shall find that any exploration of these and other class-based questions is an inherently theoretical exercise, and one which is dominated by theories deriving from the works of the three theorists whose work is so influential in organizational analysis: Marx, Weber and Durkheim. Because the distinctive class, or stratification, theories of these three writers are well known, and have been so thoroughly and frequently presented elsewhere, we shall do no more than briefly outline the distinctive and differentiating features of each approach.

Alone among the three founding fathers whose work is discussed in this book, Durkheim did not advance an explicit theory of inequality; nevertheless he has been influential in the establishment of a distinctive theory of class – or, in this case, of stratification – through his promulgation of two ideas: functional theory and the theory of industrial society.

The functionalist theory of stratification argues, essentially, that inequalities in the distribution of resources, privileges and 'life-chances' are a necessary 'device' whereby

society makes sure that the more important positions
within society – i.e., in most cases within organizations –
are filled by competent and reliable people. Those who
have, through sacrifice, hard work and lengthy training,
prepared themselves for the 'functionally important' jobs
in society, must be rewarded by a greater share of society's
resources. The criticisms of this approach are well known.
As Crompton and Gubbay point out, it ignores the problems of assessing the functional importance of positions
or jobs independently of the material rewards they currently receive. It also ignores the role of power and
ideology in buttressing and transmitting privilege, and in
legitimating the distribution of resources. Rather it
argues that such inequalities as exist, must, and should
exist. One of the most glaring weaknesses of such an
argument, as Westergaard and Resler note, is that
'rewards accrue automatically to property ownership
that require no services in return.' (Westergaard and
Resler, 1975: 13.)

The functionalist theory of stratification defines relationships between more or less privileged groups as
inherently stable and peaceful. This view follows from the
definition of levels of privilege as generally agreed rewards
for level of functional significance of different jobs. Society
is differentiated into *strata*, with all that this implies for
numerous layers, arranged hierarchically, not *classes*, with
the implication of opposition and conflict. The functional
theory of stratification is closely related to the theory of
industrial society. This theory has been referred to
frequently earlier. It maintains that the major features of
society are determined by the scientific and technical
organization of production. Within such societies, classes
and class conflict are decreasingly significant, as mono-
lithic, homogenous classes become differentiated, as
welfare and citizenship establish basic levels of provision,
rights and security, as the ownership and control of

industry forces the fragmentation of the owning class and the supercession of pure profit as a motive. The 'soulful' corporation, the corporation with a conscience, is born. Within the industrial society, consensus about the goals of the society replace political dissension and ideology. Politics, like management, becomes a technical affair – a question of balancing interest groups, of regulating conflict over the distribution of resources, and maximizing economic growth.

The theory of industrial society asserts that the introduction of modern, scientific technology establishes very definite constraints on the social structure and culture of developing societies. Although some variations are possible, the process of industrialization causes a convergence of major features of societies. The implication of this highly-disputed analysis brings us back to the functional view of stratification: the distribution of privilege has nothing to do with power or the institution of private property. In the West, and in the Soviet Union, economic and political privilege and control derive not from the private ownership of property but from the managerial, technical and bureaucratic imperatives of industrialization. The conclusion of this argument, write Westergaard and Resler 'was that something much like the existing pattern of inequality – or "stratification", to use the anodyne term favoured by sociologists – was inescapable: a "functional" necessity for any complex industrial economy.' (Westergaard and Resler, 1965: 14.)[1]

This view of the convergence of industrial society has been criticized on the grounds that it is crudely technologically determinist; that it ignores the significance of private property and profit in the West; and that it underestimates the role of the values and ideologies in determining patterns of stratification, specifically, that 'in Soviet society hierarchical differentiation is an instrument of the regime. To a significant degree stratification is *organized* in order to suit the political needs of the regime.' (Goldthorpe, 1964: 114.)

Weber's theory of class has been thoroughly described elsewhere (see, e.g., Giddens, 1973). Its essential elements are as follows. Classes are made up of people with similar 'life chances'. The supply, and security of a given level of life chances is established by the market, and by the goods or services which an individual brings to the market. People in a similar class situation do not invariably combine as a group, or seek collectively to organize for class action. Weber also distinguishes status groups, which are differentiated on the basis of subjective factors such as social honour or prestige. Status groups do not organize for collective action. Furthermore, Weber distinguished between three sorts of classes: property classes, commercial classes and social classes. The first two are distinguished by the resource they exploit in the market to establish a given level of life chances: property, goods and services. Social classes are aggregates of classes within which individuals can readily move. Weber also distinguishes the *party*, which is concerned with political action at the micro or macro level.

Weber stresses the economic basis of class, and indeed of status, since economic factors ultimately condition the possibility of a style of life within a status group. He notes that property or lack of property is the basic category of all class situations. Nevertheless, this emphasis on property and the economic is not to be confused with Marx's analysis of class and property. For Weber, property refers to the ownership of any sort of resource, skill or goods which can be deployed in the market to achieve a given level of life changes or a style of life. For Weber, property is the variable which, through the mediation of the market, explains the distribution of income and privilege. But, unlike Marx, Weber is not concerned with the forces underlying the operation of the market itself. For Marxist

critics this is the major failing of Weber's approach: that it
lacks a theory of political economy. It 'focuses on the way in
which societal rewards are *acquired*, and the manner in
which patterns of acquisition are determined by the
market.' Marx's theory, on the other hand, 'focuses on the
manner in which new values are *created*, and the social
relationships arising out of, and sustaining this process.'
(Crompton and Gubbay, 1977: 16.)

For Weber, class, status and party, the three major forms
of stratification, are aspects of market-based distribution.
For Marx, on the other hand, class is a function not of the
market or of exchange, but of relationships of production.

Weber supplies a thorough-going classificatory structure, which can be used to advantage in analysing the
complexities of social stratification within market systems.
He supplies a number of forms and sub-types; he notes the
variety of relationships between them; and considers the
different circumstances which may, empirically, affect the
development of classes, or of classes as communities. In
short, Weber's complex, multidimensional scheme offers a
useful way of understanding the complex phenomena of
class and stratification, as the numerous recent analyses in
the Weberian tradition demonstrate. But for the Marxist,
such classification and analysis – of market position and its
relationship to class structures, of changes in market and
authority relationships and their impact on the differentiating class structure, for example – simply confuse appearance for reality. For the Marxist, the reality of class lies not
in the empirical appearances so carefully catalogued by the
neo-Weberian, but in the processes underlying such
appearances: those of capitalist production, relationships
and functions. It is here that class originates. Differences in
'life chances', inequalities, however great, in the distribution of society's resources and privileges, are merely an
aspect, a demonstration of the capitalist nature of the
society: 'Property, profit and market – the key institutions

of a capitalist society – retain their central place in social arrangements and remain the prime determinants of inequality.' (Westergaard and Resler, 1975: 17.) Certainly the 'market' is important in determining life chances, but behind the market is the capitalist mode of production, within which one group – those who own the means of production – employ and exploit the labour power of those who have nothing to sell but their labour.

The Marxist view of class is, of course, directly tied to the Marxist view of capitalism. Classes are inherent in the capitalist mode of production. Within capitalism one section of the population owns the means of production: the rest – the majority – are excluded from such ownership. As a result they must sell their labour power to survive. The system operates on the basis of the creation and expropriation of surplus value. Those who own the materials of production, the machinery, purchase the labour power of the formally free labourers on the market, and use it to manufacture goods which, when sold, achieve profit. This profit comes from the labour of the employees, who can, therefore, never be paid the real value of their work. Relations between these groups – the owners of capital and the owners of labour power – are ones of conflict, not simply because they are struggling for greater shares of resources, but because the former systematically *exploits* the latter.

Clearly the Marxist theory of class is not indifferent to the differences in wealth and income between the owners of the means of production and the working class. But such differences are seen as aspects of the mutual opposition of interests, and the differences in economic power of the two groups. Differences in wealth and income are results of different positions within the capitalist mode of production (ownership of the means of production versus ownership of labour).

If Weber's analysis of class and stratification has been

criticized because it cannot grasp the pattern lying behind and structuring the complexity of detail, Marx's analysis has been taken to task on the grounds that its ambitiousness and abstraction do not supply a useful or applicable model for the analysis of the apparently highly differentiated class structure of present-day capitalism. There appear to be class divisions other than those of bourgeoisie and proletariat – clerks, technicians, managers, professionals. The category of non-owning employee seems to be differentiated in ways which, at least at the level of consumption, lifestyle, political sympathies, working conditions, income, suggest some class implications. Either the category of non-owners of the means of production requires some further sub-division and reformulation, or it is so wide and all embracing that it would seem an inadequate tool for the anlysis of actual class locations and class actions.

Marxists themselves, of course, are aware of this problem (see, for example, Alan Hunt, 1977). The Marxist theory of class is not to be seen as an attempt to identify and locate all categories of workers. It is a theory of society and economy; an analysis of the basic processes of capitalist society and their implications for basic social divisions. How these divisions, established by Marxist theory, work out in practice is a historical and empirical question. Furthermore the Marxist categories of owner/non-owner have been accepted as inadequate as a basis for understanding the empirical complexity of class structures: various refinements and sub-categories have been proposed, deriving, it is claimed, from Marx's own analysis. The use of the various proposed classifications, all of which are in terms of role and position within the capitalist mode of production, permits a more complex analysis of the class locations of such groups as professionals, technicians, managers, clerks etc. As we shall see, the various classifications on offer – from Poulantzas (1975), Crompton

(1976), Carchedi (1977), Wright (1978) and others, are concerned not with the different experiences or circumstances of the various groups, not with what Lockwood, for example, has understood to be the elements of class position – market relations and authority relationships at work – but with position and function within the capitalist mode of production as conceptualized in Marxist theory, as it is refined, reworked and rediscovered in the hands of recent writers. Inevitably, as a result, these schemes are highly abstract and general.

A major focus of class analysis – whether Marxist or Weberian in origin – is to establish the connections between class experiences and class attitudes, and, ultimately, class consciousness. For both sorts of theory this issue, although differently approached, remains a central one. For Marxism, in particular, the explanation of the low levels of radical consciousness and class action in the West is a major problem. The various efforts to establish a new theoretical taxonomy of the various axes of differentiation within the non-owning groups in terms of their functions and position within the capitalist mode of production is part of the effort to address this issue by establishing the 'real' class positions of different groups of employees. Once satisfactorily catalogued, their class attitudes and political behaviour will, it is hoped, become explicable, in terms, for example, of their 'structurally ambiguous' or 'contradictory' positions in society, or their functions as 'agents' of capital, if not as capitalists themselves.[2] Of course, such analyses are buttressed, when necessary, by reference to the operation of society-wide forces (the dominant value system, notions of consensus etc.) which also serve to interfere in the development of class consciousness.

Nevertheless, once again, if the Weberian model is open to criticism in that it fails to take into account the 'structure which . . . logically precedes both market relationships and work relationships (the elements of class position as defined by Lockwood) – the capitalist mode of production and its associated relations of production' (Crompton, 1976: 413), the Marxist models may be criticized on the grounds that they have not been notably successful in demonstrating their explanatory usefulness in interpreting the complex empirical world of class experiences and attitudes, in making the connections between class as an analytical category and classes as social structures.

We have seen, then, that each of the three theorists under discussion here has initiated a distinctive approach to the study of social classes. Each theory has application to organizations, for each is concerned, in characteristic ways, with developments in work arrangements, domination and subordination, the distribution of rewards, the functions of various categories of employee and so on. Specifically, we shall consider the application of these theories to three issues: inequalities in organization; classes within organizations; and relationships between classes within organizations.

Class and inequalities within organizations

As noted, organizations are hierarchical structures. They are structures of control, whereby each level takes orders from the level above and takes responsibility for the level below. But they are also hierarchical in terms of the distribution of rewards, deprivations and privileges. Thus, within organizations we find very great differences in the distribution of income, career possibilities, danger, working conditions and other sources of gratification or dissatisfaction. These differences are no less remarkable and problematic simply because most members of organizations themselves sometimes seem to take them for granted, unquestioningly.

The highly inegalitarian distribution of organizational resources, privileges and deprivations reveals and reflects the class nature of organizations. For these inequalities are not random, haphazard, variable. On the contrary, they are patterned; they cluster together, so that those who receive privileges on one dimension usually receive privileges on others, and *vice versa*. They are highly significant for life chances; and they are closely connected to variations in economic power (market power, position within the capitalist system of production); and they are related to political attitudes and culture. In short, these inequalities are class-based.

The inegalitarian distribution of organizational rewards raises two issues: first, what are these rewards and deprivations, and how unequally are they distributed? And secondly, how is this unequal distribution structured and patterned? What 'breaks' and clusters of privilege or deprivation are apparent? In other words, how does the distribution of organizational resources, with their implications for individuals' life chances, relate to the existence of classes?

Numerous writers have reported on the inegalitarian distribution of a number of key rewards. As far as income is concerned, Westergaard and Resler report, on the basis of an exhaustive survey, that 'It has been part of the postulate of progressive equalization that the earnings of occupational groups previously quite distinct now overlap to a large extent. The data . . . show no movement in that direction.' (Westergaard and Resler, 1975: 76.) These authors note the sharp distinction between a small group of senior managers, officials, professionals and directors who receive a highly privileged share of the organization's rewards, and the mass of employees who receive, in financial terms, a fraction of the senior members' incomes. Westergaard and Resler report that average earnings for the upper group exceed unskilled earnings by four to one.

Other writers have focused on income differences between intermediate groups – for example, between manual workers and non-manual office workers. Here again, consistent if less striking differences are apparent. Roberts *et al.* report that although some overlap between the two groups is apparent, in general, 'The most impressive feature of trends in pay differentials over time has been their stability.' (Roberts *et al.*, 1977: 26.) However, these authors point out that contrasting annual incomes of various grades of employee leads to an underestimation of the pervasiveness of inequality even with respect to financial matters.

Wedderburn and Craig, and Goldthorpe *et al.* reach the same conclusions: that manual and non-manual workers are sharply differentiated not only by level of annual income, but also by the number of hours required to make such income, by the differential granting of fringe benefits, by typical career patterns, security etc. In all these respects, manual workers fare less favourably than non-manual workers, in general. The possibility of a progressive career is a particularly important difference. As Roberts *et al.* note, manual workers have jobs, non-manual workers, in the main, have careers – some possibility of progression and incremental salaries. Furthermore, security of employment and the profiles of life earnings characteristic of the two groups differ markedly: 'manual and non-manual occupations remain fairly sharply differentiated both in respect of security and in the periods of notice given when dismissal does occur.' (Wedderburn and Craig, 1975: 67.) Typically, manual workers' incomes decline as they get older; non-manual workers' increase (Giddens, 1973: 180).

Other organizational rewards and deprivations are highly unequally distributed. The nature of work tasks themselves is a major source of fulfilment or despair and boredom. Numerous writers have described the deprivations of much working-class work (Beynon, 1973,

Braverman, 1974, Nichols and Beynon, 1977), and have noted the comparison in work design between manual work and non-manual work.[3] Fox, for example, isolates and compares what he terms high and low discretion work (Fox, 1974). Davis *et al.* report the pervasiveness of repetitive, fragmented work among shop-floor jobs (Davis *et al.*, 1972). Related to such variation in the principles of job design are frequently reported variations in the nature, and strictness of control systems and procedures (see Chapter 6). Manual jobs are controlled in overt and onerous ways which clearly articulate the 'untrustworthiness' of the manual workers (see Fox, 1974: Wedderburn and Craig, 1975). Non-manual workers are much more likely to be involved in the hierarchy of management in a way that manual workers, who stand outside of the hierarchy and in opposition to authority, are not.

Other aspects of work are similarly distributed. Manual work is more likely to be dangerous, to involve unpleasant conditions, noise, dirt, exposure to disease. For example, Wedderburn and Craig, on the basis of their research, report that: 'it might be said that the overall picture is one of considerable inequality in all aspects of the employment relationship; where the traditional dividing line between manual and non-manual occupations still represents a fairly sharp break in conditions.' (Wedderburn and Craig, 1975: 69.) The existence of such inequalities raises two problems.

First, how do such inequalities relate to *class* differences? So far we have been interested primarily in the unequal distribution of organizational rewards, but it is impossible to separate such analysis from the question of class structuration within those same organizations. What classes are, then, apparent within modern organizations? Secondly, how do we explain the overt inegalitarian distribution of organizations' rewards? We shall address these questions. Both require recourse to the theories of class described earlier.

What classes are apparent within organizations? What changes are occurring within these classes? It is generally agreed that some significant changes are occurring. But theorists vary widely in the significance they attach to them. 'All parties to the debate,' writes Low-Beer, in a recent study, 'were willing to admit that the skill composition of the labour force of the advanced societies is changing. If the rise of the semi-skilled, the clerical, and other white-collar groups has been the most noticeable change in the non-agricultural labour force before the war, the growth in the professional and technical category has been the most striking change in the postwar decades.' (Low-Beer, 1978: 8.) Changes in the composition of the labour force are generally held to be relevant to changes in class structure. But other developments are also pertinent: changes in work and market situation, changes in life outside work (patterns of sociability, leisure activities, consumption levels and patterns), cultural normative developments – i.e., such things as, for example, political or trade union and class attitudes.

However, if all parties may be willing to admit the occurrence of certain empirical changes, theorists vary considerably in their interpretation of these, and in their preparedness to regard these as evidence of changes in class structure. Definitions of classes as social groups reflect the distinctive emphasis of the theories themselves. Debate about changes in the class structuring of organizations is, ultimately, a theoretical as well as an empirical issue, as we shall see.

Before considering different, theoretical interpretations of these changes it is apposite, briefly, to sketch in the changes that have been noted.[4]

Within the working class, conventionally defined, embourgoisement supporters claim – or claimed – that changes in income levels, at least among the affluent sections, and changes in consumption patterns were leading to the fragmentation of the working class, and to sections becoming middle class. Such consequences were particularly likely for workers in new technologies and new industries, for example those working in automated factories and continuous process plants, or for affluent or skilled workers. In opposition to this view, Goldthorpe *et al.* argue for a survival of the traditional connections between manual work and working-class patterns of values and relationships, but also postulate that certain sections of the working class while still isolated from the middle class, were also distinct from traditional 'proletarian' manual workers, not least in their class-related attitudes (Goldthorpe *et al.*, 1960; see also Roberts *et al.*, 1977).

A related development is the recent emergence of what has been called the 'new working class' – technicians in modern high-technology industries. These are skilled workers. They differ markedly in income, working conditions, qualifications etc. from manual workers. Their existence sets a problem for class theories – which class do they belong to? Are they truly a *new* class of some sort?

The most important developments, however, and the ones that have given most trouble to competing class and stratification theories, have been within the middle class. This category has grown enormously since the nineteenth century. And it is undeniable that this growth has led to a process of fragmentation. A major development has been the separation of ownership and control with the consequent expansion of management as a separate organizational category. Managers themselves have been identified as a new class, able to use their control of organizations to protect and advance their interests, rather than the owners'. They have also been seen as agents of their employers – the owners – with no capacity to function except in the interests of profit. And they have been presented as detached, impartial technicians, able, by virtue of their separation from ownership, to exercise a responsible, and socially conscious restraint on the excesses of the pursuit of profit.

A broadly similar range of possibilities has been attributed to the emergence and expansion of professionals within organizations: a new interest group, vigorously pursuing its own advantage under the guise of professionalism; the agents, in a number of ways, of capitalism with its various functional requirements of expertize, legitimacy, social stability; or a new, disinterested order, offering an alternative value emphasis (on trust, and the altruistic application of expert knowledge).

Some writers have paid particular attention to the emergence of new organizational categories, and have seen in the increasing number of officials, administrators and bureaucrats, a new class. The argument is that positions within the power hierarchy of bureaucracies confer the possibility of bureaucrats pursuing their group interest. Dahrendorf, for example, remarks: 'the monopoly of authority founded in expert knowledge provides the incumbents of bureaucratic roles at a given time with a degree of exclusiveness which underlies their unity as members of the same quasi-group and may be conceived as a condition of conscious solidarity.' (Dahrendorf, 1959: 298–9.)

The most discussed development, however, is the expansion of office work – the white-collar workers. A constant problem for class theories is whether or not these workers are middle class. The facts of the expansion itself are not in doubt: what is debated is the class location of the new, white-collar groups. Montagna (1977) calculates that in the USA in 1980 twenty-four per cent of the work force are in sales and clerical work. In 1975 in the UK, twenty-six per cent was classified as engaged in clerical work.

As we have seen, a number of writers emphasize the extent to which manual and non-manual work are still clearly differentiated, and the class position of non-manual workers distinct from, and relatively privileged to, that of manual workers. However, most commentators would accept a 'blurring' of this distinction at the boundaries of the two groups, a blurring which has been interpreted by some as the 'proletarianization' of office workers. Roberts *et al.*, for example, argue:

'White-collar proletarians . . . are not mythical creatures . . . The proletarians in our non-manual sample were distinguished by their relatively depressed socio-economic conditions. They were typically employed in routine jobs at the base of the white-collar occupation hierarchy, income levels were below the average for other white-collar groups, and a relatively high proportion had received no post-secondary education whatsoever. (Roberts *et al.*, 1977: 140.)

This proletarianization argument is supported by those who choose to focus not on the distribution of organizational resources in the widest sense (for here most white-collar workers are still relatively advantaged, even though in terms of income alone, at least according to Westergaard and Resler, whole categories of white-collar workers are now no better off than manual workers) but on the organization and design of work and working conditions. In these latter terms it is possible to argue for proletarianization of much clerical work in that the work itself increasingly resembles manual work – i.e., it is without authority or responsibility, fragmented, repetitive, takes place in large offices and is mechanized or automated.

To summarize this section: the evidence suggests that organizations remain highly inegalitarian phenomena, and that the distribution of organizational resources occurs along class lines. There is also evidence, however, that traditional class categories and demarcations are changing, but there is disagreement about the extent and implications of such changes. Indeed, some writers would dispute that any change of significance is occurring at all. As noted earlier, approaches to, and assessment of, the class structure of modern organizations make use of theories of class deriving from the works of the early theorists. Each theory offers a distinctive and competing analysis, which varies not only in the interpretation of changes in, or persistence of, class structure, but also disagrees as to which 'facts' are pertinent to such conclusions. We shall consider each approach in terms of its distinctive analysis of the origins of organizational inequality and the class structuring of modern organizations (and such changes as are seen to have occurred).

Functionalism and the theory of Industrial Society

This approach to stratification within organizations offers a two-sided analysis of organizational inequality: (a) that it is diminishing, and (b) that, to the extent it persists, it is a necessary consequence of the need to motivate and reward people conscientiously to fill important and demanding positions within organizations.

The reduction of class-based inequalities is argued by Industrial Society theorists on a number of grounds: the extension of civil rights and the levelling of status differences, the achievement by working-class people of levels of consumption previously the prerogative of the middle class, the spread of welfare facilities and arrangements, increasing opportunities for social mobility.[5]

Inasmuch as some inequalities are recognized, these are attributed to the functional requirements of the industrial order: 'A certain degree of inequality is clearly inevitable and indispensable in all complex societies in order to encourage production.' (Aron, 1961: 90.) For many writers, a 'certain degree' becomes synonymous with the empirical extent of inequality existing within society. The current distribution of rewards and deprivations is seen as existing because it is necessary. An industrial society involves the application of science and technology to production. This has immediate consequences for the division of labour, organizational hierarchy and the design of jobs (see Chapter 5). Differentiated jobs have differential skill requirements. Those who fill the most demanding and important jobs must be rewarded appropriately. Service to the organization is service to society, so the organizational distribution of rewards reflects society's evaluation of the functional significance of differentiated work. Inequalities are regarded in this analysis as a necessary concomitant of industrialization: 'the management of an industrial economy requires essentially the same sort of pattern of inequality – of division of labour and authority, of fairly sharply graded incentives – whether the society in question is nominally communist or capitalist. The same logic of technological and organizational necessity would impose itself on industrial societies of both faiths.' (Westergaard and Resler, 1975: 14.)

Industrial Society theorists assert the differentiation of traditional classes, and the emergence of new class groups. The fragmentation of classes in the twentieth century follows the emergence, in the Industrial Society, of a highly differentiated occupational structure, and the expansion of skilled and middle-class occupations. 'The labour force of the industrial society is highly differentiated by occupations and job classifications, by rates of compensation, and by a variety of relative rights and duties in the work place community . . . The variety of skills, responsibilities, and working conditions at the work place *requires* an ordering or hierarchy.' (Kerr *et al.*, 1973: 48; my emphasis.) This differentiation of skills and functions (and the variations in conditions and rewards that are associated with them) gives rise to the fragmentation of previously homogeneous classes.

Overall, Industrial Society theorists perceive an up-grading of skill levels. The application of science and technology, far from demolishing skills, requires a more skilled work force. Skilled workers are always in demand: 'Increasingly complex machines require increasingly qualified designers, builders, maintenance and repair men, and even minders.' (Dahrendorf, 1959: 49.) Unskilled work is decreasing: the 'proletarian has left the scene'.

As well as the up-grading and differentiation of much working-class work, there has recently emerged a new class – the 'new middle class', which, as Dahrendorf puts it, was 'born decomposed' – i.e., it was never a homogeneous class group. This category is composed of clerks, sales staff, managers, professionals and bureaucrats. Furthermore, these people, as many writers of this school have asserted, take up an increasing proportion of the work force. Its existence further complicates the Marxist analysis, since it can be seen to stand as an intermediary group between manual workers (now themselves considerably more heterogeneous) and the bourgeoisie. Even if the new middle-class groups do not constitute a class, and if it is possible to allocate white-collar workers to the working class and bureaucrats and managers to the bourgeoisie, it is clear that these additional groups differ markedly from respectively, traditional working class and bourgeoisie. Indeed, according to Dahrendorf, the addition of clerks and bureaucrats to the two established classes so changes and complicates the original categories as to make them absurd: 'the pleasing simplicity of Marx's view of society has become a nonsensical construction. If ever there have been two large-homogeneous, polarized, and identically situated social classes, these have certainly ceased to exist today, so that an unmodified Marxian theory is bound to fail in explaining the structures and conflicts of advanced industrial societies.' (Dahrendorf, 1959: 57.)

Another major development is also given emphasis and distinctive interpretation: the separation of ownership and control. The decomposition of capital accompanies the fragmentation of labour. The capitalist class becomes fragmented as the working class does, with 'ownership' split between shareholders who now own but have little chance to control the organization, and the managers who are effectively in control, but who do not formally own what they control. This development is seen as carrying a number of implications: management is seen as playing an intermediary, technical, neutral role, humanizing and softening the crude pursuit of profit; it is also argued that since managers are 'functionaries without capital' they must develop the legitimacy of their formal superiority through sensitivity to their subordinates' aspirations and needs. The separation of ownership and control results in the search for new bases of managerial legitimacy. But the most significant interpretation of these developments is that advanced by Dahrendorf: that the separation of wealth (private ownership of the means of production) and power within organization, separates the *bases* of classes. Whereas in Marx's time, property and possession of authority were coincident; developments since have revealed that this coincidence is neither necessary nor inevitable. Class is not a question of property, *per se*, but of authority relations.

The separation of ownership and control reveals the specificity of Marx's analysis: within industrial society, classes still exist, but, being organized around the distribution of authority, they occur in more than one context. And position within a class system within any one context may differ from position in another. For example, Dahrendorf argues that 'the dominant and subjected classes of industry need no longer be part of the corresponding political classes.' (Dahrendorf, 1959: 271.) Not only are classes now differentiated internally, but the basis of classes is so defined as to enable more than one axis of class relations to be isolated.

As Scott (1979) argues, the foundation of the theory of industrial society is the separation of ownership and control, for this development underpins many of the theory's basic propositions about class structures in industrial society: namely the emergence and differentiation of management and technical specialists, the differentiation of class bases, and the emergence of a new 'sense of responsibility' among senior managers. This development is also seen as having implications for relationships between classes. The antagonism of nineteenth-century classes is replaced by more harmonious and consensual relationships between strata. Certainly conflicts still exist, but conflicts between groups are conflicts about the distribution of rewards within the logic of the societal *status quo*. They are not conflicts about the *nature* of the society itself. A number of factors are adduced to explain this diminution of class conflict. Dahrendorf points to the separation of industrial and political contexts of classes, and to the institutionalization of class conflicts, which now are governed by established, and institutionalized procedures. The reduction of inequalities, mentioned above, and the possibility of upward social mobility are also seen as important.

Other writers point to the consensual nature of modern industrial society – 'a distinctive consensus which relates individuals and groups to each other and provides an integrated body of ideas, beliefs, and value judgements.' (Kerr *et al.*, 1973: 53.) The decline of political ideologies from political life, which could inflame a direct conflict about the nature of the society itself, also explains the lack of structural conflicts between classes or strata. Politics, like management, becomes a question of *technical* decision-making about the claims of interest groups within the context of *agreed* values.

For writers within the Weberian tradition, work-based

inequalities represent the very essence of class – variations in life chances. Differences in pay, fringe benefits, and related lifestyles, in the design of work itself, and work experiences, deprivations and satisfactions, work conditions, career possibilities, are a result of differences in class position: i.e., position within the social organization of production and the constraints and life chances that follow from that location (Goldthorpe *et al.*, 1969: 82).

For neo-Weberians, class position and the life chances that this involves are determined, ultimately, by variations in market power. Following Weber, class is defined largely in terms of levels of rewards received by virtue of amount and type of marketable skills possessed. Thus Parkin, for example, argues:

At least so far as modern capitalist societies are concerned the role of the market in allocating rewards via the occupational order seems crucial to the entire stratification system . . . occupational groupings which stand high in the scale of material and symbolic advantages also tend to rank high in the possession of marketable skills . . . marketable expertise is the most important single determinant of occupational reward.
(Parkin, 1971: 20–1.)

Thus variations in organizational rewards allocated to various organizational categories – skilled workers, managers (and various grades of manager), personnel experts, janitors and so on, reflect the skill of knowledge commanded by that category of employee. The greater the skill, the greater its scarcity, the greater will be the level of reward.[6]

If market power is the ultimate basis of class, two related problems immediately present themselves: how are the variations in market power structured to give rise to *classes* rather than to a multitude of differently placed *individuals*? And how do variations in market power determine classes as social categories? Writers influenced by the Weberian tradition have given thought to both issues.

Most writers hold to the persistence of traditional demarcations between working and middle class, while accepting some changes at the boundaries of these groups, and a differentiation within the middle-class category. Parkin, for example, as noted, argues that: 'It is the highly patterned nature of the inequalities we have so far examined which enables us to portray the reward system in terms of a dichotomous or two-class model.' (Parkin, 1971: 26.) However, it is clear that moving from 'market-position' to classes as social categories involves more than merely plotting the distribution of work rewards and identifying the natural 'breaks'. For all neo-Weberians, classes as social categories are more than collections of people (usually occupational colleagues, presumably) who share the same market situation. Classes as 'structured forms' (Giddens, 1973: 104) involve 'normative' and social elements, and the process whereby these classes develop out of variations in market power requires the operation of what Giddens has termed the structuration of class relationships – the process whereby economic or market relationships become translated into 'non-economic' social structures (Giddens, 1973: 105).

For Lockwood (1958) the transition from class position, as an abstract economic category, to social classes, and class consciousness, is via three sorts of experience, all of which relate to economic and market relationships. 'Market situation' refers to 'economic position narrowly conceived, consisting of source and size of income, degree of job-security, and opportunity for upward occupational mobility' (Lockwood, 1958: 15). As Lockwood notes, those who are similarly propertyless differ in their market situations; to define such differences as irrelevant obstructs analysis and understanding. 'Work situation' refers to the matrix of social relations people are involved with in their work: 'every employee is precipitated, by virtue of a given division of labour, into unavoidable relationships with other employees, supervisors, managers or customers. The work situation involves the separation and concentration of individuals, affords possibilities of identification with and alienation from others, and conditions feelings of isolation, antagonism and solidarity.' (Lockwood, 1958: 205.) The most important aspect of work situation is location within authority relations – i.e. nearness to, involvement in, or subordination to, the exercise of power within the organization.

Finally, 'status situation' refers to the amount of social honour people attach to each other's work activities. Lockwood maintains that any given level of class consciousness is the outcome of the interplay of three sets of experiences, which persuade the individual of his separateness from or similarity with, certain sets of others. Undoubtedly, these categories are extremely useful as ways of classifying such relevant experiences (see Mackenzie, 1975).

More recently, Giddens in an important work on class theory also notes the need to relate class as an abstract, theoretical category to classes as social groups, or to class consciousness. He suggests that initially the 'mediate' structuration of classes is facilitated '*to the degree to which mobility closure exists in relation to any specified form of market capacity*.' (Giddens, 1973: 107.) Three sorts of market capacity are isolated: property, education and technical qualifications, and labour power. The actual structuring of class formations however is achieved by the operation of 'proximate' structuration factors which can be seen to be broadly similar to Lockwood's categories: the division of labour within the enterprise; authority relations within the enterprise; and the impact of distributive groupings (i.e., distinctive neighbourhoods and communities and levels and patterns of consumption). Giddens notes that the organization and design of tasks within the enterprise has an important role in the fragmentation or homogenization of the work force. The division of labour itself is strongly influenced by technology, the effect of which is to separate the conditions of labour of manual and non-manual workers. The organization of control tends to reinforce these divisions (and the process of mediate structuring of classes through mobility patterns) since those with some role in the organization's authority system are typically separate from manual workers. Those who mind machines, who execute, but do not design, procedures, tend also to be those who receive orders and do not initiate them. Similarly, at the upper levels, Giddens notes that those who own property are also those who have the 'right' and the capacity to initiate orders, to manage.

If Industrial Society theorists argue for the diminution of class inequalities, the differentiation of traditional class groups, and the up-grading of sections of the working class (see Goldthorpe *et al.*, 1969), those who employ a neo-Weberian approach not only assert the persistence of work-based inequalities, but the persistence of traditional class demarcations within organizations. Parkin, as noted, argues for the continuation of a two-class model, i.e., for the survival of the 'break' between working and middle class; Goldthorpe *et al.* argue that their researches do not support the argument that class differences and divisions between working and middle class have disappeared, and they add that such changes as have occurred can be seen not as the embourgoisement of sections of the working class, but as 'the adaptation of old norms to new exigencies and opportunities' (Goldthorpe *et al.*, 1969: 158).

For these writers, while the basis of class is a question of market power, the formation of classes as social groups, of class behaviour, identifications, consciousness, relationships and culture, is an empirical matter. Precisely how the abstract fact of market position is transformed into social categories cannot, as Giddens remarks, be 'settled in abstracto: one of the specific aims of class analysis in relation to empirical societies must necessarily be that of determining how strongly, in any given case, the "class principle" has become established as a principle of structuration.' (Giddens, 1973: 110.) As we shall see, this is a conviction which distinguishes these writers from those of a Marxist persuasion.

Relationships between the classes within organizations are seen as being governed by the impact of class experiences, and the orientations which employees bring to bear on these experiences. Conflict is a constant possibility within organizations since, as Parkin puts it, 'Inequality in the distribution of rewards is always a potential source of instability.' (Parkin, 1971: 48.) But whether or not this potential is realized depends not only on the level of deprivation experienced by a group in comparison with a superior, more privileged group, but also on the subordinate group's expectations, on its political and class culture, on the operation of various 'safety valve' factors, on opportunities for social mobility, on 'dominant' and 'subordinate' value systems (Parkin, 1971).

The impact of class experiences leads to the development of attitudes of class solidarity and class opposition. Of particular importance is the emergence of distinctive *images of class* – i.e., the views people hold regarding the number of classes, their origins and inter-relationships. In an early and influential paper, Lockwood (1966) suggested that, broadly speaking, individuals conceptualize class structure in two ways: power/conflict/dichotomous models on the one hand and prestige/status/hierarchical models on the other. The first is more common among the working class, the latter among the middle class.

Lockwood himself, however, and other more recent commentators, also note the diversity of class images even within one class, and attribute these variations to variations

in workers' 'industrial and community milieux'. Of
particular importance in producing distinctive and diverse
images of class, according to Lockwood and other writers,
are variations in the *work situation*. Variations in perceptions of class, in assessments of class interests and in class
identifications, are significantly affected by the way in
which work is organized, the conditions of work, the
distribution of work rewards etc. In other words, the social
relations at work play an important part in structuring
workers' images of class and class relations. As Mackenzie
remarks, for example: 'Given the fact that one of the
outstanding features of modern industry is the physical and
social separation of those on the factory floor and those "in
the office" it is therefore not surprising that clerks do not
identify with, or see themselves as sharing a working-class
situation with, manual workers.' (Mackenzie, 1975: 172.)
The experience of authority within the enterprise – of some
degree of participation in authority, or of subordination – is
regarded as particularly important in inculcating class
attitudes and images.

It is not possible here to do justice to the vigorous and
fruitful work on variations in class images and class consciousness and their relationship to work and community
factors (see, for example, Lockwood, 1966; Goldthorpe *et
al.*, 1968, 1969; Bulmer, 1975; Mackenzie, 1975). But the
main argument of such analyses is highly relevant to a
sociology of organizations, and can be briefly stated: that
the organization of work, the distribution of work rewards,
the organization of control, and the design of jobs, all play a
part in the development of conceptions of class, and of
relations between them. This possibility has important
implications for organizational analysis: organizational
structure is seen as not only revealing, through the
distribution of organizational rewards and deprivations,
class variations in market power, but also as being
responsible for the development of class identifications,

solidarity and opposition. Organizations are seen in such
analysis as characterized by class conflicts which are a
direct result of organizational structure. Such conflicts
follow from employees' organizational experiences, exclusion from authority, from highly visible class differentials, from the numerous ways in which the majority of
organizational members find that they are excluded from
decisions taken by a more privileged and powerful
minority. (For an important analysis of the 'fundamental
principles implicitly informing the ways in which men
organize, regulate, and reward themselves for the production and distribution of goods and services,' see Alan Fox,
1974.)

Finally, the Marxist conception of class does not start
with market relations or distributive patterns, but with
relations of production. For Marxists, inequalities *per se* do
not constitute the major feature of class. Consequently,
within class analysis, inequalities in the distribution of
organizational rewards and deprivations are seen to pertain
to class theory and class relations only in so far as they relate
to production relations. This linkage is supplied by the
fact that one major inequality – ownership and non-
ownership of the means of production – is, in Marxist class
theory, the basis of class divisions, the source of class
interests and relationships. For Marxists, inequalities at
work are seen, ultimately, to derive from the organizational
member's relationship to the means of production – i.e.,
whether the person simply sells labour power, or, through
ownership of capital, buys labour power. Those in the first
group will receive less than the value of their product, and
will have to struggle constantly to achieve any improvement. Those in the latter category will receive far more
than the value of their contribution since they expropriate
profit. Westergaard and Resler state this position as
follows: 'Private ownership of economic resources entitles
the owners to whatever surplus the resources yield, once

costs have been met. Maximization of the surplus is the main motor of economic enterprise. The prime determinant of income for those without property is the pull they can exert in the markets where they sell their labour.' (Westergaard and Resler, 1975: 237.)

Westergaard and Resler demonstrate how the ownership/non-ownership of the means of production constitutes the most decisive break between the wealthy and privileged (owners) on the one hand, and the rest (the non-owners), on the other. They note, for example, that the top one per cent of the population, who own property, take as much income as the bottom thirty per cent who of course own nothing but their labour. These authors argue that this level of inequality is the direct consequence of capitalism: 'The range and shape of income inequality in Britain reflect the fact that the economy is still, in all essentials, capitalist.' (Westergaard and Resler, 1975: 52.) And they isolate the private ownership of capital as the most important determinant of the pattern of distribution.

Nevertheless, while the ownership/non-ownership axis may represent the major division between rich and poor (as well as being the *basis* of the distinction), it is clearly insufficient as a way of isolating or explaining differences in distribution *within* the propertyless category within organizations.

Crompton and Gubbay (1977), accept the importance of private property – ownership of capital – as the ultimate basis of inequality, but they note that it is not possible to explain the details of distribution simply in terms of production relations: 'patterns of distribution in capitalist societies will show considerable variation depending on the history of the particular society, local labour market variations, the evolution of property ownership, the manner of capitalist development, and so on.' (Crompton and Gubbay, 1977: 154.)

These authors explain the unequal structure of incomes

within capitalism by reference to the development of the organization of work within capitalism and, in particular, to the differentiation of the processes of design and execution, and the increasing location of control in specialized expert groups. Those who now take on some of the differentiated specialist functions of capital are re-warded advantageously. 'Differential rewards can be explained at least in part by the need to preserve and maintain a structure of authority, and ensure that it continues to be exercised on behalf of capital.' (Crompton and Gubbay, 1977: 155.) This argument rests, ultimately, on the argument that capitalism as a form of work organization has certain specific requirements: technical expertise, management, supervision etc.; and that either those who fill these roles must be treated advantageously in order to maintain their commitment and ensure adequate levels of performance, or that they vary in their power capacity. The recalcitrance of these organizational employees would be disastrous for the capitalist. The ultimate source of the distribution of organizational rewards and deprivations is here related to the functions of capital. As such it has certain similarities with other functionalist arguments.

Ownership and non-ownership are also seen at the ultimate basis of class divisions and relationships. Once again, however, such a demarcation alone is obviously insufficient as a basis for analysis of the class structures of modern capitalist societies. Marxists themselves are aware of the need to identify the boundaries of the working class, and to establish the class location of various apparently marginal or intermediate categories (Hunt, 1977). Recently, a number of Marxist writers have offered definitions of classes in modern capitalism, which attempt to break down the basic ownership versus non-ownership of capital distinction into a number of separate axes. These analyses all share a concern to isolate class positions on the basis of the application of Marxist categories of position or function within the capitalist mode of production. They reject the neo-Weberianism of writers such as Goldthorpe *et al.* who focus on variations in experiences, life chances and conditions, on the grounds that such an approach is 'technicist' and empiricist. The allocation of employees to classes on the basis of the 'intrinsic' content of their work ('Work situation') is inadequate, remarks Poulantzas, for example, because it fails to come to grips with the different functions and positions of groups within capitalism, and confuses appearance for underlying reality (Poulantzas, 1975: 256). The problem with this criticism, of course, is that it is by no means clear just what the criteria are for allocating groups to different classes.

Two important and influential attempts to separate the functions and positions of apparently differentiated groups on the basis of Marxist theory are those of Poulantzas (1975) and Wright (1978). The former argues that the working class is composed not simply of all those who do not own the means of production. The distinction between productive and unproductive labour is also important. The working class is composed of those who are (a) productive (i.e., create wealth, surplus value) and (b) who are propertyless. These are the employees, who by virtue of these two characteristics, are most truly exploited. Poulantzas also insists that classes cannot be isolated only by economic criteria, and he puts particular emphasis on political and ideological criteria in establishing the class position of the new and traditional petty bourgeoisie – i.e., those in supervision and management, experts, administrators. Their exclusion from the working class is a result of their labour being unproductive, but their location within the petty bourgeoisie is reinforced by virtue of their maintaining authority, within the enterprise, over the working class (in the case of those organizational categories with formal managerial authority) or by their possession of expertise removed from de-skilled workers.

Poulantzas's criteria for class allocation has been extensively criticized by Carchedi (1975), Hunt (1977), and Wright (1978). Criticism has focused on the validity of Poulantzas's emphasis on the productive-unproductive distinction, on the 'narrowness' of his definition of the working class, on the implications of his introduction of political and ideological criteria of class allocation. Wright (1978) takes a much broader definition of the working class. He argues that capitalist relations of productions give rise to three processes all of which are involved in the establishment of classes: relations of control over money capital, over physical capital – i.e., the physical means of production, and over labour – i.e., management and supervision.

The use of these three axes produces two sorts of categories: class locations, which are of three kinds – capitalist class, working class and petty bourgeoisie. The first two of these are defined by having, or lacking, all three sorts of control. The petty bourgeoisie is 'outside' the capitalist mode of production since it involves production without employees. The second sort of category is described by Wright as contradictory locations within the class structure. These are groups which are in more than one class at the same time. They are not *between* classes, they are in more than one. They have a foot in both camps. Three such categories are isolated: managers and supervisors (who control labour, and the physical means of production, but not money capital); small employers; and 'semi-autonomous' employees, who are employed, but retain control over their own work. This model is illustrated in the figure opposite.

Wright's analysis shares with other Marxist attempts to develop a theory of class structure in modern capitalism the argument that modern capitalism demonstrates a differentiation of the functions of capitalism. During this

The basic class relations of capitalist society

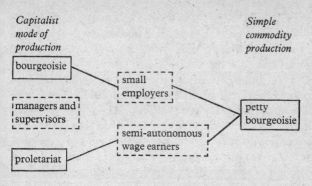

Capitalist mode of production

Simple commodity production

classes   contradictory locations within class relations

Source: Wright (1980).

century the original fusion of, for example, ownership, control and technical expertise has been fragmented. As the functions of capitalism have become differentiated they have been assumed by people who are not themselves capitalists – i.e., they are formally propertyless. Nevertheless, their involvement in the functions of capital, and, frequently, their obtaining privileged shares of organizational rewards, separates them from the working class. For many, the result is a contradictory, or 'ambiguous' class position (Crompton, 1976) sharing features of more than one class location.

Such analyses raise a number of problems. First, there is considerable disagreement within Marxism as to the appropriate criteria for establishing the boundaries of classes. Secondly, the empirical, heuristic value of such schemes is not clearly established, particularly when, with some schemes, the possibility of a looseness of 'fit' between class location and class action is posited. Thirdly, it remains unclear how far the categories and levels of organizational employees within capitalism are the result of capitalism itself. While it is widely accepted that there are strong links between the use of alienated labour to achieve profit and the design and work and the structure of organizations, Crompton is right when she notes the difficulties in ascertaining how far coordination and technique are the result of capitalism, or the result of the need to coordinate any production process. 'Because both elements have been developed within the capitalist function, it is difficult, if not impossible, to gauge the extent to which either is strictly (a) "necessary to any complex production process", (b) "necessary in order to ensure the extraction of relative surplus value" – i.e., specific to the capitalist mode of production.' (Crompton, 1976: 419.)

Relations between classes in Marxism are defined in terms of exploitation and struggle. Indeed, as Poulantzas expresses it: 'For Marxism, social classes involve in one and the same process both class contradictions and class struggle. Social classes coincide with class practices, i.e., with the class struggle, *and are only defined in their mutual opposition.*' (Poulantzas, 1975: 14; my emphasis.)

This mutual opposition follows from the definition, within Marxism, of classes in terms of two mutually opposed locations within the capitalist mode of production, relations between which are defined in terms of exploitation and expropriation. Such an analysis has certain implications for the interpretation of relationships between classes within organizations.

First, unlike Weberians, who start their analysis of inter-group relations by isolating the factors which generate class consciousness and dichotomous class imagery – who seek to explain the *existence* of class consciousness – the Marxists, by virtue of their theory of class relations, must explain its *non-appearance*. This difference is significant.

Secondly, the stark simplicity of the traditional Marxist

model of two mutually opposed classes is, as noted, hardly sufficient for analysis of the complex relations between the variety of groups within organizations – technicians, supervisors, managers, skilled workers, professionals etc. We have seen that modern Marxist theory acknowledges the insufficiency of conventional Marxist categories for understanding the class structure and class behaviour of modern societies, and advances a number of more differentiated models. A major implication of a more differentiated model of class, however, is a more complicated analysis of *class relations*. If, as many of the schemes on offer suggest, modern capitalism – and modern capitalist organizations – now consist of various groups intermediate between the two polar opposites of bourgeoisie and working class, the existence of such groups will presumably complicate relations between the two basic classes. Relations between these groups and these polar classes, and among these intermediate groups themselves, will not accord in any obvious fashion with the Marxist analysis of relations between bourgeoisie and working class. For example, Wright's analysis of the class structure of advanced capitalist societies argues for the existence of various contradictory class locations which are simultaneously placed in two classes, i.e., people in these positions within organizations – managers, professionals etc. – will have, in Marxist terms, the same interests as members of the working class as employees, but will also share an interest with the bourgeoisie, since they obtain genuine privileges from their services to the capitalist system. Wright is clear about the complicated conflicts within and between classes that can occur within advanced capitalism as a result of the differentiation of the bases of class and of the functions of capitalism. He remarks that the understanding of class categories is all the more important since it aids an understanding of the varieties of class conflicts evident within modern capitalism, conflicts which obstruct the development of socialism. But such conflicts, he adds, are real, they reflect real differences of interest. They are not confusions, mystifications, or 'false' consciousness.

Thirdly, however, many of those responsible for recent Marxist analyses of class and class relations claim their analyses have relevance to class conflicts of a more basic kind between working class and bourgeoisie. This claim rests upon the process of 'proletarianization': the exposure of employees from traditionally privileged locations within organizations to the working conditions, principles of work design, levels of reward, exclusion from authority etc. conventionally characteristic of the working class. The extent of these processes – 'de-skilling' of skilled workers, the proletarianization of clerical workers, of technicians, or even of professionals – has been much debated recently. The issue is not simply an empirical one: the 'facts' of the processes concerned can only be understood in the light of the definitions and concepts and problematics of the theories employed. Writers within the Weberian tradition, for example, regard the hypothesized proletarianization of the white-collar worker in terms of life chances, and variations in work, market and status situation. Within this tradition, analysis focuses on working conditions and authority relations.

For the Marxist, however, such analyses fail to get behind empirical detail and come to grips with the class locations and functions of these workers. Their analyses are consequently, at best, descriptive. So, for example, Crompton argues that the question of the proletarianization of white-collar workers cannot be resolved by an empirical comparison of the 'class situation' (in Lockwood's terms) of clerical and manual workers alone, but requires theoretical analysis of 'structural differences reflecting different relationships *vis à vis* the capitalist mode of production' (Crompton, 1976: 420). Such analysis, she claims, reveals a basic ambiguity in the class location of white-collar workers which is reflected in the 'heterogeneous and often contradictory forms of collective representation' adopted by members of this category.

Some Marxists see an increasing proletarianization of employees, as more and more categories of employees are 'de-skilled'. Braverman, for example, insists on the differences between contemporary clerical and office work and that of the nineteenth century, as the work becomes de-skilled, differentiated and subordinate. The proletarianization follows the increasing subordination of clerical work of which de-skilling is a major feature. It is the change in clerks' relationship to authority which is critical to their proletarianization. Wright argues the same case: that with the development of advanced capitalism, ownership has become differentiated into three sorts of control, that different groups within the enterprise; foreman, managers, clerks, technicians, may have some degree of control over one or more of the three relevant resources (see Wright, 1978: 58–87). For proletarianization to occur, increasing numbers of employees must find themselves devoid of any sort of control whatsoever.

To postulate an irreconcilable conflict of interest between two basic classes (however 'narrow' or 'broad' the definition of the working class) is not to assert that all enterprises are characterized by constant class conflict. Marxists are well aware of the importance of situational factors in affecting the visibility of class exploitation. They have noted the implications of the development of a large-scale trade union movement, and have speculated about the relationship between formal union objectives and class consciousness.[7] Furthermore, the role of out-of-work factors in limiting workers' conception of alternative forms of society, in promulgating notions of a neutral, national interest, in legitimating patterns of distribution (as a consequence of individual ability and achievement), and in dividing working-class solidarity through sexism and racism, has been frequently noted. Marxists regard modern employing organizations as characterized by, and as articulating, conflict between classes, and they regard inter-group relations as class relations, especially relations between working-class employees and senior management. But they are aware that numerous factors, at work and in the larger society, obstruct the clear perception or articulation of these conflicts of interest.

To conclude this chapter on theories of class and class relations within organizations, some general remarks about the relationship between these theories and theories of organization are appropriate. The first and most striking point about recent theories of organization is their lack of any consideration of class within organizations. Most organization theory appears indifferent to the possibility that the various organizational *roles* that are described, or *levels* that are distinguished, measured and related to some determinant variable are also class categories. The restriction of interest to the level of the organization very frequently results in a strangely de-politicized form of analysis. Inequalities within organizations are given little attention, in the face of vigorous speculation about organizational structure and its determinants; the distribution of power, and the design of jobs (elsewhere seen as elements of class situation, or as reflections of class conflicts) are conventionally regarded as outcomes of technical problems and priorities. If the possibility of conflict within organizations is granted (as it is in only some traditions of organizational analysis) it is regarded simply as a fact of organizational life, not as directly related to class relationships.

There are a number of explanations of the strange absence of reference to class in most organization theory – an absence which is all the more surprising in the face of the importance of the organization of work and the enterprise in class theories, and the fact that the founders of organization theory each advanced a distinctive theory of class.

Partly the absence is due to the institutional and social settings of much organization theory; partly to its concern with different audiences and sponsors, partly to its empiricist emphasis, its preoccupation with practical matters. (A preoccupation which, insofar as it leads to a denial of theory, is unfruitful.) But mainly the absence is the result of much organization theory implicitly adopting the class theories and concepts derived from Durkheim, albeit in such a crude form as not to do justice to the problematics of that tradition. Within most organizational analysis – even much of that which claims some derivation from Weber – the supercession of class is assumed; the irrelevance of concepts such as class conflict, exploitation and expropriation is assumed; the origins of organizational structures, the design of work, the distribution of authority and rewards in the organizational resolution of technical issues is taken for granted. Only recently have we seen a revival of interest in other forms of class theory, of a sort which have been described in this chapter, the objective of which has been to suggest some of the ways in which the major theories of class have direct relevance to an understanding of organizational processes and structures.

A theory of organizations must include reference to a theory of class. The strange omission from most organization theory of reference to class analysis may not be altogether surprising in view of the origins and audiences of much of this writing. But without the clear recognition that the design of work, the distribution of work rewards, the process of organizational control and legitimation, and relations between grades of employee within the plant reflect the class relations of the wider society our understanding of organizational process and structures can at best be partial, at worst, hopelessly unreal. It must by now be clear that a major reason for the popularity of functionalist approaches to employing organizations is precisely because they permit a classless and de-politicized conception of the enterprise. Such an unrealistic and inadequate conceptualization has done much to hinder the development of a more successful – and realistic – form of organizational analysis.

8   Conclusion

This book has been concerned with varieties of organization theory and their relationship to the classic theories of Durkheim, Weber and Marx. Its main thrust has been the irredeemably theoretical nature of organizational analyses, and the connections between modern forms of theory, however inchoate, and earlier, more coherent forms. The book has argued that each theorist established a characteristic approach to organizations (and other phenomena) which is still influential and apparent. Each approach, while being internally consistent and coherent, differs significantly, sometimes radically, from other approaches.

Yet it has also been argued throughout that each theory, despite major differences, can be seen to be concerned with broadly similar questions: the nature of the individual's work experiences in modern industrial society; a theory of organizational control and structure; and a theory of class. Within each theory these three elements are interconnected: for example, theories of 'alienation' and its origins rely on theories of the origins of organizational structure and control, and articulate notions of inter-class relations, class formations, and the origins of structured inequalities and conflicts.

In insisting on the irrevocably theoretical nature of an understanding of organizations, and in pointing to the variety of forms of theory that exist, the book has, so far, raised (but not explicitly deal with) the problem of choosing between these approaches. Such a choice cannot be made solely on the basis of each theory's adequacy at explaining the 'facts' in question. Exactly which issues and subjects are regarded as problematic is itself a result of a commitment to a theoretical position in terms of which certain *questions are seen as important* – the work attitudes of industrial workers, or the nature of bureaucratic rationality for example. This is not to say that any of the theories discussed in this book take a nominalist position, regarding reality as entirely a consequence of the language through which it is made available. But it is clear that even if some of these theoretical traditions espouse a version of positivism, a choice between them cannot be reduced entirely to an assessment of their relative competence at explaining a discrete and objective empirical world.

The theories on offer differ not only in their problematics and their characteristic interpretations, but in more basic ways. They differ, for example, in postulating either a consensus (functionalism) or a conflict (Marxism) view of organizations and society. The distinction between these two types of sociological theory once excited much attention. Indeed, recently Burrell and Morgan (1979) have argued for its continued relevance to an understanding of distinct types of sociological theory. The theories also differ in their view of sociological theory itself, and, consequently, of the relationship between sociological theory and society. For example, Marxist theories of organizations regard functionalism or theories of 'industrial society', as barely more than ideologies of capitalism, seeking to deny the essentially class-based nature of capitalist society, and replace it with the language of the requirements of technology and industrialism. In extreme forms this view argues that functionalist sociology and coercion are functional alternatives: functionalism operates to support, and disguise, capitalist domination in society or organization. The 'findings' of this form of sociology, the result of 'value-free' methods and analysis, merely serve to celebrate existing social forms and social patterns and, by ascribing to them the status of necessary, or functional, arrangements, to de-politicize capitalism, to normalize oppression, to accept rationalization and ideology as reason itself. Such a form of sociology, it is held, employs its claims to scientificity in the natural sciences' positivistic sense, to recreate within sociology the domination of institutions and classes over people, and the consequent alienation of citizens and employees which it seeks to deny. The language of functionalism is the language of oppression, alienation and constraint. The insistence on the separation of fact and value, observer and reality, makes possible an acceptance of the way things are, socially speaking, of the dominant institutions of society.

So the Marxist assesses functionalism as neither value-free nor as satisfactorily explanatory, but as an integral part of the very form of society – capitalism – within which it exists and the exploitative character of which, by its concern for industrialism and its imperative, it seeks to deny.

On the other hand, representatives of a neo-Durkheimian approach regard a Marxist sociology as deeply flawed as a result of its mixture of ideology and explanation, of philosophical and sociological elements. Marxist forms of analysis are seen as only sociologically legitimate to the extent that they reject the evaluative elements, and restore the primacy of scientific observation and method. Each of these approaches regards the other as seriously if not totally inadequate by virtue of its explicit or masked concern with retaining or transforming existing social arrangements. Clearly no attempt to choose between them can rely on empirical verification alone since the interpretation of 'verification' or 'falsification' would vary widely between supporters or critics of the theory in question, who would point to the extent to which, in sociological analysis, the concepts, subjects and methodologies of empirical research derive from the problematics or questions specific to particular theories and traditions of debate.

In an important recent exploration of types of sociological theory, Burrell and Morgan have argued that it is fruitful to categorize forms of theory in terms of two basic dimensions: sociology of regulation (order) or radical change (conflict), and an objective-subjective dimension composed of polar positions on such issues as ontology, epistemology, theories of human nature and methodology. The first dimension distinguishes between theories concerned with the need for regulation and control in society and theories interested in the realization of man's potential by means of radical change in society. The second dimension contrasts theories which attempt to define sociology and the social world in terms of the natural sciences, and theories which stress the subjective nature of social life. Using these dimensions to construct a matrix, these authors argue for four paradigms of 'basic metatheoretical assumptions' which underlie whole groups of theories. These paradigms are: the radical humanist, the radical structuralist, the functionalist and the interpretative. In terms of these paradigms, the theories under discussion in this book can be allocated to separate paradigmatic boxes: Marxism to radical structuralism: functionalism and some utilizations of Weber to the regulation/objective category; critical theory to radical humanism. Marxist sociology and Functionalist sociology differentiate most importantly in terms of their stance on the order-conflict dimension, rather than on the objective-subjective axis. As Burrell and Morgan remark, the sociology of radical change (Marxism)

. . . stands in stark contrast to the 'sociology of regulation', in that its basic concern is to find explanations for the radical change, deep-seated structural conflict, modes of domination and structural contradiction which its theorists see as characterizing modern society. It is a sociology which is essentially concerned with man's emancipation from the structures which limit and stunt his potential for development. (Burrell and Morgan, 1979: 17.)

Functionalism, on the other hand, emphasizes the need for constraint and regulation, and the dangers of radical change. Order and control are regarded as *required* by existing social forms and techniques; unity and cohesion are discovered and celebrated; and conflict, viewed as unnecessary, is minimized. Actual, current, societal arrangements are emphasized, in contrast to potentials.

It should by now be clear that the versions of Marxism and functionalism which have been found in current varieties of organizational analysis differ in precisely these terms. Returning to Burrell and Morgan's analysis, this is important for our purposes in a number of ways. First, they supply a timely categorization of the basic ways in which types of theory differ. They differ not only in their characteristic approaches and interpretations, but in more basic, sometimes underlying respects. Secondly, their work emphasizes that while it is possible to differentiate four discrete paradigms, one of these – functionalism – has until recently attracted a disproportionate share of interest. It has been the dominant paradigm within the sociology of organizations. This itself is not without sociological import. Why should a perspective on organizational analysis which emphasizes consensus and the requirements of technology be so attractive to researchers and their audiences as virtually to swamp alternative approaches and interpretations? Answers to this will vary depending on whether one works within or without this approach. Thirdly, these authors make the important point that differences between these theoretical paradigms are so great, have such influence over all aspects of the theory that it cannot be assumed that these paradigms can be incorporated into each other. They 'reflect four alternative realities. They stand as four mutually exclusive ways of seeing the world.' (Burrell and Morgan, 1979: 398.) Furthermore, each paradigm articulates a rich theoretical tradition, using ideas from 'broader intellectual traditions which have underwritten social science in the widest of terms. It is time that organization theory became fully aware of its pedigree.' (Burrell and Morgan, 1979: 401–2.) This book, too, is an attempt to rediscover and reconsider organization theory's intellectual pedigree.

However, if organization theory can be seen to reflect ideas and assumptions from classic sociology theorizing, this is not to say that current forms of analysis always do justice to their intellectual precedents. For one thing, as Burrell and Morgan note, organizational analysis has been dominated by one tradition – functionalism – to such an extent that a relatively narrow field of exploration, and an inevitably narrow intellectual approach have begun to produce diminishing marginal returns. Furthermore, the dominance of this approach has frequently caused competing positions to be couched in terms of their opposition to the dominant tradition, or their critique of it, rather than in terms of an effort fully to develop and think through the alternative form of analysis.

This book has shown that while it is possible to see relationships between current forms of analysis and earlier traditions; in many cases modern forms of organizational analysis present a bowdlerized and simplified version of the original. We have seen this in more than one instance. Many modern functionalist analyses of the meaning of work, for example, fail to do justice even to that tradition upon which they most rely – Durkheim's analysis of pathological forms of the division of labour, and of anomie, within industrial societies. Even Durkheim, who can be considered the least radical of the theorists under discussion here, the most concerned to regard existing social forms as necessary, and capable of generating consensus and integration, was aware that the individual costs of industrialization were to some degree the result of the non-spontaneous division of labour, and the role of class privilege in distorting the distribution of differentiated jobs among the population. Furthermore Durkheim's concept of anomie was directed at a critical analysis of the impact of industrialization on culture and values. In industrialization, self-interest, market-based values and commercialized relationships assume dominance. These are the conditions under which egoism and the pursuit of individual interest are unchecked; appetites are unlimited and anomie flourishes. Yet in modern research into work attitudes, Durkheim's emphasis on the causal role of industrialization is interpreted in terms of technology, and his insistence on the damaging personal consequences and costs of the values of capitalist forms of industrialization, and on the role of class in influencing the persistence of inequality at work, is forgotten. The 'operationalization' of anomie spells the elimination of any degree of outrage at the impact of modern work forms, or of any concern to question the values and interests which are revealed in work and organizational design. Unlike the masters whose work is used to legitimate such analyses, much modern research into the meaning of work shows no interest at all in judging the society, merely in (one-sidedly) describing it. Weber too has been seriously misinterpreted in similar directions. All too often his work has been used to initiate discussion of the pathologies (i.e. inefficiencies) of bureaucracy, or in empirical analyses of dimensions of bureaucracy and their variation with selected internal or external variables. Both these modern traditions misunderstand Weber's notion of rationality, and fail to appreciate his argument that modern work or organizational domination and organizational hierarchy are legitimated by reference to an increasingly pervasive cultural value – rationality – which destroys previous cultures and relationships and

238 Class and the Corporation

replaces them with an emphasis on calculation, impersonality, formality and science. The notion of rationality as a pervasive legitimation of new structures of domination, and as a form of analysis with particular inter-connections with capitalist priorities and problems, is noticeably absent from the many studies within organizational analysis which take as their starting point the *efficiency* of organizations under various circumstances. In other words, modern utilizations of Weber frequently offer a de-politicized version of his analysis. Questions of power, inequality and legitimation if they arise at all are treated empirically in terms of inter-relationships between organizational arrangements and various determinant variables. The cultural context of work – the bodies of knowledge and criteria of evaluation – that make such structures sensible or possible, and the forces which assert the inevitability and dominance of such rationalities, are overlooked.

More precisely, the major deficiency of much that passes for organization theory is its striking rejection, or ignorance, of class analysis. Clearly theories of organization, from whatever tradition, depend upon a theory of class which explains and categorises the nature of relations between organizational employees of various types, which analyses the distribution of organizational rewards and deprivations, which relates organizational structures of power and privilege to the stratification (or class structuration) of society. It will be clear from Chapter 7 that the three theories of class examined each attempt these tasks. Yet a surprising proportion of theories of organization either ignore these developments completely, or employ some naïve version of a functionalist stratification theory (itself a seriously defective form of analysis, as Chapter 7 indicated).

Yet it is obvious that analyses of organizations not only require class analysis, their analyses are frequently relevant to theories of class, although such connections are rarely drawn by the organization theorists. And nowhere is this more evident than in discussions of organizational control.

We have shown the centrality of control to organizational structure, and the relevance of processes of control to theories of organization. Theories of organizational control assume distinctive explanations of the origins of these processes, and their implications for inter-group relations. These assumptions derive from theories of class. Yet those who write about power and control in organizations from within the academic speciality of organization theory, are apparently constrained by the traditions of their topic and style of enquiry from apprehending the obvious implications of their analyses.[1]

For example, it must be obvious that the design of work, and of organizational structure and hierarchy, and the distribution of work rewards (and deprivations) have enormous significance for class structuration and class relations. Yet numerous organizational theorists are prepared, in the characteristic language of conventional organizational analysis, to attribute variation in organizational structure in terms of such variables as 'configuration' and 'formalization', or to the operation of de-humanized variables and processes, such as size, or technology, without apparently realizing that in so doing they are effectively explaining class formations in terms of necessary and neutral organizational 'adjustments' to modern technology, and growing organizational size.

Some research into organizational control, however, is directly relevant to class analysis, although even here the authors are frequently unwilling to see the implications of their analyses. Of particular importance is that growing body of work on varieties of organizational control systems. This literature makes two major points: that senior members of organizations utilize a wide variety of control methods, ranging from the unobtrusive to the overtly repressive and alienative, and that these controls are the object of struggle and resistance. Furthermore these forms of control are continually surrounded by efforts to justify and mystify them. Numerous mechanisms of control have been isolated: technology, employment and payment systems, training, recruitment and selection, careers, budgetary controls, limits on decision-making etc.

The important point about these variations in forms of control, as noted by numerous writers, is that they relate to class differences. Although few organization researchers are prepared to make the point explicitly, it is clear that the decision to apply different forms of control to different categories of organizational employee is directly related to the class position of the employees. Working-class employees who are inherently untrustworthy, from management's point of view (Fox, 1974), are controlled in ways which are explicitly oppressive. Middle-class and professional employees are controlled in more insidious and unobtrusive ways. This partly reflects the greater centrality and importance of their functions (and therefore the importance of retaining their commitment), partly it reflects the capacity of middle-class employees to resist the application of 'rationalized' work-design principles.

The literature on forms of organizational control reveals the reality of class differences within organizations. It also reveals class conflicts: those who are exposed to attempts to fragment and standardize and cheapen their jobs seek to resist such efforts. For example, it is a well-established finding of organizational research, as it is of organizational life, that de-skilling means a loss of autonomy and of intra-organizational power. Precisely because the retention of informal power on the shop floor constitutes a major barrier to management's efforts to redesign work in ever more intensive, i.e., efficient ways, a constant struggle for control takes place around questions of, for example, work design, or the application of new technology etc. For the same reason senior management develops less obtrusive and onerous modes of control to apply to those employees whose commitment is important, and is contingent upon them retaining some apparent work autonomy.

It is a central argument of this book that it is possible to see connections between certain discussions of processes of, and reactions to, varieties of organizational control and class analysis. This requires that I make explicit the view of class analysis which is being employed. Since a theory of class is just one of the elements of an overall theory of organizations and alienation, this will require a brief exposition of the approach to organizational analysis which seems to the writer to be most useful for understanding the issues and problems that both the public and the professional would seem to be defining as crucial at this point in the development of capitalism, e.g., those of productivity, industrial conflict, new technologies, competitiveness of manufacturing industry. For the present writer this means a Marxist approach to organizations, but one which incorporates elements from the Weberian tradition.

The first stage within this approach to organizational analysis requires an affirmation of the continued existence and relevance of capitalism. Certainly the capitalism of contemporary, advanced capitalist societies differs significantly from nineteenth-century capitalism. But it remains capitalism, in that production is organized around one class of people selling their labour power to those who own and control the means of production, who then own the products. Production is for profit; international competition forces the application of new work technologies, the mobility of capital requires the rationalization of work organization. Modern forms of capitalism differ in a number of ways from earlier forms, but the essentials remain. In advanced capitalist societies, the middle class has grown considerably. The once unitary role of capitalist/manager has been fragmented into a number of discrete specialities and functions: managers, experts, professionals (personnel, training, systems analysis etc.); white-collar workers. Secondly, the characteristic form of organization has grown. Thirdly, the state now plays a crucial role in the economy, and in ameliorating some of the consequences and social costs of this form of economic system (Crompton and Gubbay, 1977). These developments are pertinent to any analysis of the relationship between capitalism and forms of work organization. But they do not alter the fact that Western societies are not only industrial, they are also capitalist.

Unquestionably, within advanced capitalist societies significant developments in the size and consequently of ownership and control of corporations have occurred. The characteristic form of the modern business enterprise is remarkable for its size: a small number of enormous corporations dominate national economies. Within the UK, fifty corporations employed twenty-five per cent of the labour force as early as 1963 (Westergaard and Resler, 1975: 150). An increasing proportion of employees work for large companies – by 1963 over seventy per cent of the UK work force was employed by corporations with at least five hundred employees (Westergaard and Resler, 1975: 152). Increased organizational size is frequently accompanied by increased bureaucratization of employment. Presthus calculates that by 1970 ninety per cent of Americans were employees. Only ten per cent worked for themselves. Roughly half the employees, 'perhaps as many as forty million, worked in environments that can be called "bureaucratic settings". The conditions of their work often included large size, standardization, impersonality, exquisite specialization, hierarchy and dependence.' (Presthus, 1979: 58.)

Some of these giant bureaucratic organizations can no longer be contained within national boundaries, and some control more assets than entire national economies.

As already mentioned, the increasing preponderance of large-scale employing organizations is related to the differentiation of management and expert functions within the organizations and to the ways in which large corporations are typically owned. Large corporations are not owned by individuals; they are owned by a number of shareholders. The owners are too numerous and dispersed to control the enterprise they 'own', therefore it is claimed the functions of ownership must be performed by managers. Ownership and control are split. Power is seen as split off from wealth.

The undoubted dispersal of ownership of corporations has been used to justify the thesis that the modern corporation differs radically from its nineteenth-century predecessor. Since the modern company is controlled by non-owners, and since the real owners are dispersed, control will remain with the managers who will employ it in pursuit of goals other than profits, who will seek 'socially responsible' objectives, who will try to 'satisfice' performance criteria, not maximize them.

This argument is important, as we have seen, for our purposes because if true it seriously weakens the argument that within capitalism the forces of competition and the need for profit have direct implications for work design and organizational structures.

However, I would argue that the notion of the separation of ownership and control is invalid for two major reasons.

First, it is in sociological terms doubtful if it is possible to make any clear-cut distinction between senior managers and capitalists – i.e., owners. Senior managers are usually from wealthy sections of society; they are frequently themselves owners of shares; and they pay themselves high fees and salaries out of profits. While it would not be possible to claim that the share-holdings of senior management are sufficient to enable them to exert overall control, they are big enough to ensure that they are not likely to 'give low priority to considerations of profit, because they have little personal stake in it through share-ownership' (Westergaard and Resler, 1975: 161).

Furthermore, similarities of social background, culture, social and family relations and education ensure overall similarity of outlook between owners and controllers. 'The two groups are equally wedded to the instrumental and moral value of company profitability and the principle of production for profit as such, together with an associated corpus of conservative ideas.' (Crompton and Gubbay, 1977: 66.)

Secondly, even *if* a company were to be controlled by managers with a commitment to objectives other than profit, their organizations would not survive if these goals were actually achieved. 'No company can dissociate itself from the objective constraints of the market, and these constraints will often be backed up by the board representation of ownership and banking interests.' (Scott, 1979: 144.) Put simply, companies which do not make profits will not survive. The thesis that an apparent split between ownership and control has resulted in the emergence of non-profit, 'soulful' goals is undermined by the fact not only that such a separation is more apparent than real but also by the continuing primacy of profit for organizations no matter how they are controlled. A number of writers, for example, have noted the distinction between operational and strategic control. The former may have passed to middle managers and expert advisers and includes decisions involved in the implementation of corporate strategy. The latter is still retained by senior managers/owners, and involves establishing 'the basic parameters within which the corporations forming a particular unit of capital are to act' (Scott, 1979: 37). Strategic control is firmly oriented towards the imperatives of profit and competitive advantage – i.e., survival: 'The corporation is . . . a long-term profit seeker. It attempts to secure a relation of revenue to costs which will give it the best chance of survival in the market.' (Scott, 1979: 140.)

The modern corporation exists – and seeks to survive – within a capitalist economy. The pressures of the market force each corporation to accumulate capital in order to install new plant and equipment, develop more efficient work systems, develop new products, gain market penetration, install new expertise. If a company fails to achieve profit, and thus to accumulate capital, it will lose competitive advantage, and become vulnerable to bankruptcy or take-over.

The need to maximize profit has direct repercussions on internal organization and company decision-making. It results in the need constantly to monitor and improve the efficiency of the work process. This requires expert attention to the design of work with a view to reducing the time taken to produce a unit of production. This entails attention to technology, work design, payment systems, work flow, the 'rational' fragmentation and coordination of the labour process. The efficiency of these processes for profit is constantly under inspection by expert managers and technicians.

This is not, however, to argue that these efforts are always successful. The overall goals may have primacy, but the experts and managers may disagree as to the optimum means of achieving the goal, or the relative advantage of short- versus long-term maximization. There may be disagreement about the best way to channel investment, or the most efficient way to reorganize work, or to handle labour unrest. But these disagreements concern operational matters, not questions of strategic control. It would be quite wrong to view the professionals and experts employed within large-scale corporations as concerned, ultimately, with anything but the efficient achievement of the overall company goal: profitability. The internal structure of large-scale employing organizations, and the design of work and control are a result of senior and expert organizational members' attempts, within the context of their knowledge and assessment of operational goals, and of available techniques, to achieve the necessary organizational goal – increased profitability. Failure to achieve competitive advantage is equivalent to competitive failure. The decision not to maximize profits is a decision to invite bankruptcy.

There is evidence that within the UK the pressures of international competition and of rising wage rates have resulted in declining profits (Glyn and Sutcliffe, 1972). This trend also applies to other advanced capitalist societies, but is particularly evident in the UK. Under these circumstances, the internal organization of work, control technology; the rationalization of work flow and work procedures become even more important, and one would expect to find an increasingly direct relationship between the search for company profitability and internal organizational arrangements and the control of employees – i.e., the *intensification* of the exploitation of labour. Increasingly, too, this search for ever more rational and efficient forms of work organization becomes the object of professional, expert analysis and theory.

It has been argued that the increasing intervention of the state in the economies of advanced capitalist societies is related to the falling rate of profit in these economies. Certainly state intervention is directly concerned with supporting capitalist economies and with taking responsibility for areas of stagnation, and with supplying services. Scott isolates three forms of state involvement in the economy: collective provision (of welfare, housing, transport etc.); demand management through manipulation of such variables as money supply, taxation, state spending etc.; and central planning. As Scott notes, 'these and other activities are increasingly taken over by the state when they are essential supports of economic activity which cannot be met by private capital, whether this is because of the sheer scale of the expense involved or because such provision is not sufficiently profitable for private initiative.' (Scott, 1979: 147.) The main point to appreciate in this connection is established by Scott (1979), Crompton and Gubbay (1977), Westergaard and Resler (1975), Milliband (1969) and others: within modern, advanced capitalist societies, the state plays a necessary and pervasive role in support of the capitalist economy. Without state regulation, provision and direct state participation in production as employer or financier, mature capitalist societies would collapse.

It follows from this brief mention of the role in the state in ensuring the private accumulation of capital that internal organizational arrangements and the design of work and control are likely to be affected by state activity, both indirectly, through state management of the economy, or through state intervention in employment practices and conditions, in legislation concerning labour relations, income policies etc., and directly through employment in state-owned enterprises.[2] In the latter case it is not the case that employment by the state removes the urgent priority for managers of state-owned enterprises to achieve the same goals of privately-owned corporations – profits. Many state-owned enterprises are required to operate commercially, 'as if' they were privately owned. Many state-owned enterprises face considerable market competition, at home or internationally. These enterprises must remain competitive, or re-organize (e.g., British Airways, BL Motors, British Steel, Chrysler, Amtrak). As Westergaard and Resler remark, since the 1960s 'the nationalized industries have been required in effect normally to pursue a commercial profit . . . these requirements . . . reinforce other pressures on the nationalized industries each to act as a separate and commercially directed enterprise, chasing

its own profit in the market like any private corporation.'
(Westergaard and Resler, 1975: 208.)

Nevertheless, if it remains true that in the advanced
capitalist societies, work organizations must reflect the
over-riding primacy of profit, and competitive pressures, it
must be noted that the relationship is mediated in various
ways, not all of which have yet been fully explored. First,
capitalism itself experiences cycles of activity and reces-
sion. It is likely that the requirement to rationalize work
design and control systems will vary over time in accord
with such things as levels of economic activity, rates of
profit, or the international situation. For example, the fact
that enterprises within the UK are only currently being
forced to rationalize and modernize work practices and
design is a consequence of the fact that during the early
period of industrialization it was possible for organizations
to achieve high rates of profit without much consideration
being given to the intensive organization of work simply
because Britain's lead in the level of industrialization gave
competitive advantage. This advantage has now been all
but lost, hence the more obvious connection between
competition and internal structure.

Secondly, it is unlikely that all sectors of the economy
will be faced with competitive pressures of equal intensity.
It is possible that some sectors might be relatively
protected, at least for a period. Some sectors might be more
competitive than others. Some may, to some degree, be
insulated by traditional management practices, by state
intervention (see Friedman, 1977).

Thirdly, the reactions of employees themselves to
proposed alterations in, or intensification of, the efficiency
of work design and practices play a considerable part in the
need for such alterations, and the possibility of their
installation. For example, at a time of falling rates of profit,
worker recalcitrance (real or assumed) may become
increasingly expensive to management, who may be

impelled to break shop-floor resistance in set-piece confrontations between modern work arrangements and technologies on the one hand and 'luddite' workers on the other. Alternatively, the necessity, in order to retain or regain competitiveness, to install new work systems or technologies which will intensify the utilization of labour and further fragment and de-skill shop-floor work, is likely to occasion a major struggle about the shifting frontier of control. Certainly within an increasingly competitive milieu with deteriorating rates of profit, the question of labour attitudes and of management's capacity to redesign work and reorder organizational structure in order to maximize profitability become of major importance.

Fourthly, the relationship is mediated not only by management's *capacity* to alter organizational systems and structure (i.e., by worker strength and awareness) but by management *knowledge*. To argue for the continuing relationship between capitalism as a form of economic system based on class conflict and class interest and organizational structure and the design of work is not to assert that this relationship will be automatically achieved. It is mediated through what at any time stands for management and expert knowledge of what constitutes the most efficient form of organizational structure (in both senses outlined by Gordon, 1976). Such 'knowledge' is always incomplete and, in 'pure' terms, relatively defective. It can always be argued over by specialists of differing schools. It is always capable of generating precisely the effect that was most feared. The point is that if Child has drawn attention to the significance of strategic choices by the dominant collation within organizations, he has also shown that the knowledge and expertise on which such choices are made is always inadequate and partial, serving, for example, both technical and ideological purposes, glossing over contradictions, accepting its own rhetoric (Child, 1973).

Furthermore, it is clear that any assertion of the relationship between capitalism and the organization of work must take cognisance of the *variety* of work arrangements which currently exist. In the course of this book reference has frequently been made to the forms of work organization characteristically emphasized by the three theorists under discussion, and the ways in which each distinctive theory developed a concern for particular conceptions of work arrangements. But we must remember also that the work arrangements specified have empirical application, and to some extent differences between the theorists reflect different work forms: bureaucracy, scientific management, human relations, professionalism, all exist as alternative strategies of work organization and control. The application of each of these strategies of work represents changing historical periods (in that the characteristic work arrangements of capitalism change over time as the costs and inefficiencies of each form are recognized and new strategies developed), and changing class locations at any one time (in that different class locations within the capitalist system of production, for example, the clerk versus the manual worker – i.e., different class positions – are likely to be controlled in different ways, to be exposed to different forms of work organization). Friedman (1977), for example, distinguishes two broad forms of strategy used by senior managers to exercise control over labour – 'Responsible Autonomy' and 'Direct Control'.

The Responsible Autonomy type of strategy attempts to harness the adaptability of labour power by giving workers leeway and encouraging them to adapt to changing situations in a manner beneficial to the firm. To do this top managers give workers status, authority and responsibility. Top managers attempt to win their loyalty, and co-opt their organizations to the firm's ideals (that is, the competitive struggle) ideologically. The Direct Control type of strategy tries to limit the scope for labour power to vary by coercive threats, close supervision and

minimizing individual worker responisibility.
(Friedman, 1977: 78.)

Similar distinctions have been made by Fox (1974) and, in a
managerial context, by Burns and Stalker (1961).

Friedman goes on to suggest that these strategies have
varied over time, with the deficiencies of Direct Control
strategies causing a shift of emphasis to the Responsible
Autonomy strategy, as the growing expert nature of
management opens up the possiblity of more sophisticated
control systems, and as the limitations and contradictions
of Direct Control (e.g., Scientific Management) become
increasingly apparent. He also suggests that control
strategies will vary with different sectors of the economy –
i.e., in the *monopolistic* sector some degree of insulation
from the need to intensify the efficiency of labour is
achieved by the capacity to pass on wage increases as price
increases, while in the competitive industries sector this is
not possible (O'Connor, 1973).

Clegg (1979) also emphasizes the varieties of forms of
control of the labour process – Taylorism, Mayo and
Human Relations etc., and argues that each is an attempt to
'correct' the increasingly evident inadequacies of the
preceding. Thus Mayo's solution to the problems of
managerial control 'was the proposal of persuasion in the
guise of new forms of social solidarity to replace those
destroyed by the industrial processes of de-skilling and
isolation introduced by the combined efforts of Taylorism
and Fordism.' (Clegg, 1979: 132.)

Furthermore, both Clegg and Friedman argue that the
forms of control they distinguish exist simultaneously but
are applied to different sectors of the economy in terms of
importance to the labour process. Technical rules or Direct
Control are applied to peripheral workers (i.e., workers,
like clerks, whose labour is not immediately crucial to the
overall operation of the plant) and social-regulative rules or

Responsible Autonomy will be applied to more central workers (i.e., workers like maintenance engineers whose work is absolutely central and critical to the whole work process, whose withdrawal would halt the entire operation). As numerous writers have noted, these differences are partly the result of the relative ease, or difficulty, of applying Taylorist principles to different sorts of jobs. Not all jobs are equally amenable to fragmentation and differentiation, as Fox notes (1974). Perrow argues that of crucial importance in this context is the extent to which a job involves knowledge and intuitions which are not amenable to fragmentation, and the sort of 'exceptional cases' which occur. When these are unfamiliar and unpredictable, the job is difficult to standardize (Perrow, 1972). Finally, as many writers have noted, the more important workers are to the overall goals of the enterprise, the more critical it becomes that they are not disgruntled. The greater the functional significance of type of organizational employee, the greater the cost of his or her withdrawal of commitment. It is these 'strategically contingent' types of worker that are likely to be controlled in 'insidious' or unobtrusive ways. We have seen that within organizations a variety of control mechanisms exist. We have seen, for example, that centralization of decision-making and the delegation of decisions to employees who have been exposed to such processes of selection, recruitment, induction, appraisal and professional programming that they can be relied on to make sensible decisions, may be functional alternative methods of control. It is now clear that these variations in methods of control are determined by the anticipated cost that will be incurred should the employees in question withdraw their commitment to the priorities of the enterprise, as these are seen by senior management.

This is not to say that all forms of control are equally successful, or that all disguised forms consistently and successfully mislead those to whom they are applied, or that within any system of control there will not be some space for the controlled to establish some influence over important decisions and processes (from the point of view of senior managers) which can be used as a basis for some intra-organizational power (Crozier, 1964; Hickson *et al.*, 1973). What is being argued here, however, is that in general terms an account of varieties of organizational strategies of control rests upon an analysis of the differing functional significance of those who are controlled; on their 'worth' to those who own/control the enterprise. Clearly, then, organizational control is directly related to the existence, within organizations, of classes.

A few writers are very unambiguous regarding this connection. Clegg, for example, argues that 'power in organizations derives from control of the means and methods of production' (Clegg, 1979: 123). But the majority of social scientists show little interest in relating internal organizational inequalities, or relations of super- or sub-ordination to class structures. This is particularly puzzling as recent developments in class theory make it abundantly clear that the time is now ripe for the false dichotomy between the analysis of classes and that of organizations to be abandoned.

Processes of organizational control reveal conflicting class groups and interests and opposing class rationalities. Increasingly, attempts by senior management to install new work technologies on shop-floor workers (with clear implications for job autonomy and skill) which are accompanied by elaborate statements of the necessity for such 'rationalizations', and associated reductions in manpower, are often met not only by organized shop-floor resistance, but by alternative statements of what con-stitutes rationality under the relevant market and competi-tive circumstances. It is increasingly clear to organizational employees that methods of organizational control, ex-

perience of organizational hierarchy, the unequal distribution of rewards and deprivations, and the policies
pursued by organization decision-making machinery (the
dominant coalition) reflect class interests and groups. Such
a connection is also evident to sociologists.

We have noticed that Marxist and neo-Weberian
theories of class are usually held to differ radically.
Weberians are criticized for failing to understand the
relations of production that lie behind and make possible
the predominance of the market, for supplying *descriptive*
categories of class, but not *explanatory* analyses. Marxist
class theory is vulnerable for its problems in relating
elegant (but disputed) theoretical models to empirical class
formations, notably in the case of new, intermediate class
categories; and for its explanatory inadequacy in analyses
of class conflicts. Yet despite these problems and the very
real differences they reflect, it is possible to see both forms
of theory as increasingly concerned with the relationship
between processes of organizational control and class
groups and class conflict.

Despite the highly abstract and general nature of much
Marxist class analysis – in terms of the differentiated
functions of capital within the enterprise – actual attempts
to establish the class position of various class groups
frequently refer to positions within the organization's
control system as a means of establishing class location.
With the increasingly obvious inadequacy of the
property/propertyless distinction for establishing class
boundaries, particularly in the case of intermediate groups,
Marxist class analyses frequently base their distinctions on
location within the organizational control systems. This is
particularly clear in the case of Braverman, for example,
who asserts a tight relationship between work design
(expert versus de-skilled), job control and class position.
This analysis asserts a coincidence of type of work, level of
control, and class, which is the result of organizational

structures themselves being designed explicitly to achieve control and exploitation of the working class through the expert work of privileged agents of capital.

Similarly Poulantzas and Carchedi justify their inclusion of experts and managers within the bourgeoisie on the grounds not of their owning property (for this is usually not the case) but on the grounds of their location within, and contribution to, the achievement of control and regulation of the work force in the interests of capital. The key to this attribution lies in the assertion that such employees are performing *control functions* which are the consequence of the capitalist nature and objectives of the enterprise. As Parkin has noted, this argument does raise questions as to the relative primacy of property or authority within Marxist theory (Parkin, 1979: 616).

Furthermore, Wright, for example, bases his entire analysis of class relations, and particularly of contradictory locations within the class system, on 'three central processes underlying the basic capital-labour relationship: control over the physical means of production; control over labour power; control over investments and resource allocation . . . these three processes are the real stuff of class relations in capitalist society.' (Wright, 1978: 73.)

In practice, then, Marxist analysis, in attempts to relate Marxist theory to developments within the modern corporation, is increasingly basing the attribution of class categories to actual organizational groups on location within organizational control structures, as revealing the class functions of these groups. In this respect it is similar to neo-Weberian analyses which regard location with organizational authority systems as a major determinant of work situation, and therefore of class position.

As we have seen neo-Weberians define class in terms of the market, and differential control over resources or services required by productive enterprises. Within a capitalist economy, three types of resources/skills are distinguished – ownership of the means of production, possession of educational or technical qualifications and skills, and possession of labour-power (Giddens, 1973: 107.) Possession of any one of these resources establishes (within variable limits) differential life chances. Furthermore, ownership of various resources grants, or denies, certain rights of command or control within the enterprise. As Giddens notes, ownership of property in particular, 'confers certain fundamental capacities of command, maximized within the "entrepreneurial" enterprise in its classic form.' (Giddens, 1973: 108–9.)

This writer goes on to distinguish three major factors responsible for the structuring of class relationships: division of labour; authority relations; and distributive groupings. He remarks that the task of any class analysis must be to discover, empirically, how these factors inter-relate under different economic and social conditions. As he notes, these questions cannot be settled *in abstracto*. In this, clearly, Giddens differs from those Marxist writers who establish the class location of organizational categories by reference to the theoretically derived notions of contribution to the differentiated functions of global capital.

Furthermore, within this tradition of analysis, position within, and experience of, organizational authority systems is used as a major dimension of class *experience*, and therefore of class position (as defined by Lockwood, for example). As Mackenzie remarks, position within organizational or bureaucratic control systems is an important determinant of class attitudes and imagery. Such experiences constitute an element of what is meant by class position itself (Mackenzie, 1975). For writers within both traditions, then, location within organizational authority structures represents a central element of class – a means of assessing class position either by reference to such location in terms of class functions within capitalist systems of production, or by reference to rights associated with certain market resources, or to relative strength or weakness associated with market position.

Since organizational hierarchy and processes of organizational control are regarded as directly related to class groups, relations and interests, it follows that organizational statements of the necessity for such processes and the neutrality of organizational hierarchy must be regarded as ideologies. Most common are statements couched in terms of technocratic rationality within which capitalist and dominant class priorities and interests, and the organizational and technical means for their achievement, are presented as classless, neutral, national and general. It follows that the means for their attainment are seen as following inevitably from the application of societally approved methods to agreed tasks. This rationality allows organizational and bureaucratic forms, processes and outcomes to be seen as unquestionable and sensible. Forms of organization not only articulate forms of thinking with a definite class function; they are explicitly buttressed by these forms of knowledge.

The task now for a sociology of organizations and work design is to demonstrate clearly and precisely the class nature of organizations and the ideological nature of their supporting rationalities, this in turn to open the way for a consideration, by researchers, employers and employees alike, of the real nature of organizational structure and the purposes, interests and classes they serve.

Notes

3 Alienation and the Meaning of Work

1. For a thorough discussion of management's changing interest in workers' attitudes towards, and involvement in, the enterprise and its hierarchy, see Anthony (1977, Ch. 11). This treatment is particularly useful for its analysis of the role of social scientists in assisting management to measure and manipulate workers' attitudes and behaviour. The sort of work under consideration here constitutes part of the larger managerial concern 'with inducing a cooperative attitude among the employees' (Bendix, 1963: 338).

2. Like many others who have attempted to isolate types of technology, Blauner's categorization is clearly problematic in that it is not simply an analysis of differences in technology alone, but contains elements of (a) the social organization of work; (b) control systems; and (c) work-flow arrangements. The difference between machine minding and assembly-line work is not simply a technological one. These difficulties will be discussed in Chapter 4.

3. See Eldridge (1971) for a useful discussion of this view with respect to Blauner's study. The transformation, in Faunce's usage, of a *class-based* concept into one based on *status* is particularly revealing.

4. Orientations to Work

1. See Aronowitz (1973) for a similar analysis of anti-school cultures and anti-intellectualism – especially Chapter 2.

2. Turner and Lawrence (1966) report significant differences between the work aspirations of city and small-town workers. Town workers like autonomy and variety. City workers, apparently, prefer jobs with low skill.

3. For a useful review of the situation in North America, see Montagna (1977).

4. This is not to argue that such processes are entirely successful. They are not. But, together, they constitute a massive obstacle that any opposition to current work forms – and principles they articulate – has to overcome. For a useful analysis of the relationship between aspirations and work systems, see Fox (1971).

5. Alienation and the Design of Work

1. Walker and Guest (1952) summarize the characteristics of mass-production jobs as follows: (1) mechanical pacing; (2) repetitiveness; (3) minimum skill requirements; (4) predetermination of tools and processes; (5) minute subdivision of jobs; (6) surface mental attention.

2. For classification of industrial applications of technology, and these skill requirements, see Bright (1958).

3. Bright's analysis of the impact of automation on skill levels is well summarized in Braverman (1974: Ch. 9).

4. These findings have been supported by other researches, many of which are summarized in Blumberg (1968: Ch. 4).

5. Lockwood (1958) gives an important, if now slightly out-of-date, analysis of changes in the class location of clerical workers. Klingender (1935) offers an analysis based not on the work and market situations of clerical workers, but on their propertylessness, which they share with manual workers.

6. For thorough and useful analyses of the mechanization of the office, see Lockwood (1958), Braverman (1974), Mills (1956), Shepard (1971), Crozier (1971).

7. The alienation of the modern employed professional is discussed more fully in Salaman (1979).

8. For a useful, critical discussion of these approaches see Mouzelis, (1967). Brown (1967) develops a thorough critique of one influential British tradition within this management-oriented group.

9. For an excellent and critical summary of the systems approach in organization theory, see Silverman (1970).

10. See also Galbraith on the development of the 'technostructure', and Bell who emphasizes the relationship between the expansion of these expert groups and the development of new forms of information technology. For writers in this tradition, management and management sciences are a neutral application of neutral forms of knowledge to technical problems of planning and integration.

11. Significantly, many of the writers who adopt this position insist that industrial societies show increases in the number of skilled jobs – at shop-floor level, and, most importantly, in the growth of professional occupations.

12. This distinction was first developed by Lockwood (1964).

6. Organization and Control

1. These issues are dealt with thoroughly and sympathetically in Eldridge (1971).

2. For an analysis of the role of social science in this process of ideological development, see Baritz (1975). For a critique of systems theory within organization theory see Silverman (1970).

7. Organizations, Class and Conflict

1. For a thorough criticism of these views see J. H. Goldthorpe (1964) and Westergaard and Resler (1965).

2. As Hunt (1977) notes, 'Any fundamental criteria of class determination must meet one essential test. Does it succeed in revealing the most fundamental and pervasive boundaries within the social structure? It must reveal real differences between classes and their members.' (Hunt, 1977: 92.)

3. This is not to deny the proletarianization of much low-grade non-manual work, nor to assume the coincidence of the manual/non-manual distinction with the working-class/middle-class distinction. These questions are considered below later in this chapter. The point being made here is to emphasize that regardless of where the dividing line is drawn, organizational jobs vary widely and systematically in the principles underlying their design.

4. Low-Beer (1978) presents a useful summary of various theoretical analyses of changes in class structure.

5. Representatives of other theoretical persuasions, of course, dispute both the extent and the interpretation of these developments offered by the Industrial Society theorists. These criticisms will be presented later in this chapter.

6. Parkin acknowledges the device whereby groups attempt to increase their scarcity and thus their 'reward-power'. But he argues that on the whole it is only those occupations which already control scarce skills or vital services which are likely to be notably successful at this sort of strategy.

7. Hyman quotes Gramsci with good effect on the paradox of trade unionism: 'Trade unionism is evidently nothing but a reflection of capitalist society, not a potential means of transcending capitalist society.' (Hyman, 1971: 12.) Some writers regard trade unionism as an obstacle to the development of class consciousness, encouraging economism and incorporation. In this case, spontaneous shop-floor struggles are seen as much nearer to genuine class struggles. Others regard any conflict between workers and employers as indicating some degree of class conflict through their ultimate concern with questions of control and resistance (see Hyman, 1971).

8. Conclusion

1.   This limitation is not characteristic of more recent writers who approach organization theory from outside the speciality and regard it in terms of the theories and problematics of general sociology (see Burrell and Morgan, 1979; Clegg, 1979; Clegg and Dunkerley, 1980). Nor is it always a feature of those writers who approach organizations from the viewpoint of Marxist or 'radical Weberian' theory.

2.   For a valuable discussion of the goals and implication of state-owned enterprises, see Crompton and Gubbay (1977: Ch. 6).

Bibliography

The dates of works cited are those of currently available editions and not necessarily of first publication.

AIKEN, M., and HAGE, J. (1970): 'Organizational Alienation: a Comparative Analysis', in Grusky, O., and Miller, G.A., *op. cit.*, pp. 517–26.

ALBROW, MARTIN (1970): *Bureaucracy*, Macmillan, London.

ANTHONY, P. D. (1977): *The Ideology of Work*, Tavistock, London.

ARGYLE, MICHAEL (1953): 'The Relay Assembly Test Room Retrospect', *Occupational Psychology*, vol. 27, pp. 98–103.

ARON, RAYMOND (1961): *Eighteen Lectures on Industrial Society*, Weidenfeld and Nicolson, London.

ARONOWITZ, STANLEY (1973): *False Promises: the Shaping of American Working-Class Consciousness*, McGraw-Hill, New York.

AVINERI, SHLOMO (1968): *The Social and Political Thought of Karl Marx*, Cambridge University Press.

BABBAGE, CHARLES (1835): *On the Economy of Machinery and Manufactures*, Charles Knight, London.

BALDAMUS, W. (1961): *Efficiency and Effort*, Tavistock, London.

BARAN, PAUL A., and SWEEZY, PAUL M. (1968): *Monopoly Capital*, Penguin Books, Harmondsworth.

BARITZ, L. (1975): 'The Servants of Power', in Esland, Geoff, *et al.*, *op. cit.*

BEECHEY, VERONICA (1977): 'Some Notes of Female Labour in Capitalist Production', *Capital and Class*, no. 3, pp. 45–66.

BELL, DANIEL (1974): *The Coming of Post-industrial Society*, Heinemann, London.

BENDIX, REINHARD (1963): *Work and Authority in Industry*, Harper and Row, New York.

BERLE, A. A., and MEANS, G. C. (1933): *The Modern Corporation and Private Property*, Macmillan, New York.

BEYNON, HUW, and BLACKBURN, R. M. (1972): *Perceptions of Work*, Cambridge University Press.

BEYNON, HUW (1973): *Working for Ford*, Penguin Books, Harmondsworth.

BLAU, PETER M., and SCHOENHERR, RICHARD A. (1971): *The Structure of Organizations*, Basic Books, New York.

BLAU, PETER M. (1972): *The Dynamics of Bureaucracy*, Chicago University Press.

BLAUNER, R. (1960): 'Work Satisfaction and Industrial Trends in Modern Society', in Galenson, W., and Lipset, S. M., eds., *Labour and Trade Unionism*, Wiley, New York.

BLAUNER, R. (1964): *Alienation and Freedom*, University of Chicago Press.

BLUMBERG, PAUL (1968): *Industrial Democracy*, Constable, London.

BRAHAM, PETER (1975): 'Immigrant Labour in Europe', in Esland, Geoff, *et al.*, eds., *op. cit.*, pp. 119–33.

BRAVERMAN, HARRY (1974): *Labor and Monopoly Capital*, Monthly Review Press, New York.

BRAVERMAN, HARRY (1975): 'Work and Unemployment', *Monthly Review*, 27.

BRIGHT, JAMES R. (1958): *Automation and Management*, Harvard Business School, Boston.

BROWN, R. K. (1967): 'Research and Consultancy in Industrial Enterprises', *Sociology*, vol. 1, no. 1, pp. 33–60.

BULMER, MARTIN, ed. (1975): *Working-Class Images of Society*, Routledge and Kegan Paul, London.

BURNS, T., and STALKER, G. M. (1961): *The Management of Innovation*, Tavistock, London.

BURRELL, GIBSON and MORGAN, GARETH (1979): *Sociological Paradigms and Organisational Analysis*, Heinemann, London.

CARCHEDI, GUGLIELMO (1977): *On the Economic Identification of Social Classes*, Routledge and Kegan Paul, London.

CAREY, ALEX (1967): 'The Hawthorne Studies: a Radical Criticism', *American Sociological Review*, vol. 32.

CHILD, JOHN (1973): 'Organization Structure, Environment and Performance: the Role of Strategic Choice', in Salaman, Graeme, and Thompson, Kenneth, eds., *op. cit.*, pp. 91–107.

CHILD, JOHN (1976): 'Organization Structure and Strategies of Control', in Pugh, D. S., and Hinings, C. R., eds., *op.cit.*, pp. 27–44.

CHINOY, E. (1964): 'Manning the Machine – the Assembly-Line Worker', in Berger, P. L., ed., *The Human Shape of Work*, pp. 51–82, Macmillan, New York.

CHINOY, E. (1965): *Automobile Workers and the American Dream*, Beacon Press, Boston.

CLEGG, STEWART (1979): *The Theory of Power and Organizations*, Routledge and Kegan Paul, London.

CLEGG, STEWART, and DUNKERLEY, DAVID (1980): *Organization, Class and Control*, Routledge and Kegan Paul, London.

COHEN, B., and JENNER, P. (1968): 'The Employment of Immigrants', *Race*, X.

COOMBS, ROD (1978): 'Labour and Monopoly Capital', *New Left Review*, 107, pp. 79–96.

COTGROVE, STEPHEN, and VAMPLEW, CLIVE (1972): 'Technology, Class and Politics', *Sociology*, vol. 6, no. 2, pp. 169–86.

COTGROVE, STEPHEN (1972): 'Alienation and Automation', *British Journal of Sociology*, vol. XXIII, no. 4, pp. 437–51.

CROMPTON, ROSEMARY (1976): 'Approaches to the Study of White-collar Unionism', *Sociology*, vol. 10, pp. 407–26.

CROMPTON, ROSEMARY, and GUBBAY, JON (1977): *Economy and Class Structure*, Macmillan, London.

CROZIER, MICHAEL (1964): *The Bureaucratic Phenomenon*, Tavistock, London.

CROZIER, MICHAEL (1971): *The World of the Office Worker*, tr. David Landua, University of Chicago Press.

DAHRENDORF, R. (1959): *Class and Class Conflict in Industrial Society*, Routledge and Kegan Paul, London.

DANIEL, W. W. (1969): 'Industrial Behaviour and Orientation to Work', *Journal of Management Studies*, 6, pp. 366–75.

DANIEL, W. W. (1971): 'Productivity Bargaining and Orientation to Work', *Journal of Management Studies*, 8, pp. 329–35.

DAVIS, CELIA, DAWSON, SANDRA, and FRANCIS, ARTHUR (1973): 'Technology and Other Variables: Some Current Approaches in Organization Theory', in Warner, Malcolm, ed., *Sociology of the Workplace*, pp. 149–63, Allen and Unwin, London.

DAVIS, LOUIS E. (1971): 'Job Satisfaction Research', *Industrial Relations*, 10, May.

DAVIS, LOUIS E., CANTER, RALPH R., and HOFFMAN, JOHN (1972):

'Current Work Design Criteria', in Davis, Louis E., and Taylor, James C., eds., *Design of Jobs*, pp. 65–82, Penguin Books, Harmondsworth.

DAWE, ALAN (1971): 'The Two Sociologies', in Thompson, Kenneth, and Tunstall, Jeremy, eds., *Sociological Perspectives*, pp. 542–54, Penguin Books, Harmondsworth.

DOBB, MAURICE (1963): *Studies in the Development of Capitalism*, Routledge and Kegan Paul, London.

DORE, RONALD (1973): *British Factory, Japanese Factory*, Allen and Unwin, London.

DUBIN, R., HEDLEY, ALAN, and TAVEGGIA, C. (1976): 'Attachment to Work', in Dubin, R., ed., *Handbook of Work, Organization and Society*, pp. 281–342, Rand McNally, Chicago.

DUNKERLEY, DAVID, and SALAMAN, GRAEME, eds., (1980): *The International Yearbook of Organizational Studies*, vol. 1, Routledge and Kegan Paul, London.

DURKHEIM, EMILE (1957): *Professional Ethics and Civic Morals*, tr. Cornelia Brookfield, Routledge and Kegan Paul.

DURKHEIM, EMILE (1958): *Socialism*, tr. Charlotte Sattler, Antioch Press, Yellow Springs.

DURKHEIM, EMILE (1964): *The Division of Labour in Society*, tr. George Simpson, Free Press, New York.

EDWARDS, R. C., GORDON, D. M., and REICH, M., eds. (1975): *Labour Market Segmentation*, D. C. Heath, Lexington.

ELDRIDGE, J. E. T., (1971): *Sociology and Industrial Life*, Michael Joseph, London.

ESLAND, GEOFF, SALAMAN, GRAEME, and SPEAKMAN, MARY-ANNE, eds., (1975): *People and Work*, Holmes McDougall, Edinburgh.

ETZIONI, AMITAI (1961): *A Comparative Analysis of Complex Organizations*, Free Press, New York.

FAUNCE, W. A. (1968): *Problems of an Industrial Society*, McGraw-Hill, New York.

FOSTER, JOHN (1974): *Class Struggle and the Industrial Revolution*, Methuen, London.

FOUCAULT, M. (1977): *Discipline and Punish*, Allen Lane, London.

FOX, ALAN (1971): *A Sociology of Work in Industry*, Collier-Macmillan, London.

FOX, ALAN (1974): *Beyond Contract*, Faber and Faber, London.

FOX, ALAN (1980): 'The Meaning of Work',

in Esland, Geoff, and Salaman, Graeme, eds., *The Politics of Work and Occupations*, pp. 139–91, Open University Press, Milton Keynes.

FREUND, JULIEN (1968): *The Sociology of Max Weber*, Allen Lane, London.

FRIEDMAN, L. ANDREW (1977): *Industry and Labour*, Macmillan, London.

FRIEDMANN, GEORGES (1961): *The Anatomy of Work*, Heinemann, London.

GALBRAITH, J. K. (1969): *The New Industrial State*, Penguin Books, Harmondsworth.

GALLIE, DUNCAN (1978): *In Search of the New Working Class*, Cambridge University Press.

GERTH, H. H., and MILLS, C. WRIGHT (1948): *From Max Weber: Essays in Sociology*, Routledge and Kegan Paul, London.

GIDDENS, ANTHONY (1968): 'Power in the Recent Writings of Talcott Parsons', *Sociology*, vol. 2, no. 3, pp. 257–72.

GIDDENS, ANTHONY (1973): *The Class Structure of the Advanced Societies*, Hutchinson, London.

GIDDENS, ANTHONY (1978): *Durkheim*, Fontana Paperbacks, London.

GLYN, A., and SUTCLIFFE, B. (1972): *British Capitalism, Workers and the Profit Squeeze*, Penguin Books, Harmondsworth.

GOLDMAN, PAUL, and VAN HOUTEN, DONALD (1980): 'Managerial Strategy in Turn-of-the-century American Industry', in Dunkerley, D., and Salaman, G., eds., *op cit.*, pp. 108–41.

GOLDTHORPE, JOHN H. (1964): 'Social Stratification in Industrial Society', in Halmos, Paul, ed., *The Development of Industrial Societies*, Sociological Review Monograph no. 8, pp. 97–122.

GOLDTHORPE, JOHN, LOCKWOOD, DAVID, BECHHOFER, FRANK and PLATT, JENNIFER (1968): *The Affluent Worker: Industrial Attitudes and Behaviour*, Cambridge University Press.

GOLDTHORPE, JOHN, LOCKWOOD, DAVID, BECHHOFER, FRANK and PLATT, JENNIFER (1969): *The Affluent Worker in the Class Structure*, Cambridge University Press.

GORDON, DAVID, M. (1976): 'Capitalist Efficiency and Social Efficiency', *Monthly Review*, vol. 28, pp. 19–39.

GORZ, ANDRÉ (1972): 'Technical Intelligence and the Capitalist Division of Labour', *Telos*, no. 12, pp. 27–41.

GOULDNER, ALVIN (1954): *Patterns of Industrial Bureaucracy*, Free Press, New York.

GRUSKY, O., and MILLER, G. A., eds. (1970): *The Sociology of Organizations*, Free Press, New York.

HALL, RICHARD (1972): *Organizations: Structure and Process*, Prentice-Hall, New Jersey.

HICKSON, D. J. (1973): 'A Convergence in Organization Theory', in Salaman, Graeme, and Thompson, Kenneth, eds., *op. cit.*, pp 109–19.

HICKSON, D. J., HININGS, C. R., LEE, C. A., SCHNECK, R. E., and PENNINGS, J. M. (1973): 'A Strategic Contingencies' Theory of Intraorganizational Power', in Salaman, Graeme, and Thompson, Kenneth, eds., *op. cit.*, pp. 174–89.

HOBSBAWM, E. J. (1968): *Labouring Men*, Weidenfeld and Nicolson, London.

HOOS, IDA (1961): 'The Impact of Automation on Office Workers', *International Labour Review*, 82, pp. 363–88.

HORTON, JOHN (1964): 'The Dehumanisation of Anomie and Alienation: a Problem in the Ideology of Sociology', *British Journal of Sociology*, vol. XV, no. 4, pp. 283–300.

HUNT, ALAN (1977): 'Theory and Politics in the Identification of the Working Class', in Hunt, Allan, ed., *Class and Class Structure*, pp. 81–112, Lawrence and Wishart, London.

HYMAN, RICHARD, and BROUGH, IAN (1975): *Social Values and Industrial Relations*, Basic Blackwell, Oxford.

HYMAN, RICHARD (1971): *Marxism and the Sociology of Trade Unions*, Pluto Press, London.

INGHAM, GEOFFREY (1967): 'Organizational Size, Orientation to Work and Industrial Behaviour', *Sociology*, vol. 1, pp. 239–58.

KATZ, D., and KAHN, R. I. (1967): *The Social Psychology of Organizations*, Wiley, New York.

KERR, CLARK, DUNLOP, JOHN T., HARBISON, FREDERICK, and MYERS, C. A. (1973): *Industrialism and Industrial Man*, Penguin Books, Harmondsworth.

KLINGENDER, F. D. (1935): *The Condition of Clerical Labour in Great Britain*, Martin Lawrence, London.

KUMAR, KRISHAN (1978): *Prophecy and Progress*, Penguin Books, Harmondsworth.

LANDES, D. S. (1969): *The Unbound Prometheus*, Cambridge University Press.

LEAVITT, HAROLD J. (1973): 'Applied Organisational Change in Industry', in Vroom, V. H., and Deci, E. L., eds., *Management and Motivation*, Penguin Books, Harmondsworth.

LEVISON, ANDREW (1974): *The Working Class Majority*, Coward, McCann and Geoghegan, New York.

LITTERER, JOSEPH (1961): 'Systematic Management: the Search for Order and Integration', *Business History Review*, 35, pp. 461–76.

LITTLER, CRAIG R. (1978): 'Understanding Taylorism', *British Journal of Sociology*, vol. XXIX, no. 2, pp. 185–207.

LITTLER, CRAIG (1980): 'Internal Contract and the Transition to Modern Work Systems', in Dunkerley, D., and Salaman, G., eds., *op. cit.*, pp. 157–85.

LOCKWOOD, DAVID (1958): *The Blackcoated Worker*, Allen and Unwin, London.

LOCKWOOD, DAVID (1964): 'Social Integration and System Integration', in Zollschan, G. K., and Hirsch, W., eds., *Exploration in Social Change*, Routledge and Kegan Paul, London.

LOCKWOOD, DAVID (1966): 'Sources of Variation in Working-class Images of Society', *Sociological Review*, vol. 14, pp. 249–67.

LOW-BEER, JOHN (1978): *Protest and Participation*, Cambridge University Press.

LUKES, STEVEN (1967): 'Alienation and Anomie', in Laslett, Peter, and Runciman, W. G., eds., *Philosophy, Politics and Society*, pp. 134–56, Basil Blackwell, Oxford.

LUKES, STEVEN (1973): *Emile Durkheim: His Life and Works*, Penguin Books, Harmondsworth.

MACKENZIE, GAVIN (1975): 'World Images and the World of Work', in Esland, Geoff, *et al.*, eds., *op. cit.*, pp. 170–85.

MALLET, SERGE (1963): *La Nouvelle class ouvrière*, Editions du Seuil, Paris.

MANN, FLOYD C. (1962): 'Psychological and Organisational Impacts', in Dunlop, John T., ed., *Automation and Technological Change*, pp. 43–65, Prentice-Hall, New Jersey.

MARCUSE, HERBERT (1972): *One-Dimensional Man*, Abacus/Sphere Books, London.

MARGLIN, S. A. (1976): 'What do Bosses Do?', in Gorz, André, ed., *The Division of Labour*, pp. 13–54, Harvester Press, Brighton.

MARX, KARL (1954): *Capital*, vol. I, Progress Publishers, Moscow.

MARX, KARL (1959): *Capital*, vol. III, Progress Publishers, Moscow.

MARX, KARL and ENGELS, FREDERICK (1970): 'Manifesto of the Communist Party', in *Selected Works*, Lawrence and Wishart, London.

MELMAN, SEYMOUR(1951): 'The Rise of Administrative Overhead in the Manufacturing Industries of the United States, 1899–1947', *Oxford*

Economic Papers, vol. III.

MERTON, R. K. (1957): *Social Theory and Social Structure*, Free Press, Chicago.

MILLER, GEORGE A. (1970): 'Professionals in Bureaucracy', in Grusky, Oscar, and Miller, George A., eds., *op. cit.*, pp. 503–16.

MILLIBAND, R. (1969): *The State in Capitalist Society*, Quartet, London.

MILLIBAND, R. (1978): 'A State of De-Subordination', *British Journal of Sociology*, XXIX , no. 4, pp. 399–409.

MILLS, C. WRIGHT (1956): *White Collar*, Galaxy, New York.

MONTAGNA, PAUL D. (1977): *Occupation and Society: Towards a Sociology of the Labor Market*, Wiley, New York.

MORRIS, R. J. (1979): *Class and Class Consciousness in the Industrial Revolution, 1780–1850*, Macmillan, London.

MOUZELIS, NICOS (1967): *Organization and Bureaucracy*, Routledge and Kegan Paul, London.

NELSON, DANIEL (1975): *Managers and Workers*, University of Wisconsin Press.

NICHOLS, THEO (1969): *Ownership, Control and Ideology*, Allen and Unwin, London.

NICHOLS, THEO, and ARMSTRONG, PETER (1976): *Workers Divided: A Study in Shopfloor Politics*, Fontana Paperbacks, London.

NICHOLS, THEO, and BEYNON, HUW (1977): *Living with Capitalism*, Routledge and Kegan Paul, London.

NISBET, ROBERT, A. (1967): *The Sociological Tradition*, Heinemann, London.

O'CONNOR, J. (1973): *The Fiscal Crisis of the State*, St Martin's Press, New York.

PARKER, S. R. (1964): 'Work Satisfaction: a Review of the Literature', *Government Social Survey*, Paper M115.

PARKER, S. R., BROWN, R. K., CHILD, J. and SMITH, M. A. (1977): *The Sociology of Industry*, Allen and Unwin, London.

PARKIN, FRANK (1971): *Class Inequality and Political Order*, MacGibbon and Kee, London.

PARKIN, FRANK (1979): 'Social Stratification', in Bottomore, Tom, and Nisbet, Robert, eds., *A History of Sociological Analysis*, Heinemann, London.

PARSONS, TALCOTT (1970): 'Social Systems', in Grusky, Oscar, and Miller, George E., eds., *op. cit.*, pp. 75–82.

PEACH, CERI (1968): *West Indian Migrants to Britain*, Oxford University Press.

PERROW, CHARLES (1972): *Complex Organisations: a Critical Essay*, Scott, Foresman, Illinois.

PIORE, MICHAEL J. (1972): 'Notes for a Theory of Labor Market Stratification', *Working Paper* no. 95, Dept. of Economics, MIT Press, Cambridge, Mass.

POLLARD, SIDNEY (1965): *The Genesis of Modern Management*, Edward Arnold, London.

POULANTZAS, NICOS (1975): *Classes in Contemporary Capitalism*, New Left Books, London.

PRESTHUS, ROBERT (1979): *The Organizational Society* (revised edition), Macmillan, London.

PUGH, D. S. and HICKSON, D. J. (1973): 'The Comparative Study of Organizations', in Salaman, Graeme, and Thompson, Kenneth, eds., *op. cit.*, pp. 50–66.

PUGH, D. S. and HININGS, C. R., eds. (1976): *Organizational Structure: Extensions and Replications*, Saxon House, Farnborough.

PUGH, D. S. and HICKSON, D. J., eds. (1976): *Organizational Structure in its Context*, Saxon House, Farnborough.

PUGH, D. S., and HININGS, C. R. (1976): 'Introduction', in Pugh, D. S., and Hinings, C. R., eds., *op. cit.*, pp. vii–xviii.

PUGH, D. S., and PAYNE, R. L., eds. (1977): *Organizational Behaviour in its Context*, Saxon House, Farnborough.

ROBERTS, K., COOK, F. G., CLARK, S. C., and SEMEONOFF, ELIZABETH (1977): *The Fragmentary Class Structure*, Heinemann, London.

ROSE, MICHAEL (1975): *Industrial Behaviour*, Allen Lane, London.

ROY, S. F. (1973): 'Banana Time: Job Satisfaction and Informal Interaction', in Salaman, Graeme, and Thompson, Kenneth, eds., *op. cit.*, pp. 205–22.

SALAMAN, GRAEME (1978): 'Towards a Sociology of Organizational Structure', *The Sociological Review*, vol. 26, no. 3, pp. 519–54.

SALAMAN, GRAEME (1979): *Work Organizations: Resistance and Control*, Longman, London.

SALAMAN, GRAEME, and THOMPSON, KENNETH, eds. (1973): *People and Organizations*, Longman, London.

SCHACHT, RICHARD (1970): *Alienation*, Allen and Unwin, London.

SCOTT, JOHN (1979): *Corporations, Classes and Capitalism*, Hutchinson, London.

SEEMAN, MELVIN (1959): 'On the Meaning of Alienation', *American Sociological Review*, XXIV, pp. 783–91.

SEIDMAN, STEVEN, and GRUBER, MICHAEL (1977): 'Capitalism and Individuation in the Sociology of Max Weber', *British Journal of Sociology*, vol. XXVIII, no. 4, pp. 498–508.

SENNETT, RICHARD, and COBB, JONATHON (1973): *The Hidden Injuries of Class*, Vintage Books, New York.

SHEPARD, JON (1971): *Automation and Alienation*, MIT Press, Cambridge, Mass.

SHEPARD, H. L., and HERRICK, N. Q. (1972): *Where Have all the Robots Gone?*, Collier-Macmillan, London.

SILVERMAN, DAVID (1970): *The Theory of Organizations*, Heinemann, London.

STINCHCOMBE, ARTHUR (1970): 'Bureaucratic and Craft Administration of Production', in Grusky, Oscar, and Miller, George, A., eds., *op. cit.*, pp. 261–72.

STONE, KATHERINE (1974): 'The Origins of Job Structures in the Steel Industry', *Review of Radical Political Economics*, vol. 6, pp. 113–73.

SWADOS, HARVEY (1957): 'The Myth of the Happy Worker', *Nation*, CLXXXV, pp. 65–9.

SYKES, A. J. (1965): 'Economic Interest and Hawthorne Researches: a Comment', *Human Relations*, vol. 18, pp. 252–63.

TARLING, R., and WILKINSON, F., (1978): 'The Social Contract: Post-War Income Policies and their Inflationary Impact', *Cambridge Journal of Economics*, vol. I, pp. 395–414.

THOMPSON, E. P. (1967): 'Time, Work and Discipline, and Industrial Capitalism', *Past and Present*, no. 38, pp. 56–97.

THOMPSON, E. P. (1968): *The Making of the English Working Class*, Penguin Books, Harmondsworth.

TOURAINE, ALAIN (1971): *The Post-industrial Society*, Random House, New York.

TURNER, A., and LAWRENCE, P. (1966): *Industrial Jobs and the Worker*, Harvard University Press.

UDY, STANLEY H. (1959): '"Bureaucracy" and "Rationality" in Weber's Organisation Theory', *American Sociological Review*, vol. 24, pp. 791–5.

URE, ANDREW (1861): *The Philosophy of Manufactures*, Bohn, London.

WACHTEL, H. M. (1975): 'Class Consciousness and Stratification in the Labour Process', in Edwards, D. C., *et al.*, eds., *op. cit.*

WALKER, C. R., and GUEST, R. H. (1952): *Man on the Assembly Line*, Harvard University Press.

WARNER, W. L., and LOW, J. O. (1947): *The Social System of the Modern Factory*, Yale University Press.

WATSON, TONY J. (1977): *The Personnel Managers*, Routledge and Kegan Paul, London.

WEBER, MAX (1930): *The Protestant Ethic and the Spirit of Capitalism*, Allen Unwin, London.

WEBER, MAX (1964): *The Theory of Social and Economic Organization*, Free Press, New York.

WEBER, MAX (1968): *Economy and Society*, 3 volumes, tr. and ed. by Guenther Roth and Claus Wittich, Bedminster Press, New York.

WEDDERBURN, DOROTHY, and CRAIG, CHRISTINE (1975): 'Relative Deprivation in Work', in Esland, Geoff, *et al.*, eds., *op. cit.*, pp. 59–69.

WESTERGAARD, J. H. (1970): 'The Rediscovery of the Cash Nexus', in Milliband, R., and Saville, John, eds., *The Socialist Register*, Merlin, London.

WESTERGAARD, J. H., and RESLER, HENRIETTA (1975): *Class in a Capitalist Society*, Heinemann, London.

WILLIS, PAUL (1977): *Learning to Labour*, Saxon House, Farnborough.

WILSON, H. T. (1977): *The American Ideology*, Routledge and Kegan Paul, London.

WOODWARD, JOAN, ed. (1970): *Industrial Organizations: Behaviour and Control*, Oxford University Press.

WORSLEY, PETER (1964): 'The Distribution of Power in Industrial Society', in Halmos, Paul, ed., *The Development of Industrial Societies*, pp. 15–34, *Sociological Review* monograph, University of Keele.

WRIGHT, ERIC OLIN (1978): *Class, Crisis and the State*, New Left Books, London.

ZIMBALIST, A. (1975): 'The Limits of Work Humanisation', *Review of Radical Political Economics*, vol. 7, pp. 50–9.

Work in America, Report of Special Task Force to the Secretary of Health, Education and Welfare (1973), MIT Press, Cambridge, Mass.

Index

accumulation, 78, 135–7, 245; *see also* capitalism

Aiken, M. and Hage, J., 124

Albrow, M., 131

alienation: Marx's concept of, 47, 62, 64–5, 68, 73–5, 89, 95–6, 100, 129, 139; and meaning of work, 72–98, 111–12; and social theory, 72; Weber on, 74; Blauner defines, 89–92, 96, 114; Faunce defines, 94–6, 99; and purposes of enterprise, 99–100; and design and control of work, 113–42; and automation, 117; and bureaucratization, 121–5; of professionals, 123–5, 133; and workers' attitudes, 129–30; and rational organizational control, 133; Durkheim and, 133; and humanizing work, 184–5; *see also* Durkheim, E., Horton, J., *and* Lukes, S.

Amtrak, 247

anomie: and division of labour, 45–7, 147, 236; and social theory, 75; and morality of work, 88–9, 91; and meaning of work, 88–9, 91; Durkheim on, 147–8, 236–7; *see also* Horton, J., *and* Lukes, S.

Anthony, P. D., 103, 259 n1

Argyle, M., 148, 150

Aron, R., 207

Aronowitz, S., 84, 101, 161, 176, 259 n1 (Ch. 4)

assembly lines, 82, 86–7, 90, 115

Aston school (of organization studies), 132, 161–3

automation, 90–4, 116–21, 169

Avineri, S., 65

Babbage, C., 40

Baldamus, W., 180–1

Baran, P. A. and Sweezy, P. M., 78–9, 87–8, 129

Baritz, L., 261 n2

Beechey, V., 108–9

Bell, Daniel, 123, 151–2, 261 n10

Bendix, R., 33, 37–9, 184, 259 n1

Berle, A. A., and Means, G. C., 129

Beynon, H., 100–1, 115, 201

Beynon, H., and Blackburn, R. M., 108

Blau, P. M., 157–9, 162

Blau, P. M. and Schoenherr, R. A., 124–5, 131, 162–3, 185

Blauner, R., 80–2, 84, 259 nn2–3; on alienation, 89–93, 96–7, 114; on automation, 117

Blumberg, P., 260 n4 (Ch. 5)

bourgeoisie, 63, 221, 223, 225; *see also* class

Braham, P., 109

Braverman, H., 93, 114, 117, 119, 121, 133, 138, 202, 260 nn3 (Ch. 5), 6; on meaning of work, 100;

INTO UNKNOWN ENGLAND 1866-1913

SELECTIONS FROM THE SOCIAL EXPLORERS

Edited by Peter Keating

How did the poor live in late Victorian and Edwardian England? In the slums of London and Birmingham? In the iron-town of Middlesbrough? In a Devon fishing village? In rural Essex?

This is a fascinating sequence of extracts from the writings of those individuals, journalists and wealthy businessmen, a minister's wife, and a popular novelist, who temporarily left the comfort of their middle-class homes to find out how the other half lived. Peter Keating includes material from Charles Booth, Jack London, B. S. Rowntree and C. F. G. Masterman as well as by such lesser-known figures as George Sims, Andrew Mearns and Stephen Reynolds.

'. . . a brilliant and compelling anthology . . . *Into Unknown England* is not only an education in itself, throwing into three-dimensional chiaroscuro the flat statistics of "scientific" history, but a splendid example of prose which is always immediate and alive.'
Alan Brien, *Spectator*

'The writers collected here used all the techniques they could to solicit sympathy. Their descendants are a thousand television documentaries.'
Paul Barker, *The Times*

'. . . a rich collection of passages, intelligently presented.'
The Guardian

Fontana Paperbacks

Fontana is a leading paperback publisher of fiction and non-fiction, with authors ranging from Alistair MacLean, Agatha Christie and Desmond Bagley to Solzhenitsyn and Pasternak, from Gerald Durrell and Joy Adamson to the famous Modern Masters series.

In addition to a wide-ranging collection of internationally popular writers of fiction, Fontana also has an outstanding reputation for history, natural history, military history, psychology, psychiatry, politics, economics, religion and the social sciences.

All Fontana books are available at your bookshop or newsagent; or can be ordered direct. Just fill in the form and list the titles you want.

FONTANA BOOKS, Cash Sales Department, G.P.O. Box 29, Douglas, Isle of Man, British Isles. Please send purchase price, plus 8p per book. Customers outside the U.K. send purchase price, plus 10p per book. Cheque, postal or money order. No currency.

NAME (Block letters)

ADDRESS

While every effort is made to keep prices low, it is sometimes necessary to increase prices on short notice. Fontana Books reserve the right to show new retail prices on covers which may differ from those previously advertised in the text or elsewhere.